TED LASSO
AND PHILOSOPHY

No Question Is Into Touch

T0283814

The Blackwell Philosophy and Pop Culture Series
Series editor: William Irwin

A spoonful of sugar helps the medicine go down, and a healthy helping of popular culture clears the cobwebs from Kant. Philosophy has had a public relations problem for a few centuries now. This series aims to change that, showing that philosophy is relevant to your life—and not just for answering the big questions like "To be or not to be?" but for answering the little questions: "To watch or not to watch South Park?" Thinking deeply about TV, movies, and music doesn't make you a "complete idiot." In fact, it might make you a philosopher, someone who believes the unexamined life is not worth living and the unexamined cartoon is not worth watching.

TED LASSO
AND PHILOSOPHY

No Question Is Into Touch

Edited by

Marybeth Baggett
David Baggett

WILEY Blackwell

Library of Congress Cataloging-in-Publication Data
Names: Baggett, David, editor. | Baggett, Marybeth, editor. | John Wiley &
    Sons, publisher.
Title: Ted Lasso and philosophy : no question is into touch / edited by
    David Baggett, Marybeth Baggett.
Description: Hoboken, New Jersey : Wiley-Blackwell, [2024] | Series: The
    blackwell philosophy and pop culture series | Includes index.
Identifiers: LCCN 2023037911 (print) | LCCN 2023037912 (ebook) | ISBN
    9781119891932 (paperback) | ISBN 9781119891949 (adobe pdf) | ISBN
    9781119891956 (epub)
Subjects: LCSH: Ted Lasso (Television program). | Television–Philosophy.
Classification: LCC PN1992.77.T38435 T43 2024 (print) | LCC
    PN1992.77.T38435 (ebook) | DDC 791.4501–dc23/eng/20231018
LC record available at https://lccn.loc.gov/2023037911
LC ebook record available at https://lccn.loc.gov/2023037912

Cover Design: Wiley
Cover Image: © thanasak/Adobe Stock Photos; © owngarden/Getty Images

Set in 10.5/13pt Sabon by Straive, Pondicherry, India

SKY10065277_011824

For Earl

Contents

A Taste of Athens

Nate's favorite restaurant means a great deal to him. Not because it's cool. In fact, A Taste of Athens is dumpy and sad, and their dips look like piles of vomit. The good news is, they taste a lot better than they look. The restaurant is also where the Shelley family celebrates birthdays, anniversaries, and every other important event in their lives. All of that makes it even better than cool.

A Taste of Athens, like Sharon's transformer bike, reminds us there's often more to most things than meets the eye. You might even say that the restaurant provides a window (table) into issues relevant to another Athens, the birthplace of philosophy.

The comparison's no joke. We can't wait to unpack it with you.

The colorful and charming *Ted Lasso* premiered amidst a pandemic so dire you'd think the Wichita State Shockers tried to end a game in a tie. The show's optimism and sweetness during those dark days came as a bit of a tonic. This fizzy water went down surprisingly smooth, and soon the beloved characters and clever writers captivated audiences, earning *Ted Lasso* lots of beautiful, shiny awards and loads of critical acclaim. At moments it almost seemed to be an antidote to the acrimony and angst of our time.

For a series in so many ways easy to watch—usually light and lots of fun—*Ted Lasso* features more nuance, depth, and philosophical resonance than its vibrant veneer suggests. The nature of true success, the role of mental health, sportsmanship, revenge versus justice, the importance of friendship, the imperative of respect for persons, humility, leadership, identity, character growth, courage, journalistic ethics, belief, forgiveness, and what love looks like: these are all topics broached by the show, plus much more.

That said—not to tinkle on anyone's toenails—the show is far from perfect. At times, it's uneven (looking at you, Season 3). It has its highs and lows, its depths and superficialities, its epiphanies and blind spots. By turns it can be inspiring and predictable, iconoclastic and formulaic. *Ted Lasso* has attracted die-hard fans, as loyal as Basil, Jeremy, and Paul are to the Greyhounds. But it also has its detractors who counter the accolades with charges of shallowness and schmaltz.

Fortunately, this book is not about the philosophy of *Ted Lasso*. Rather, it's *Ted Lasso* and philosophy. In the great dartboard scene in Season 1's "Diamond Dogs," Ted talks about how people had long underestimated him. They let judgmentalism crowd out their curiosity and shut down fruitful questions. Philosophy by contrast celebrates questions and begins in wonder. It peels back all the juicy layers of appearance to discover the reality that lies beneath. That's exactly what we intend to do here: using the show, whatever its faults, as a springboard for philosophical reflection.

Those who have watched *Ted Lasso*, featuring biscuits-with-the-boss, finger allergies, and exorcisms of training rooms, find its defiance of low expectations more than fitting. Like a candy bar little Ronnie Fouch might offer you on the playground, it invites further investigation.

Ted Lasso is surely a book you don't want to judge by its cover, lest you miss out on an undiscovered mega-talent. On its surface, it's about (English) football and a cheerful, guileless, displaced American working abroad. But as Trent Crimm wisely observes, sport is a meta-phor for life. There's certainly more to Ted Lasso himself than first appears. Relentlessly optimistic and happy-go-lucky, Ted navigates complicated feelings and deep trauma from his past. For those like Dr. Fieldstone "only interested in the truth," this book can help diagnose Ted's tears, and a whole lot more.

Other characters are equally complex. At first Nathan Shelley seems an unimpressive kit man, awkward and bumbling, when in fact he turns out to be a football genius. Rebecca Welton initially acts like she sees something in Ted that her team needs to get to the next level, when in fact her motivation is to hire Ted to destroy its prospects. Jamie Tartt begins as an obnoxious self-absorbed superstar, but he eventually reveals his deep yearning for meaningful connections with others.

Sometimes appearance/reality gaps in *Ted Lasso* result from revising history, sometimes from intentional deception, and sometimes from too static a conception of characters. Our worst moments don't define us, and there's a great dynamism in *Ted Lasso* when it comes to the maturation of its characters. Ted, especially, helps those around him to become better people, the best versions of themselves both on and off the field.

Ted himself has to come to terms with aspects of his past that make him as haunted as Richmond's training room. He too needs help from his surrogate family. This makes the show fascinating from a psychological perspective, but also from a philosophical one. It's a show that continually challenges viewers to look beyond surface differences and misleading appearances that too often divide or prove destructive. It also resists too-simple categorizations, reminding us as Beard might say that "all people are different people" ("Goodbye Earl"). For those with eyes to see, *Ted Lasso* can help us look right.

We're sad to see *Ted Lasso* come to a close. Nelson Road is a delightful world to inhabit. The creators do have a tendency to surprise us, though, so whether or not this truly is the end remains to be seen.

The chapters to come, whose titles at times are intentionally as opaque as Keeley's office window, are divided into five sections: (a) *Do the Right-est Thing*, which touches on Augustine, Taoism, precursive faith and the ethics of belief, and ethical egoism; (b) *The Best Versions of Ourselves*, dealing with issues of fear, competitive excellence, psychological health, and coach/athlete friendships; (c) *Man City*, canvassing masculinity, gender, the relative importance of winning, and "bullshit"; (d) *Mostly Football Is Life*, touching on music in *Ted Lasso*, the possibility we're in a simulation, insights from *Candide* and Camus, and Chestertonian optimism; and (e) *Smells Like Potential*, covering journalistic ethics, Stoicism, respect for others, and whether Rupert is beyond redemption. "Beard's Bookshelf" closes the volume by chronicling the books Coach Beard (and others) are reading throughout the series.

We're indebted to our wonderful contributors who met deadlines tighter than Coach Beard's thong. We're also grateful to the team at Wiley Blackwell who believed in this project from the start, and especially to William Irwin, whose support has been characteristically both brilliant and unstinting. And we'd be remiss not to recognize our friend Michaela Flack whose early delight in *Ted Lasso* sparked our own and whose enthusiastic support of our work enriched this project.

So pull up a seat. A taste of Athens awaits, no reservation required. Look past the seemingly rude hostess, the annoying manager, and the snooty diners, and you'll find a feast for the heart and mind. The baklava, we've heard, is divine.

Metaphor? Exactamundo, Dikembe Mutombo.

Part I
DO THE RIGHT-EST THING

1

On the Pitch with Saint Augustine

Sean Strehlow

"What do you love?"

Ted asks Trent Crimm this simple question during the third episode of Season 1. Ted follows up with his own answer: "I love coaching. For me, success is not about the wins and losses. It's about helping these young fellas be the best versions of themselves on and off the field" ("Trent Crimm: The Independent"). This notion that coaching can prepare athletes for life *on and off the field* echoes a strong cultural sentiment that participation in sport builds character. But when setting out to define "character," concrete definitions are difficult to pin down. Ted's definition of the offsides rule may well apply here: "I'm gonna put it the same way the US Supreme Court did back in 1964 when they defined pornography. It ain't easy to explain, but you know it when you see it" ("Biscuits").

One reason character is such an elusive notion is that it is rarely reducible to its readily observable dimensions. As a simple exercise, imagine one of several scenes in *Ted Lasso* where the Richmond team is working out in the weight room. We can assume that every athlete enters the weight room with a set of *intentions*, or goals, for their workout. Some athletes may be working on rehabbing an injury, while others may be looking to strengthen a particular muscle. Each athlete also shares a larger goal of improving his individual and team performance. Some (ahem… Jamie Tartt) may be more concerned with their physical appearance than anything else. How these intentions are ordered shapes the way the athletes engage in their workout.

Ted Lasso and Philosophy: No Question Is Into Touch, First Edition.
Edited by Marybeth Baggett and David Baggett.
© 2024 John Wiley & Sons, Inc. Published 2024 by John Wiley & Sons, Inc.

As the above scene illustrates, our behaviors are made meaningful by our intentions, our goals or purposes that provide motivations for our actions. These lie close to our affective center. When evaluating a person's character, we might begin with behaviors we can directly observe, or the reasoning that led to those behaviors. But what is infinitely more complex, and what forms our cognitive and behavioral patterns, is what Ted's opening question highlights. More than anything, our character is defined by our heart—it is dictated by what we love.[1]

What Is Love?

One of the challenges and opportunities for philosophy and the clarity and rigor it seeks is the transient nature of language across time and place. Or, as Ted would advise, best not to smother English biscuits in gravy ("Biscuits"). Today, images related to love and the heart typically evoke a kind of sentimentality one might find in a Hallmark card or romantic comedy ("rom com"). Love is a rather degraded notion in common parlance. Reviews of *Ted Lasso* regularly feature a similar "heartwarming" emotivism.[2] When ancient philosophers refer to the heart, though, it often carries the same weight as the Greek word *kardia,* which more accurately might be described as the soul—the spiritual epicenter of our deepest, most fundamental, longings and desires.

The heart (*kardia*) is an unavoidable part of the human experience. By asking Crimm about what he loves, Ted communicates the philosophical truth that the key question is not *whether* we love, but *what* we love. Perhaps no one knew this better than Saint Augustine of Hippo (354–430), a North African Bishop whose writings remain essential to the Western philosophical tradition. Augustine belongs to a long line of philosophers, beginning with Aristotle (384–322 BC), who see happiness as the ultimate human aim. This is to say, all human activity is aimed at achieving a state of stable and sustainable happiness, understood in a robust and substantive way. For Augustine, happiness is inextricably tied to what we love.

To complicate matters, we have many loves that compel us to think and act in different, often conflicting or dissonant, ways. Consider the morally ambivalent Rebecca, whose desire to enact revenge against Rupert eventually clashes with her growing affinity for the Richmond Football Club and for Ted himself. As these two passions fluctuate in Rebecca's heart, her actions realign with the one that takes primacy.

This prioritization is what Augustine refers to as the *ordo amoris*, the ordering of loves, which

> requires one to be capable of an objective and impartial evaluation of things; to love things, that is to say, in the right order, so that you do not love what is not to be loved, or fail to love what is to be loved, or have a greater love for what is to be loved less, or equal love for things that should be loved less or more, or a lesser or greater love for things that should be loved equally.[3]

Drawing on this concept, we can think of our heart as an ecosystem of desires that are constantly competing for our attention. Augustine described our desires as having their own gravitational pull that prompts us to think and act in certain ways: "My love is my weight! I am borne about by it, wheresoever I am borne."[4] When faced with difficult decisions or moral dilemmas, our most deep-seated desires "win out" to provide the motivation for our actions.

The *Ordo Amoris* in Ted Lasso

"Two Aces" most vividly captures this spirit in *Ted Lasso*. This is the episode of the training room curse. More importantly, it is the episode introducing the ebullient Dani Rojas. If Ted is the show's most loveable character, Dani must be a close second. His infectious joy seems to permeate the entire show, demonstrating that one can, in fact, "give away joy for free" ("Diamond Dogs"). Avid *Ted Lasso* fans will be familiar with Dani's mantra, "Football is life!" But there is another Richmond player who wears this mantra on his sleeve, even if he doesn't say it out loud—Jamie Tartt. In fact, Ted says this explicitly while yelling at Jamie for missing practice:

> We're talking about practice. You understand me? Practice. Not a game. Not a game. Not the game you go out there and die for. Right? Play every weekend like it's your last, right? No, we're talking about practice, man. Practice!

Indeed, both Dani and Jamie love football as if it is life itself, but in very different ways.

Augustine can strengthen our analysis here. Jamie's love for soccer resembles what Augustine refers to as *cupiditas* or cupidity, a disordered love. This kind of love is self-serving because its intention is self-gratification, even at the expense of others. Ted's tirade about missing practice is a crucial moment because, for the first time, Jamie is directly confronted about this disordered affection. Notice what happens immediately after Ted puts Jamie in his place. Colin takes a jab at Jamie for being a "second-teamer" and Isaac backs him up. Until that moment, they idolized Jamie, another example of *cupidity*. With Jamie's change of fortunes, among a group of athletes with their own desires bouncing every which way, the gravitational center of their collective desires shifts ever so subtly toward the good of the team.

Immediately afterwards comes Dani Rojas, whose love for football is enlivened by a different intention. This type of love is what Augustine refers to as *caritas*, a rightly ordered love that finds pleasure and satisfaction in the good of others. Not only does Dani repeat his mantra. He also demonstrates it to the coaches ("You say it, I do it, coach!") and to his teammates by attributing his goal to their efforts. Dani further shows this kind of love during his post-practice shootout with Jamie—admiring Jamie's shots and attributing his own success to luck. We might more accurately interpret Dani's mantra as "football is life *giving*." This newfound source of talent, energy, and concern for others leaves a noticeable impression on the team and the center of gravity shifts yet again.

Later, when the Richmond team gathers for the ceremony to get rid of the ghosts in the training room, Rebecca inaugurates another affective shift. In her obsession with getting revenge on Rupert, Rebecca had exemplified what Augustine calls *cupiditas*—a disordered love of something that should not be loved at all. Throwing the newspaper with Rupert's headline into the trash can symbolizes a shift to prioritizing Ted and the Richmond team, even if it takes a little while to stick.

Jamie, too, uncharacteristically opens up about his painful past. We see his disordered love for football begin to shift ever so slightly. In fact, we can look at everyone's sacrifices, even the silly ones (like Richard's memento from his maiden voyage with a supermodel), as a reordering of loves. Each object represents a source of self-gratification and comfort that their owners had valued above all else. The ghosts in this episode may not have been real, but there is something quite enchanting and transcendent, even supernatural, about an entire group of people giving up what means most to them for something that might benefit the group.

Worship at Crystal Palace

Ordering our loves is never a linear process, however. Jamie retreats back into himself when he's recalled by Manchester City. Rebecca still waffles back and forth in her desire for revenge. Even Nate finds his own dark path in his disordered love for status and respect. In Season 3, we also see a disordered collective love, centered on Zava. In this instance, the team seems to think the Russian phenom will save their season, but in fact, the redemptive arc does not begin until the team learns to play without him.

A challenge to an Augustinian analysis of *Ted Lasso* is that Augustine's philosophy was painstakingly theocentric. For Augustine, without a proper love of God, even our most noble and selfless intentions can become disordered. In the opening paragraph of his *Confessions*—a spiritual autobiography written as a form of prayer—Augustine describes humans as restless creatures. He proclaims to God, "You have made us for yourself, and our heart is restless until it rests in you."[5] Without God, by Augustine's lights, when one desire fails to deliver on its promise to make us happy, we wander "restlessly" to the next.

Augustine saw *liturgy*, a ritualized form of public worship, as a way to train and transform the heart so that it desires God and God's will above all other desires. For this reason, the contemporary philosopher James K. A. Smith urges us to think about our seemingly banal routines as cultural liturgies that shape our desires and order them toward some ultimate intention. One only need observe the religious language ("church," "pray," "transubstantiation," "collection plate") used to describe Roy's favorite kebab shop to get a sense of how important our routines can be. Smith argues that "thick" ritual practices (like sports) constitute liturgies because of their ability to "inscribe" a vision of the good life onto our hearts.[6] In this way, professional sports are extremely formative liturgies. At bottom, highly competitive sport can inculcate a desire to win that reorders our entire lives.

The pub-crawling trio—Paul, Baz, and Jeremy—are the perfect representatives of a large swath of sports fanatics who live and die by the success of their team. Week in and week out they adorn themselves with special attire and gather in droves at houses, pubs, and stadiums to begin the opening ceremonies. There is a rhythm to their practice: a time to sit and stand, to scream, to sing, to embrace others around you, to celebrate, and to mourn. Keeley has memorized it, even though she never really cared for football herself. Still, she knows "how to act at a match," including when to dub a referee a turnip ("The Hope That Kills You"). Through these rituals, we learn to hope (or not to hope) in a highly anticipated future. That future is an image of victory—of the good life—that is "willing to make room for *additional* loyalties, but it is not willing to entertain *trumping* loyalties."[7]

This image is never just about sports. It includes a wide range of narratives that define what it means to be fully human. Writing on the tight coupling between winning and national identity in capitalist societies, Hugh Mackay once observed of Australia, his home country:

> Our sporting impulse encourages us to think about economic growth or globalization, or industrial relations reform, in terms of winning; our spiritual impulse drives us to think about equity, fairness, and justice, and about the impact of our success on the poor, disadvantaged, the marginalized. In a culture that almost deifies competition, the sporting urge prevails most of the time.[8]

What better image of this in *Ted Lasso* than the ideological clash between Cerithium Oil and Sam's civic identity as a Nigerian? ("Do the Right-est Thing"). By protesting Dubai Air, his club's sponsor, Sam challenges the longstanding virtues and values embedded in one of England's richest cultural liturgies. These moral assumptions are also embodied in Edwin Akufo, whose unbridled capitalistic ambition is certainly a disordered love. Sam's moral courage in the face of Dubai Air and Akufo shows that without a more transcendent narrative, outcomes—on the field or in the market—become disordered as an ultimate concern.

When winning becomes an ultimate concern, the liturgy of competitive sport reinforces the myth that our worth and value stem from what we are able to produce, rather than an inherent human dignity that we all share. In Augustine's tradition, the tendency to find one's value in a sub-ultimate good, like athletic success, is a form of idolatry. Though not everyone would describe this tendency in those terms, the negative effects are obvious. Take Roy's initial inability to come to terms with his retirement. This phenomenon, known by social scientists as *identity foreclosure*, is prevalent in highly competitive athletes when they reach the end of their career.[9] Without counter-liturgies to remind us of our worth and value, we are extremely dependent on relationships with other people who can remind us of these truths.

Saints and Scamps

Augustine was well aware of the influence that others can have on us. In his *Confessions*, he recalls a friend, Alypius, who allowed others' disordered love for the violent spectacle of Roman gladiatorial games to draw him in. Alypius arrived in Rome with an aversion to these games, but "[h]is friends and fellow students whom he chanced to meet as they were returning from dinner, in spite of the fact that he strongly objected and resisted them, dragged him with friendly force into the amphitheater on a day for these cruel and deadly games."[10] Not only did Alypius become a willing participant in this activity. He also became one who, like his friends, recruited others to join.

The lesson here is that ordering loves always takes place in community. To some extent, the character of the individual will start to resemble the character of the communities they become a part of. Other chapters in this volume explore the influence of coaches and peers in some form or fashion as one illustration. The example here is a different relationship: fathers and father figures.

The pain of an absent father is a common Hollywood trope, and one that *Ted Lasso* employs on a variety of levels. The theme is so pervasive it can even be seen in the appearance of John Wingsnight, Rebecca's underwhelming date in "Goodbye Earl." During their outing with Roy and Keeley, John mentions Roy's retirement speech, noting: "It's the first time my father's forwarded me an email in the last five years that wasn't about the scourge of immigration. And that really meant a lot to me, so thank you." This universal longing of a son for a connection with his father fuels most cinematic takes on the father-son relationship (including my personal favorite, *October Sky*).

Sadly, in *Ted Lasso* this longing often goes unsatisfied. Nate's development from timidity to overconfidence makes sense only in light of his father's reluctance to offer encouragement and affirmation. His arc also shows the ease with which the right amount of love can, by quick turns, be missed by either excess or deficiency in the same person. This theme is especially prominent in Jamie's development. During the de-ghosting ceremony in "Two Aces," he finally reveals the neglect of his father as the root of his behavior. Toward the end of the first season, and later in the second, we get a graphic picture of this reality when we meet the abrasive and abusive James Tartt and witness his impoverished moral character. It is suddenly easy to imagine how Jamie became the way he presents himself throughout most of the show. Deprived of the unconditional love of their fathers, both Nate and Jamie look for ways to fill the void.

We also see several positive examples of fatherhood in the show, the most obvious of which might be Ted's love for his own son, despite their painful physical distance (4,438 miles to be precise). Or the relationship between Sam Obisanya and his dad. The first hint of this relationship appears before Richmond's first game against Crystal Palace during a surprise birthday celebration for Sam. In a brief endearing moment with Ted, Sam recalls a memory of his father sparked by Ted's kindness toward him (that Jamie scoffs at). In Season 2, Sam's father reappears to reprimand Sam for his involvement with Dubai Air, and, by extension, Cerithium Oil. In this exchange, Sam's father is teaching a valuable lesson about what really constitutes the good life, and his disappointment in Sam is not connected to his performance, but his priorities. This is evident in a later phone call between Sam and his father in "Man City," near the end of Season 2. Sam's father expresses how proud he is of Sam and ends the call with a heartfelt "I love you." The director again calls attention to Jamie's disappointment and jealousy upon overhearing the conversation.

What we learn from these examples is that, in the face of cultural liturgies that conflate winning and worth, fathers have an outsized ability to help young men order their loves. Good fathers teach their sons to be a part of something larger than themselves. The great ones teach their sons to look beyond sports and toward something more ultimate. C. S. Lewis (1898–1963) echoed this sentiment when describing his mentor, George MacDonald (1824–1905): "An almost perfect relationship with his father was the earthly root of all his wisdom. From his own father … he first learned that Fatherhood must be at the core of the universe."[11]

Ted Lasso: The Father We Never Had

Like Jamie and Nate, Augustine didn't have much of a father growing up. Augustine's father, Patricius, sported a history of alcoholism, abuse, and infidelity before his late conversion to faith on his deathbed. Augustine was only seventeen years old when his father died, but he found a father figure in Saint Ambrose, the bishop of Milan, who was a fierce advocate for the church against the heresies of the day. Ambrose nurtured Augustine into the formidable philosopher and theologian he eventually became, but it began with a kindness and compassion that drew Augustine in. There's the family we're born with and the family we gain along the way.

Ambrose was a father figure to Augustine in a similar way that Ted acts as a father figure to his athletes. What is most striking about

Ted is his lack of regard for the one thing that most other characters in the show value above anything else: winning. Years of engaging in the formative liturgy of soccer had trained the Richmond team to reject Ted for his demeanor and attitude toward the sport. Slowly, though, Ted wins their affections through a relentless and thorough-going kindness that all children long to receive from their fathers.

The parallel between the father-son and coach-athlete relationships is most evident during Ted and Roy's conversation at the kebab shop in "Rainbow." The store owner mistakenly takes Ted and Roy as father and son. When Ted clarifies that he is Roy's former coach, the distinction is brushed off: "It's all the same thing." The interaction prompts the owner to reflect on his relationship with his own father, which echoes a similar dynamic between Ted and Roy. Ted notices potential in Roy that all good fathers recognize in their own sons, and he gently and lovingly guides Roy to see what he sees.

Fathers and father figures play a central role in the ordering of loves throughout the show. Just as Ted is a father figure to Roy in Season 2, Roy assumes a similar role for Jamie in Season 3. When the pair go out for a beer in "So Long, Farewell," Jaime tells Roy: "Thank you for your help too, you know. For motivating me, encouraging me. I haven't really had that from the older men in me life." In the same way, the mended relationship between Nathan and his father is the catalyst for the Wonder Kid's redemption in the final season. In both of these instances, the presence of a father figure helped the characters reorder their loves and loyalties in a way that helped them, and the Richmond club, flourish.

In the last analysis, Augustine would not much approve of the commercialized and politicized nature of sport as portrayed in *Ted Lasso*. He would likely be repulsed at the vanity and vulgarity of it all. At the same time, Augustine would be fascinated by the coach-athlete relationship as a vehicle to care for the fatherless. Because of his openness to something transcendent, Augustine might well smile down on coaches like Ted Lasso. Indeed, he understood how the love of an earthly father can open a child's eyes to deeper truths.

Notes

1 Although I will be drawing directly from St. Augustine in this analysis, the works of contemporary philosopher and Augustine interpreter James K. A. Smith have also greatly influenced my own thoughts in this chapter.

2   Proma Khosla, "Everyone's an MVP in Heartwarming 'Ted Lasso' Season 2," *Mashable*, July, 23 2021, at https://mashable.com/article/ted-lasso-season-2-review-apple-tv.

3   Augustine, *Teaching Christianity* or *De Doctrina Christiana*, trans. Edmund Hill (New York: New City Press, 1996), 118.

4   Augustine, *Confessions*, trans. John K. Ryan (New York: Doubleday, 1960), 341.

5   Ibid., 43.

6   James K. A. Smith, *Desiring the Kingdom* (Grand Rapids: Baker Publishers, 2009), 82–83.

7   Ibid., 106–107, emphasis original.

8   Hugh Mackay, *Turning Point: Australians Choosing Their Future* (Sydney: Pan Macmillan Australia, 1999), 234–235.

9   Britton W. Brewer and Albert J. Petitpas, "Athletic Identity Foreclosure," *Current Opinion in Psychology* 16 (2017), 118–122.

10   Augustine, *Confessions*, 144.

11   C.S. Lewis, *George MacDonald: An Anthology* (New York: HarperCollins, 2009), xxiii.

2

Isaac Finds His Flow

Elizabeth Schiltz

One of the most iconic moments in *Ted Lasso* occurs in the episode "Man City," when Sam requests, and receives, his once-a-season "Isaac cut."

The team gathers in hushed anticipation as the strains of "La Virgen de la Macarena" swell and Isaac readies his clippers. The mood, however, shifts into joyous appreciation as Isaac begins to demonstrate his skill. He seems to have a deeply intuitive sense of where and how to cut, and he carries out his work with a flourish and rhythm that matches the glorious Mahalia Jackson's "Down by the Riverside" playing in the background. The Greyhounds erupt into cheers, applause, and laughter at every exquisite sweep of the clippers and snip of the scissors. Even an initially skeptical Jan Maas can't resist an enthusiastic response. As Colin says: "It's like Swan Lake!"

This is indeed a thrilling scene, one that represents both an important moment in Isaac's character arc and a significant signal in the development of a unified AFC Richmond. At the beginning of Season 1, we meet Isaac as part of the gang who harass a defenseless Nate to amuse a smirking Jamie Tartt. By the end of Season 2, he is the artful captain whose gentle tap on the "Believe" sign inspires our Greyhounds to a rebound against AFC Brentford, and to a promotion back to the Premier League. How should we think about this transition? How does Isaac's mastery with his clippers reflect his developing approach to soccer—and life? What does this approach signal for his leadership of our team?

Our beloved team captain is certainly exceptional, but there are classical antecedents for his character, development, and skill. Consider

Ted Lasso and Philosophy: No Question Is Into Touch, First Edition.
Edited by Marybeth Baggett and David Baggett.

this description of a masterful butcher from the 4th century BC
Daoist philosopher Zhuangzi:

> Wherever his hand touched, wherever his shoulder leaned, wherever
> his foot stepped, wherever his knee pushed—with a zip! With a
> whoosh!—he handled his chopper with aplomb, and never skipped a
> beat. He moved in time to the "Dance of the Mulberry Forest," and
> harmonized with the "Head of the Line Symphony." Lord Wenhui said,
> "Ah excellent, that technique can reach such heights!"[1]

This chapter will argue that we can usefully understand Isaac's character arc in terms of an ongoing development of his Daoist sensibilities. Further, Isaac's virtuosity—as a barber, player, and leader—reflects
the potential utility of a kind of Zhuangzist approach to the world.

The *Dao* of Isaac

Isaac, like Zhuangzi, is an original.

Isaac is a unique presence on the Richmond team. Ted's first, astonished assessment is a good one: Isaac is truly a "Rodin sculpture in
cleats." He combines physical and skilled defensive work with a keen
understanding of the game in such a way as to allow him to play a
key role in the Greyhounds' success. In "The Signal," it is Isaac who
organizes the team into "parking the bus," and so sets the stage for
the Tottenham error that leads the Greyhounds to a thrilling FA Cup
quarterfinals win. In "The Hope that Kills You," Isaac's quick assessment of the opportunity created by an extra time free kick—and his
spontaneous organization of the team into the "Lasso Special" trick
play—garners the crucial equalizer. In "So Long, Farewell," it is
Isaac's "superhuman foot" that sends the penalty kick through the
net, and sets our Greyhounds up for a glorious victory over Rupert
and West Ham.

In similar ways, Zhuangzi is an atypical philosopher. The text that
purports to present his thinking, called the *Zhuangzi*, stands out
among the works in the philosophical canon.[2] Instead of straightfor-
ward theses or systematic essays, the *Zhuangzi* confronts us with fantastical beasts, silly stories, cheeky conversations, and mystifying
claims, expecting us to draw our own philosophical conclusions. The
text also introduces us to Zhuangzi himself. We see Zhuangzi puzzling,
perplexing, and disorienting those he meets, and, by extension, his
readers as well. His singular style is all to the good, however. As Roger

Ames asserts, the *Zhuangzi* is "one of the finest pieces of literature in the classical Chinese corpus ... an object lesson in marshaling every trope and literary device available to provide rhetorically charged flashes of insight into the most creative way to live one's life in the world."[3]

Isaac and Zhuangzi don't just share an originality in their vocations. They also have some important personal characteristics in common. Both seem utterly candid in their responses to events and people, and are not at all bothered at the prospect of appearing silly or confounding expectations as a result. Think, for example, of "Two Aces," where we see Isaac's honest reaction to learning both about the ghosts in the training room, and about Ted's surprising plans to honor them. That look of genuine puzzlement finds its analogue in Zhuangzi's response to a dream about being a happy butterfly—which has left him unsure whether he is Zhuangzi awakening from a dream that he was a butterfly or is a butterfly now dreaming he is Zhuangzi. In the same way, Zhuangzi, whose friends were astounded to find him beating on a tub and singing during what should have been a period of mourning, could surely have appreciated Isaac's star turn as an unconventional Santa in a magnificent red velour suit in "The Carol of the Bells".

In addition, both Isaac and Zhuangzi are kind to others and deeply responsive to their individual qualities and needs. They are often particularly attentive to those whose status is lower than their own. While Isaac initially picked on Nate, the team's timid kit man, we see him quickly develop care and compassion for him. By the fifth episode of the series, we find him silently making room for a surprised Nate on the team bench, and then carefully carrying the inebriated kit man out of a karaoke bar. Further, in "Make Rebecca Great Again," he gently encourages Nate to deliver his pre-game speech. The speech, as it turns out, inspires the team to a long-awaited victory over Everton. In a similar way, the *Zhuangzi* provides sympathetic, philosophical portraits of many who might not have been esteemed by society, such as the invalid, the amputee, and the "Out-of-Step Woman." This attention, too, is both meritorious and valuable. In their recent *New York Times* editorial, "Was This Ancient Taoist the First Philosopher of Disability?" John Altmann and Bryan Van Norden argue that "Zhuangzi is an important and insightful guide ... to challenge our conventional notions of flourishing and health."[4]

The commonalities go deeper. Isaac and Zhuangzi also have a similar approach to the world: both avoid unnecessary complexity. As a player and as a person, Isaac seems to focus on one thing at a time. He is utterly dedicated to the success of the team, and, when, as in "The

Diamond Dogs," he is pushed to name another thing he likes, he names "Rolos … Just Rolos, yeah." Isaac's speech is always direct and brief. He is a man who will not give a long speech when a "You've got this bruv" will work. In fact, he will not use any words at all when an angry expression or chair through a TV will make his point just as well. He is also completely without guile. As we learn in "La Locker Room Aux Folles," he is transparent in a way that renders him incapable of keeping secrets. He is forthright to a fault.

Zhuangzi reflects a similar mistrust of complexity. His commitments do not involve Rolos, but rather the single and ultimate *dao*. Alas, this is a slightly more abstruse concept, one that has developed in multifarious ways. The word "*dao*" initially referred to a road or path. In early Chinese thought, however, its meaning expanded from a reference to actual paths or "ways," to a "way" the world is.[5] This *dao* is not static, though. Like the world, it is constantly changing. As the earlier Daoist philosopher Laozi put it: the Way is like water, "flowing to the left and the right."[6]

The idea that there is a *dao,* then, was not unique to Zhuangzi. Many Chinese philosophers sought to describe both this "Way," and how we can best live in accord with it. The Confucians, for instance, encouraged the thoughtful and appropriate participation in traditional arts, rites, rituals, and properly hierarchical relationships as a means of achieving harmony with "the Way." The *Analects* show Confucius engaged in deep conversations about the utility of these means for our development of crucial virtues such as benevolence and righteousness. As such, the text points us towards a particular style of human life: "The Master said, Set your heart on the *dao*, base yourself in virtue, rely on benevolence, journey in the arts."[7]

Zhuangzi, however, develops the idea of the *dao* in a different and fascinating way. In the text that bears his name, we see him suggest that this *dao* is not human, but natural. Further, while it is conceptually linked to "Heaven," he insists that it is inherent in our world: "Where is this so-called Way?" A question he quickly answers: "There's nowhere it isn't."[8]

Of course, if, like Roy Kent, the *dao* is here, there, and everywhere, we don't need to employ extensive analysis or ornate procedures to access it. Indeed, insofar as language relies on drawing fixed distinctions between things, it is hard to see how it could capture the flowing *dao*. Even worse, since language is a complex human innovation, engaging in lengthy elaborations and detailed discussions may well serve to lead us away from the simplicity and naturalness of the *dao*.

Instead, the *Zhuangzi* suggests a process of forgetting all of that. Ted's goldfish has nothing on our new friends:

> Yan Hui said, "I'm improving."
> Kongzi said, "How so?"
> "I've forgotten benevolence and righteousness."
> "Good, but there's more."
> Yan Hui saw him again the next day and said, "I'm improving."
> "How so?"
> "I've forgotten rites and music."
> "Good, but there's more."
> Yan Hui saw him again the next day and said, "I'm improving."
> "How so?"
> "I sit and forget ... leave my form, abandon knowledge, and unify them in the great comprehension."[9]

I am, of course, not suggesting that Isaac is a student of Zhuangzi's Daoism, though who knows? The man is a mystery. The suggestion is simply that Isaac reflects the kind of Daoist sensibility we have been discussing. One can imagine Isaac as just the person Zhuangzi is looking for:

> A snare is for rabbits: when you've got the rabbit, you can forget the snare. Words are for meaning: when you've got the meaning, you can forget the words. Where can I find someone who's forgotten words so I can have a word with him?[10]

Isaac, like Zhuangzi, is about the meaning, not the words. Further: we can understand our captain's character arc in terms of a continuing development of his Daoist sensibilities.

"Do without Ado," McAdoo!

Of course, the ultimate point of the *Zhuangzi* isn't to present and defend a view of "the Way." Instead, all of these stories and suggestions aim at poking and prodding us into figuring out how we, as individuals, can best live in accord with the flowing *dao*. To that end, Daoist thinkers introduce a new and challenging suggestion: we should engage in *wu-wei*, or "effortless" action.[11]

Think about it like this: sometimes, when we try very hard at something, we get in our own way, and end up failing even more spectacularly than if we hadn't tried at all. Remember, for instance, in "Midnight Train to Royston," when Nate demonstrates to Keeley and Rebecca how he would confidently request a window table for his parents' anniversary. His earnest attempts to communicate assertiveness, as it turned out, communicated exactly the opposite. Even worse, succeeding through determined effort would be doubly challenging if what we were trying to do was to live in accord with the flowing *dao*: all of our human effort, concentration, and studied practice would actually work *against* our goal of going with the flow of nature. We would, in fact, be much better served by not trying, by forgetting all of that, and intuitively reacting to circumstances.

This, then, is the sage ideal that Daoists characterize as *wu-wei*. While the Confucian thinkers emphasize *wei*, or "deliberate effort" "to pattern [human nature] and order it and make it exalted,"[12] our Daoist friend Laozi suggests that we should "act without action, do without ado."[13] For his part, Zhuangzi emphasizes spontaneous—and often playful and mischievous—responses to circumstances: don't overthink it, don't try to force it, and don't take yourself too seriously. He highlights the behavior of a charming group of unconventional friends, instead: "Bemused, they wander about beyond the dirt and dust and play at the business of effortless action."[14] As Ted tells the team in "Smells Like Mean Spirit," "Guys, all we gotta do is remember to stay connected to one another and let anything we don't need flow right through."

While Isaac demonstrates a natural, Daoist sensibility, in "Rainbow" we find that he has lost his way. Chris Kamara observes, with uncanny accuracy, that Isaac has become "a shadow of himself." It's not, of course, that Isaac isn't trying to play well, but yelling "We need to stop playing like shit!" at his teammates isn't the most effective strategy. The Greyhound coaches notice, too. Ted describes Isaac as "a wigwam in a teepee," too tense. While Roy is not generally noted for his relaxed, whimsical approach to life, he here gives the proper Daoist diagnosis: "He's all up in his head, isn't he?"

Interestingly, it's also Roy who provides the right prescription: a night of no-stakes pickup games with players from his own old neighborhood. Isaac initially displays a properly Confucian resistance to playing with amateurs. However, Roy pushes him back toward *wu-wei* as only he can. In a truly epic rant, Roy not-so-gently encourages Isaac to forget his overthinking, and get back to treating soccer as a game that is played for fun. The plan works. By the end, Isaac is simply reacting to the game, playing with abandon, and celebrating with joy. Who can forget his funky, chicken-themed dance moves, especially when paired with Ted's appreciative call for the ages: "McAdoodle doo!"

Isaac has moved from *deliberate effort* to *effortless action*, and freed himself from his overly tense and rigid approach to soccer. We soon see Isaac laughing, dancing, and exchanging silly handshakes with his teammates. We can all agree with Kamara that "it's good to see McAdoo with a smile on his face!" This relaxed approach clearly affects the rest of the team as well. The commentators are soon noting the team's remarkable turnaround, and our Greyhounds find themselves in a position to make a run at promotion back to the Premier League.

Barbers, Butchers, and Football Players, or "Football Is Life!"

Wu-wei doesn't just make things more fun. According to Daoists, it also manifests in a state of wisdom that confers a kind of skillful ability to respond appropriately to our circumstances. As the series progresses, we see that Isaac isn't just able to buoy the team's collective spirits. Importantly, our captain is also increasingly able to respond skillfully and effectively to a range of difficult situations.

As it turns out, this is one way of understanding the pair of portraits with which we started. What, exactly, allows Isaac and the butcher to ply their crafts so masterfully? The butcher explains, "What your servant values is the Way, which goes beyond technique." It's not just that our virtuosos know how to ply their tools or what an optimal cut would look like, although both surely do. It's rather that certain masters can achieve a harmony with the *dao* that allows them to wield those tools in such a way as to work effortlessly *with*, rather than *against*, the conditions that confront them. As the butcher has it: "I rely on the Heavenly patterns, strike in the big gaps, am guided by the large fissures, and follow what is inherently so."[15]

Zhuangzi frequently points to craftsmen, like our butcher, as exemplars of this *wu-wei* in action. However, it is intriguing to note that soccer is also a particularly apt arena in which to demonstrate *wu-wei*. Unlike certain other sports, the game of soccer itself requires skillful and flowing response to the events that unfold on the field. Kind of like Total Football. While our Greyhounds practice foot skills, build fitness, and implement strategies, many of their best moments of play require employing these techniques in the moment, on the field, in free-flowing, intuitive response to conditions as they present themselves.

Of course, Zhuangzi's concern isn't just with skilled craftspeople, and we aren't only concerned with talented barbers and soccer players. As the impressed Lord Wenhui responds to the ox-cutting demonstration: "Excellent! I have heard the words of a butcher and learned how to care for life!"[16] What Zhuangzi is suggesting is not just that we should work, but also that we should *live* in harmony with the *dao*. As Philip Ivanhoe explains, Zhuangzi is describing exemplars who "follow the hidden seams deep in the pattern of nature and by so doing are able to lead highly effective yet frictionless lives. Such individuals accord with rather than collide with the things and events they encounter in life and manage to pass through them all without incurring or causing harm."[17]

Perhaps Dani Rojas is right: football really *is* life.

How to Cook a Small Fish

Our developing Daoist isn't just any player or sage, however. He is also our Greyhound captain. As such, we might worry that Isaac's Daoist sensibility doesn't lend itself to effective leadership. Indeed, the *Zhuangzi* itself is ambivalent about even engaging in governance at all. The text, for example, includes a (quite funny) account of the time that the king sent for Zhuangzi to "administer his kingdom." Zhuangzi surprises the king's emissaries by asking about the shell of a long-dead turtle, kept by the king for sacred rituals: "Would that turtle rather have its bones treasured in death, or be alive dragging its tail in the mud?... Go! I'll keep my tail in the mud, too."[18]

For his part, Laozi seems less conflicted about leadership. He sketches out a vision of Daoist governance, which, as you might expect, is decidedly of the "less-is-more" variety. On the one hand, Confucius had emphasized the role of a leader as an active moral exemplar: "If you guide them with Virtue, and keep them in line by means of ritual, the people will have a sense of shame and will rectify themselves."[19] On the other hand, Laozi suggests that a good leader refrains from the kind of deliberate activity that attempts to impose an order that diverges from the Way. He memorably asserts: "Ruling a great state is like cooking a small fish"—too much interference causes trouble. Rather, the spontaneous responses of a Daoist leader allow the people to develop naturally and act intuitively:

> The greatest of rulers is but a shadowy presence ...
> [The greatest rulers] are cautious and speak but rarely.
> When their task is done and work complete,
> Their people all say, "This is just how we are."[20]

As Sam Crane characterizes it, the Daoist approach suggests that a leader "should not impose a preferred result or force a specified option. Rather, the leader's role is to facilitate whatever possibilities inhere in a specific context."[21]

Unsurprisingly, most of the Chinese emperors tended toward the Confucian approach. Beginning in the 2nd century BC, they prioritized the study of Confucianism in the training and selection of government officials. However, Seasons 2 and 3 of *Ted Lasso* shows that our developing Daoist demonstrates a seemingly effortless and intuitive response to challenges that is a strength rather than a weakness for the team. Few of us would envy the plight of a captain who had to respond to a team member's noble—but potentially disastrous—decision to tape over the team sponsor's name on his jersey, as Sam did in "Do the Right-est Thing." Isaac, however, seamlessly works *with*, instead of *against*, the moment. He wordlessly leads his teammates into an honorable and good-hearted show of solidarity that issues in a genuine improvement in both the team and the world.

In the same way, in "No Weddings and a Funeral," Isaac provides a spontaneous and appropriate response to news of the death of Rebecca's father. We could all imagine a captain carefully weighing the relative value of supporting the team owner against resting the team at a crucial point in its season—or at least carefully considering whether or not to subject their feet to the abject horrors of dress shoes. Isaac's response demonstrates that he intuitively understands both the importance of the situation and the significance of such a gesture. And, of course, he is right. Upon seeing the team arrive at the funeral, Rebecca is astonished to note that "none of them are wearing trainers!" She surely understands the import of the action even before Higgins explains: "That's how much they care about you."

Still, it's possible to admire Isaac's deftness in facilitating appropriate responses to challenging situations, while at the same time wondering if it is apt to produce a Greyhound team that can actually win soccer games. It's all well and good to hold that a Daoist leader "should not impose a preferred result" when, say, the decision is about how to spend a free evening in Amsterdam. But this is a Premier League soccer team. A captain's job is to pursue pre-established markers of success. This, of course, mirrors the puzzle at the heart of the show: Is the goal of AFC Richmond to produce good people, or to win games?

We know where Coach Lasso stands. As he explains to an incredulous Trent Crimm, he doesn't measure success in terms of wins and losses. But in "All Apologies," Beard reminds us that they aren't in Kansas anymore: "Those were kids and these are professionals and

winning does matter to them. And it matters to me. And that's okay."
Losing has real repercussions, both for individual careers, and for the
team as a whole. Beard argues that, ultimately, failing to prioritize
winning is a kind of imposed preference in its own right: "If you
wanna pick a player's feelings over a coach's duty to make a point....
Well, I don't want to drink with someone that selfish."

As it turns out, the Richmond Way involves subverting these
conventional distinctions altogether. Isaac shows that we don't need
to be constrained by such rigid divisions or false dichotomies. By marshaling the personal and professional potentials of his team, Isaac's
quasi-Daoist leadership enables them to form a cohesive unit and
thread the needle between seemingly disparate goals. To put it another
way, Isaac shows the Greyhounds how to kick right through the net.

Notes

1 *The Zhuangzi*, trans. Paul Kjellberg, in *Readings in Classical Chinese Philosophy*, edited by Philip J. Ivanhoe and Bryan W. Van Norden (Indianapolis: Hackett Publishing, 2001), 3.
2 How much of the *Zhuangzi* is the handiwork of Zhuangzi himself is a matter of scholarly debate. The tradition often distinguishes between the text's first seven or "inner" chapters, which are thought to have been actually written by Zhuangzi, and the text's remaining "outer" and "miscellaneous" chapters, which are thought to have been added by his followers.
3 Roger Ames, *Wandering at Ease in the Zhuangzi* (Albany: State University of New York, 1998), 1.
4 John Altmann and Bryan Van Norden, "Was This Ancient Taoist the First Philosopher of Disability?" *New York Times*, July 8, 2020.
5 Paul Kjellberg, "Introduction to The *Zhuangzi*," in *Readings in Classical Chinese Philosophy*, edited by Philip J. Ivanhoe and Bryan W. Van Norden (Indianapolis: Hackett Publishing, 2001), 208.
6 Laozi, The *Daodejing*, trans. Philip J. Ivanhoe, in *Readings in Classical Chinese Philosophy*, edited by Philip J. Ivanhoe and Bryan W. Van Norden (Indianapolis: Hackett Publishing, 2001), 78, 34.
7 Confucius, *The Analects*, trans. Robert Eno, 7.6, available at https://chinatxt.sitehost.iu.edu/Analects_of_Confucius_(Eno-2015).pdf. I sub-stitute the English "benevolence" for the original "*ren*."
8 The *Zhuangzi*, 22.
9 The *Zhuangzi*, 6.
10 The *Zhuangzi*, 26.
11 While this concept is often translated as "nonaction," I here follow Slingerland and Eno's felicitous rendering of it as "effortless action."

12   Xunzi, *The Complete Text*, trans. Eric L. Hutton (Princeton: Princeton University Press, 2014), XIX.

13   *Daodejing*, 63.

14   The *Zhuangzi*, 6. To preserve consistency, I here again substitute Eno's "effortless action" for Kjellberg's "nonaction."

15   The *Zhuangzi*, 3.

16   The *Zhuangzi*, 3.

17   Philip J. Ivanhoe, "Zhuangzi on Skepticism, Skill, and the Ineffable Dao," *Journal of the American Academy of Religion* 61 (1993): 643–644.

18   The *Zhuangzi*, 17.

19   Confucius, The *Analects*, trans. Edward Gilman Slingerland, in *Readings in Classical Chinese Philosophy*, edited by Philip J. Ivanhoe and Bryan W. Van Norden (Indianapolis: Hackett Publishing, 2001), 2.3.

20   *Daodejing*, 17. For clarity, I substitute Eno's "speak but rarely" for Kjellberg's "honor words."

21   Sam Crane, *Life, Liberty, and the Pursuit of Dao* (Hoboken: Wiley & Sons Inc., 2013), 162.

3

Ted Talk, Precursive Faith, and the Ethics of Belief

David Baggett

Like a candy bar little Ronnie Fouch offers you on the playground, *Ted Lasso* is so much more than meets the eye. But in a good way. This is definitely a treat you'll want to eat, but it's not mere junk food. For a show so easy to watch, usually light and lots of fun, it contains enough food for thought you'll think you had two entrees. An important example is the way Ted believes in people. Indeed, belief is a central motif of the show and a wonderfully rich philosophical concept.

Belief in Belief

Ted Lasso is a believer. He believes in belief, hopes in hope. Rather than tending toward doubt, Ted's default is belief, belief in all sorts of things. Even spirit guides and aliens. When asked if he believes in ghosts, he affirms that he does, though adding it's more important "they believe in themselves." Rebecca's stymied response of incomprehension and incredulity is priceless.

Of course this is a joke, but a telling one. Ted shifts there from *believing that*, propositional knowledge, to *believing in*, which includes but goes beyond the factual. To believe in something calls to mind a positive disposition, an expectation of good things, for the believer and for others. Without being blind to corruption or cruelty, Ted is adamant about believing in the best of people, making him relentless in his kindness and resilient in the face of opposition. From the start Ted shows a positive expectation for winning, success, and

Ted Lasso and Philosophy: No Question Is Into Touch, First Edition.
Edited by Marybeth Baggett and David Baggett.
© 2024 John Wiley & Sons, Inc. Published 2024 by John Wiley & Sons, Inc.

good results. Unfazed by Roy's disdain, he tells Beard, "If he's mad now, wait until we win him over" ("Pilot"). Winning in one form or another—winning games, winning even if outscored, winning over people—is Ted's default attitude.

Even the posters Ted prominently displays on his office walls herald success in the face of daunting odds. Muhammed Ali's iconic knock-out of Sonny Liston in the rematch after the underdog defeated the seasoned champion in their first bout. The 1980 "Miracle on Ice" in which the US Men's Hockey team defeated the heavily favored Soviet squad. Jimmy Valvano's 1983 NC State surprise win over Houston in the NCAA Men's Tournament, one of the greatest upsets in college basketball history. And James Buster Douglas's 1990 David-versus-Goliath knockout of Mike Tyson.

Ted envisions winning, cultivates a positive attitude of expectancy, and anticipates success—in games and in his relationships with his players. He recognizes that in order to win, or at least to have a real-istic shot at winning, we typically need to be able to envision victory clearly and distinctly, to cop a phrase from Descartes (1596–1650).

Ted combines unrelenting optimism with a self-help regimen of envisioning the possible. Watching him is a little like watching Mister Rogers as a soccer coach, an intentional decision by Jason Sudeikis. Roy coaching little girls not so much, especially with pesky concerns about brain development and all. From the first episode, the impor-tance of believing in oneself is on full display with Ted's quiet self-assurance and laudable courage in the face of chronic condescen-sion and a chorus of derogatory epithets.

Ted's resilient and charming optimism might be thought to err on the side of credulity, if not wishful thinking. It's practically Pollyannaish, some might think, and intellectually irresponsible for Ted's convictions to go beyond the available evidence. His faith might be thought of as vision impaired, if not downright blind. Let's consider such a case.

The Ethics of Belief

In "The Ethics of Belief," an article famous for being almost famous, the mathematician and philosopher W. K. Clifford (1845–1879) advocates for an "evidentialist" conviction: One should believe only those propositions that there's sufficient evidence for.[1] On this analy-sis, the strength of one's beliefs should match the amount of evidence for its truth. Propositions without enough evidence should not be believed at all.

Imagine a shipowner is about to send a ship to sea. He knows that she's old and often needs repairs. Doubts about her seaworthiness prey on his mind until he succeeds in overcoming them by rationalizing his way into believing she's ready. By dint of effort he acquires a comfortable conviction that his vessel is safe and seaworthy. He watches her departure with a light heart and benevolent wishes for her success. Then collects his insurance money when she goes down mid-ocean and tells no tales.

The shipowner has no right to his belief, however strong the belief is. Clifford's takeaway is simple: "It is wrong always, everywhere, and for anyone, to believe anything upon insufficient evidence."[2] Imagine someone holding a belief he was taught in childhood or that he acquired later. He pushes away any doubts about it, purposely avoiding any books or conversations that call it into question. He regards as impious any challenges to it. "The life of that man," writes Clifford, "is one long sin against mankind."[3]

Ted's reticence to admit Dr. Sharon's preternatural effectiveness as a therapist. Jamie's hardened conviction, contrary to most appearances, that Ted had done him wrong in his transfer back to Man City. Nate's indignation and insolence over Ted's "mistreatment" of him. Beard thinking Jane's the right person for him despite ample evidence—and Higgins's frankness—that suggest otherwise. All of these are examples of potentially bad beliefs that result from neglect of available evidence.

As tempting as it is to think such examples fall outside the scope of Clifford's point, he would insist that even the Richmond fans imbibing and pontificating at The Crown & Anchor are required to consider the evidence. "It is not only the leader of men, statesmen, philosopher, or poet, that owes this bounden duty to mankind. Every rustic who delivers in the village alehouse his slow, infrequent sentences, may help to kill or keep alive the fatal superstitions which clog his race."[4]

Attending to the relevant evidence is vital. We have a rational responsibility to follow the evidence where it leads and not to go beyond it. We should carefully apportion the strength of our beliefs to the quality of the evidence, at least to the extent we're able. Failure to do so can be disastrous. Even when it isn't, our failure is still blameworthy. Lucking out doesn't absolve us of responsibility.

Notice that Clifford's point is not just about a logical or intellectual duty to pay attention to the evidence. The suggestion is that there is also an *ethical* duty at play here. We have a moral responsibility to be attentive to the evidence. To drive home this point, Clifford uses nothing less than the rhetorically thick category of "sin" to describe the failure to do so.

Precursive Faith

Some might suppose that *believing in* another person, or a particular outcome, or oneself, is more a psychological matter than a philosophical one, but this is a false dichotomy. The great American philosopher William James (1842–1910), for example, often shares insights with both philosophical and psychological import. Might James help vindicate Ted?

In his discussion of "precursive faith," James challenges Clifford's notion that all of our beliefs need to be based on adequate prior evidence.[5] Precursive faith, as he understands it, involves believing *ahead of* the evidence. Such belief, or faith, bears an uncanny resemblance to Ted's irrepressible optimism. James would agree with Clifford that the shipowner was wrong and irresponsible, but not every case of belief is the same. In some cases, belief that exceeds or goes beyond the evidence is permissible, even important.

Such cases require certain conditions to be satisfied. To begin with, the decision in question needs to be forced, live, and momentous. A *forced* option is a choice we can't opt out of. No third option is available. Performing the action or not performing it exhausts the alternatives. Either Ted will play Sam the second half of the game, or not. A forced option. A *live* option is a practical choice one is able to make. Psychologically impossible or impracticable options, for example, are not live, but dead. For most of us, making our favorite kabob shop our place of worship probably isn't a live option. A *momentous* option is a decision on which something important depends.[6] Higgins's choice to stand up to Rebecca, even to the point of quitting, is not trivial, but a momentous decision, one involving a serious risk to his livelihood and family's welfare.

A decision that's all three—forced, live, and momentous—is what James calls a "genuine option." When faced with a genuine option, James says, one is entitled to go beyond the evidence and exercise precursive faith by making a "passional decision" if one more condition is satisfied: the evidence is indecisive. The evidence for the options on offer is too close to settle the matter or coerce the intellect.

James offers a few telling examples. Take social coordination cases, where, for example, only by acting in unison can a group stop a single train robber or terrorist. Or a soccer team perfecting their dance routine for Sharon's going-away party. Such NSYNC action requires boldly dancing without the assurance of cooperation ahead of time, no strings attached one might say. Acting in unison might not guarantee the desired result, though it likely will. Inactivity will lead to Bo Jackson diddly squat and leave Sharon empty-handed ("Midnight Train to Royston").

Sam's decision to stand up against a corrupt corporate sponsor is a good example. He either will or won't, so the decision is forced. Both options are living, and a great deal depends on his call. The decision also involves social coordination, as his teammates, in a show of solidarity, join him in the symbolic, risky action. Sam doesn't know ahead of time that they will, though, so his decision to tape over the sponsor's logo takes courage and going ahead of the evidence. His decision could backfire or yield bad results, but it is hardly blind faith. It is a principled and admirable stance, and Jamie's show of solidarity is the occasion of their reconciliation.

James would agree. "Wherever a desired result is achieved by the co-operation of many independent persons, its existence as a fact is a pure consequence of the precursive faith in one another of those immediately concerned. A government, an army, a commercial system, a ship, a college, an athletic team, all exist on this condition, without which not only is nothing achieved, but nothing is even attempted."[7]

Or consider personal relations, where success demands more than strict evidentialism. Romantic relationships require taking an initiative before knowing that feelings will be mutual and reciprocated.[8] Consider Roy and Keeley, or even Sam and Rebecca. If both potential partners wait for the other to show definitive romantic interest, the relationship is not likely to get off the ground. But taking initiative and showing interest invites risk. Not usually the risk of leaving oneself open to attack, as Sassy says, but the risk of rejection, most certainly ("Goodbye Earl").

Gotta Look Right

Believing in themselves, Richmond stands a chance against Everton, despite their decades-long track record of losses to them. To have a chance at winning, a team may well have to believe they *can* do it, on at least some level or at least to some degree. And they might have to believe without decisive or even good evidence that it's true, as in this case. Such precursive faith will not ensure the desired result, but it may well be needed for its realistic possibility.

After Richmond pulls off the upset, Roy comments that nobody believed they could win, not even themselves. This could be taken to mean that the team lacked the precursive faith they needed after all. One explanation might be an inconsistency between James's analysis and the writing of the show, but there might be a better one. It seems pretty likely that though Richmond had previously doubted they could win, the unusually candid and motivating pregame pep talk delivered by Nate sufficiently changed their minds.

This sort of belief is closely related to *hope*, another recurring theme of the show and one of the classical theological virtues. The pessimistic mantra cynically repeated by Richmond fans that "it's the hope that kills you" lowers expectations and anticipates the worst for the sake of self-protection. Ted's irrepressible optimism retains soaring hope, a hope that may or may not disappoint. Like life itself, soccer involves risk, but to avoid risk by not playing (or cheering on) is too steep a price to pay. Just as a victory may be lost for lack of precursive faith, and rich enjoyment lost by playing it safe, so might truth itself be lost if we fear error so much that we aren't willing to take some risks.

As James puts it, "We may regard the chase for truth as paramount, and the avoidance of error as secondary; or we may, on the other hand, treat the avoidance of error as more imperative, and let truth take its chance. Clifford ... exhorts us to the latter course. Believe nothing, he tells us, keep your mind in suspense forever, rather than by closing it on insufficient evidence incur the awful risk of believing lies."[9]

James counsels a different course:

> For my own part, I have also a horror of being duped; but I can believe that worse things than being duped may happen to a man in this world: so Clifford's exhortation has to my ears a thoroughly fantastic sound. It is like a general informing his soldiers that it is better to keep out of battle forever than to risk a single wound. Not so are victories either over enemies or over nature gained. Our errors are surely not such awfully solemn things. In a world where we are so certain to incur them in spite of all our caution, a certain lightness of heart seems healthier than this excessive nervousness on their behalf.[10]

Consider that a Yank crossing the street in England takes a risk. Recall Ted's entrenched American habit of looking to the left before stepping off the curb. To keep him safe, Beard has to hold him back. "Gotta look right," Beard reminds him. Our habits can help us or hurt us. It takes intentionality to break bad habits, negative self-talk, a losing mentality, self-sabotaging behaviors, or a defense that's death.

A winning attitude requires more than the fear of losing, and seeking truth requires more than avoiding error. It may demand enough passion for finding the truth to take a risk.

James can't bring himself to submit to Clifford's "agnostic rules for truth-seeking," if only for this reason. "A rule of thinking which would absolutely prevent me from acknowledging certain kinds of truth if those kinds of truth were really there, would be an irrational rule."[11] Passional decisions, though not without risk, are not always blind faith. Sometimes they are just looking right.

Faith and Practice

Imagine finding yourself lost in the woods, and there's a leap ahead to cross a chasm. It's bigger than you'd prefer, you might be able to do it, but there's no guarantee. It's getting dark, a snow storm is brewing, and there's no time to turn back. So a decision has to be made. Choose not to jump and you're sure to freeze to death. Believing you can make the jump, you just might be able to. You've been training a lot, and you're in the best shape of your life, so you have reasons to think you may well be able to make the leap, but there's still a risk. Your faith and the training, in this case, go hand in hand.

Now, recall when Richmond was to face Man City, and Nate says that Richmond cannot win. An interesting contrast with his earlier having said that Richmond could do anything, by the way ("Make Rebecca Great Again"). This time his attitude is pessimistic. Concerned such a mentality will be self-fulfilling, Ted reminds Nate of the need for belief. Even Beard, however, chimes in that "belief doesn't score goals" ("The Hope That Kills You"). One might suggest that the sort of belief Ted's encouraging here is at odds with what it practically takes to win, but that seems patently wrong. After all, Ted calls the meeting in order to elicit fresh ideas and find innovative strategies to make victory possible. Which he soon does with a litany of trick plays: The Sandman, Lasso Special, Pepper Shakers, Beckham's Todger, Midnight Poutine, Chitty Chitty Bang Bang, The Broken Tap, Loki's Toboggan, The Upside Down Taxi, Hadrien's Wall, and Dirty Martini.

The scene reminds us, though, that some might see faith or trust as contrasting with hard work or adequate preparation. But this bears no resemblance to *Ted Lasso*. In the show, like in the leaping example and life itself, belief is intimately tied to action.[12] Nowhere does Ted encourage faith *instead of* hard work, or practice. If he did, he wouldn't have been so upset with Jamie for missing and trivializing practice. The scenario, imitating (while inverting) a real-life Allen Iverson press conference, reveals the importance Ted ascribes to practice, and the marriage between belief and work.[13] The team's renewed belief in the finale is combined at a crucial juncture with Nate's False Nine—another integration of belief and strategy.[14]

Rightness, Religion, and Relations

Does any of this have application to the great questions of philosophy— morality or religion, for example? Or is it mainly limited to sports and, on occasion, death-defying leaps? James thinks it does apply philosophically. He puts it this way regarding morality:

> The question of having moral beliefs at all or not having them is decided by our will. Are our moral preferences true or false, or are they only odd biological phenomena, making things good or bad for us, but in themselves indifferent? How can your pure intellect decide? If your heart does not want a world of moral reality, your head will assuredly never make you believe in one.... Moral skepticism can no more be refuted or proved by logic than intellectual skepticism can. When we stick to it that there is truth (be it of either kind), we do so with our whole nature, and resolve to stand or fall by the results. The skeptic with his whole nature adopts the doubting attitude; but which of us is the wiser, Omniscience only knows.[15]

James thinks that fundamental moral questions are paradigm cases of decisions that call for passional decisions. The evidence by turns for reductionist analyses of morality and for robust moral objectivity is ambiguous. Both stories have their appeal. For many neither option is dead, and the decision between them is forced and momentous. Since the evidence is ambiguous, a passional decision, James says, is not just lawful but required.

In many ways *Ted Lasso* is a deeply moral show, showcasing kindness, love, and the cruelty of marital infidelity. The dignity and value of persons is nonnegotiable, except, arguably, for some of its sexual ethics. The Diamond Dogs, for example, see Ted's one-night stand through a myopic and tragically simple lens: Did he and Sassy have fun?

The point is not prudish or provincial. Treating people as ends in themselves with dignity and respect may require more substantive reflection about something as important, consequential, and intimate as sexuality. There seems a disconnect between the show's celebration of intrinsic human worth, on the one hand, and its reduction of casual uncommitted sexuality to harmless recreation, on the other.

Even Higgins, a staunch family man who's ostensibly religious, falls into the trap, which raises another question: Is precursive faith relevant to the question of God? To be clear, religion plays no prominent role in *Ted Lasso*. The writers in fact seem intent on distancing the show from religion in numerous respects. The Higginses are Roman Catholic, and one of their sons, the eldest, is a priest, but his mother is careful to point out that he was born out of wedlock, making him a "cool priest" who can "explore life's little gray areas" ("The Hope that Kills You").

Roy himself seems conflicted. Where once he noted that Jamie's innate talent made him question his own faith, in the later funeral episode, he seems to adopt a philosophy of atheistic materialism where death is the end of the story. Coach similarly endorses atheism[16] (despite his prayer in "Beard After Hours"), and in the final season Rebecca makes a crack about losing money by becoming inordinately religious.

When the show broaches whether it's appropriate to pray during a game, Ted asks, "But to what God, and in what language?" Ted also quips that if God had wanted ties, she wouldn't have invented numbers. While Ted believes all sorts of things, he also explicitly disavows knowing what exists beyond this material world. The show bends over backwards to avoid anything religiously heavy handed, content to settle for fuzzy talk of faith in faith instead.

James, however, sees a religious application. Interestingly enough, although Clifford doesn't explicitly say his essay is about religious faith, James thinks he discerns its subtext. "When the Cliffords tell us how sinful it is to be Christians on such 'insufficient evidence,' insufficiency is really the last thing they have in mind. For them the evidence is absolutely sufficient, only it makes the other way. They believe so completely in an anti-christian order of the universe that there is no living option: Christianity is a dead hypothesis from the start."[17]

James says that if the "religious hypothesis"—the quintessential personal relationship—is dead rather than living, then it's not a genuine option. Some consider the problem of evil to be absolutely decisive evidence against God's existence, the final nail in the ashes (as Tartt would say). James suspects that, for Clifford, religion is out of the question, just as unbelief may for certain rationalist theists be a dead option in light of the decisive deliverances of evidence.

But for many if not most, the evidential battle over God's existence and the nature of ultimate reality is not so clear cut. The evidence is ambiguous. Some in favor, some against. Though Blaise Pascal (1623–1662) doesn't think the evidence on both sides is equal, he still recognizes and discusses the significance of the ambiguity.[18] Problems of evil and hiddenness are locked in a zero-sum game with arguments from design and contingency, history and morality. For James, if the evidential match is anything near a tie—which Ted would of course hate—if both belief and unbelief are live options, and if the decision between them is forced and momentous, then a step of precursive faith and a passional decision are perfectly appropriate, despite Clifford's protests.

Whether or not this vindicates Ted's faith in faith, aliens, or spirit guides, it might help vindicate faith in God.

Notes

1   William K. Clifford, "The Ethics of Belief," available at https://people.brandeis.edu/~teuber/Clifford_ethics.pdf.
2   Ibid., 5.
3   Ibid.
4   Ibid., 4.
5   William James, "The Will to Believe," in *Essays in Pragmatism* (New York: Collier Macmillan Publishers, 1948).
6   Ibid., 89–90.
7   Ibid., 104.
8   Ibid.
9   Ibid., 100.
10 Ibid.
11 Ibid., 107.
12 "For as the body without the spirit is dead, so faith without works is dead also." James 2:26. Significant to note is that though we have direct volitional control over our actions, we lack such control of our beliefs.
13 Iverson's press conference is available at https://www.youtube.com/watch?v=eGDBR2L5kzI.
14 The reassembled "BELIEVE" sign near the end of the third season is rife with significance. Earlier in the season Tish had mentioned *kintsugi* for its use of gold to repair and enhance broken objects. As the closing montage pans across the screen to Nate's work reassembling the poster, a bottle of gold glitter is on his work table as he stirs together the compound to put the sign back together. Belief takes on a new dimension with this image invoked from this Japanese aesthetic—belief of the whole team (re)united working harmoniously together, resonating nicely

with James's image of precursive faith involving cases of social coordination. See https://wabisabimusings.blogspot.com/2023/06/an-impermanence-for-coach-beard-and.html?m=1.

15 James, "The Will to Believe," 103–104.

16 Yet Beard is still somehow a citizen of Vatican City ("So Long, Farewell").

17 Ibid., 97.

18 Blaise Pascal, *Pensées and Other Writings* (Oxford: Oxford University Press, 1995).

4

Is Ted an Egoist?

Robert Begley and Carrie-Ann Biondi

Ted Lasso is so darn nice, and it's not an act. His relentless optimism is as refreshing as a cold glass of lemonade after a hot curry dinner. Beneath the coach's cheerful exterior is a complex, thoughtful person who has a positive impact on people in his life. Even cynical journalists like Trent Crimm of *The Independent* are won over and "can't help but root for him" because Lasso "really means it" ("Trent Crimm: The Independent").

Some might mistake Lasso's seemingly endless flow of time, energy, and kindness toward others as selflessness. Contrary to appearances, though, Lasso embodies egoism, much like architect Howard Roark—the hero of Lasso's favorite book, Ayn Rand's *The Fountainhead* ("Lavender"). Being egoistic is what fuels his life, enables him to be a good coach and friend, and inspires those around him to become the best versions of themselves.

Perhaps you're scratching your head and wondering, "How could Lasso be an egoist? After all, he's kind to everyone, gives his soccer players books to read, bakes biscuits every day for his boss, and clearly loves his family." Roark's frenemy Peter Keating is similarly puzzled, when he doesn't understand how Roark can be both an egoist and a kind person, implying that one can't be both.[1] As Lasso says, we "know it's a curveball, but [we] can explain" ("Lavender"). We think that Roark is onto something, when he replies to Keating, "Maybe the concepts don't make sense. Maybe they don't mean what people have been taught to think they mean."[2] So we'll start with clarifying the concept of egoism and then show how Lasso may be more like the hero of his favorite book than meets the eye.

Ted Lasso and Philosophy: No Question Is Into Touch, First Edition.
Edited by Marybeth Baggett and David Baggett.
© 2024 John Wiley & Sons, Inc. Published 2024 by John Wiley & Sons, Inc.

The Nature of Enlightened Egoism

Two popular myths about egoism need to be dispelled. The first is that an egoist is always a narcissistic jerk like *Ted Lasso* arch-villain Rupert Mannion, who enjoys hurting people and will play any dirty trick to get what he wants. Buying into this myth is probably why Crimm writes in his article about Lasso that "in a game where ego is celebrated, Ted reins his in" ("Trent Crimm: The Independent"). The second myth is that selfish egoism is immoral whereas selfless altruism is moral. This is why narcissistic Mannion tries to hide his bad deeds under the banner of altruism. For example, he seeks one-upmanship by donating one million pounds "for the children" to a fundraiser run by Rebecca Welton, his ex-wife and new owner of the AFC Richmond soccer team ("For the Children").

To pull back the curtain on these myths, we need to define egoism. Thinkers in the virtue ethics tradition as far apart in time as Aristotle (384–322 BC) and Ayn Rand (1905–1982) can help us here. Derived from the ancient Greek word for "I" (*ego*), egoism focuses on oneself. Aristotle holds that the human good is one's own happiness (*eudaimonia*), and Rand argues that each person's highest moral purpose is to achieve his or her own happiness.[3] What they mean by happiness is not the fleeting euphoria that AFC Richmond's kit manager-turned-assistant-coach Nate Shelley gets when people "like" social media posts about him or the pleasure he feels when something bad happens to someone he dislikes.[4] Aristotle means the deep satisfaction one experiences from excellently using one's reason, and Rand explains happiness as the "state of consciousness which proceeds from the achievement of one's values ... a state of non-contradictory joy."[5] For both, values and happiness cannot be attained without acting virtuously throughout one's life. The *way* goods are acquired, not just their acquisition, matters.

To complicate things, there are different types of egoism: psychological and ethical. Psychological egoism—defended most famously by philosopher Thomas Hobbes (1588–1679)—is a descriptive theory about how people *do* act.[6] As contemporary philosopher Gregory Salmieri explains, it claims that "people always and inevitably act egoistically—that there are no actions that are ultimately motivated by anything other than self-interest."[7] This would implausibly make nonegoism impossible, as philosophers Francis Hutcheson (1694–1746) and Bishop Joseph Butler (1692–1752) have argued.[8] Hobbes's view rides roughshod over the sincere protests of altruists like Mother Teresa.

Aristotle and Rand instead defend ethical egoism, which is a normative theory about how people *should* act. Ethical egoism recognizes that people can act against their self-interest, but it urges each person to hold himself or herself as the ultimate beneficiary of his or her actions. "Ultimate" doesn't mean "only." Aristotle's moral exemplars and Rand's fictional heroes risk their lives for the sake of values they hold dear. Those values include their loved ones, who are chosen as integral parts of their good. Threats to them would be threats to one's happiness. This is what Roark means when he tells his best friend, Gail Wynand, "Gail, if this boat were sinking, I'd give my life to save you. Not because it's any kind of duty. Only because I like you, for reasons and standards of my own. I could die for you. But I couldn't and wouldn't live for you."[9] Roark rejects altruistically sacrificing his life for others (or having others sacrifice for him), since doing so would be to give up a higher value for a lesser one.[10] Courageously risking death to save his best friend is not a sacrifice to Roark. As Aristotle argues about "character friends," having Wynand in his life as a "second self" valued for his own sake is part of what makes Roark's life worth living.[11] He couldn't live with himself if he failed to fight for his values: *that* would be a "living death."

Egoists also love themselves. Not the way self-absorbed star soccer player Jamie Tartt can't stop preening in front of mirrors. Tartt (at least in Season 1) is what Aristotle would call a base or pseudo-self-lover. He is superficial and reduces himself to a hedonistic slave to his desires by, for example, having sex without love and treating women as interchangeable partners. What Aristotle would call a proper self-lover is someone who sees himself (and other humans) as a rational being who can (and should) think long-range about what is good for him, who has forged a character he's proud of, and who can look himself in the eye. A self-lover embraces his humanity while integrating his reason and emotion. He has a wholehearted commitment to making his life the best it can be because he knows he's worth it and he's earned it.[12]

This inner wholeness makes an egoist the sort of person who can live in harmony with others. Contrary to popular belief, egoism requires the best—not the worst—of us. Mannion's cutthroat tactics are *not* advantageous. It is in one's self-interest to treat others well, which Rand calls a "principle of trade": "[T]here is no conflict of interests among men who ... deal with one another as *traders*, giving value for value.... A trader ... does not treat men as masters and slaves, but as independent equals."[13] Creating value comes first. Before cooperating or trading to get goods, egoists need to bring something to the table that others find valuable. That could be a trustworthy character like Lasso or a new product like Keeley Jones's dating app Bantr ("Rainbow"). The best of oneself creates and sustains relationships that bring out the best in others.

Folks like Mannion, (Seasons 1 and 2) Shelley, and (Season 1) Tartt are not egoists. They are like Keating of *The Fountainhead*, who is obsessed with others' opinions of him and lies, cheats, and steals his way to the top of the architecture profession. When we scratch below the surface of these guys, we find hollow men who despise themselves and have little sense of their own selves. Mannion is as second-handed as Keating and Shelley. His fragile sense of self is massaged only by tabloid reports of his ex-wife's troubles and pictures of himself with different fashion models. Hedonists and narcissists, not egoists, treat others like interchangeable tools to be used for any ends they wish. A person of healthy self-esteem would not do this.

Is Ted Lasso an Egoist?

Keeping in mind the view of egoism we just sketched, we'll make a case that Lasso is an egoist. He tells AFC Richmond's new sports psychologist, Dr. Sharon Fieldstone, that *The Fountainhead* is his favorite book ("Lavender"). There must be something Lasso admires about Roark's moral character and the novel's overall message of egoism, independence, and self-creation for it to be his top pick. He's a straight shooter, so we'll take his word for it. As Lasso advises Welton in the case of disheveled musician Cam Cole, "You do not want to judge this book by its cover" ("For the Children"), so let's dive right in. As we'll see, there are four major reasons to see Lasso as an egoist.

First, Lasso is aware of how important it is to be oneself and love oneself. In a brief exchange with Tartt, Lasso jokingly asks him, "Hey, Jamie, what would you rather be? A lion or a panda?" Tartt immediately replies, "Coach, I'm me. Why would I wanna be anything else?" A pleasantly surprised Lasso, who has so far seen only the worst of Tartt, responds, "I'm not sure you realize how psychologically healthy that actually is" ("Biscuits").[14] For all his flaws, Tartt doesn't want to imitate anyone, which Lasso sees as a good thing and a sign of potential growth for Tartt. It's obvious throughout the series that Lasso also is comfortable in his own skin and has his own style. This is similar to how Roark "has always liked being Howard Roark" and doesn't compare himself to anyone else, even rejecting the suggestion of having a statue made of himself: "I don't wish to be the symbol of anything. I'm only myself."[15] The parallel between Roark and Lasso on this point is underscored at the very end of the *Ted Lasso* series, when Crimm changes the title of his book manuscript from *The Lasso Way* to *The Richmond Way* because of Lasso's feedback: "One small suggestion.... I'd change the title. It's not about me. It never was" (So Long, Farewell").

Second, Lasso—like Roark—is a creator who loves his work. Instead of building beautiful skyscrapers, he empowers people and builds team spirit. Roark notes the connection between creation and egoism: "The creators were not selfless. It is the whole secret of their power—that it was self-sufficient, self-motivated, self-generated. A first cause, a fount of energy, a life force, a Prime Mover."[16] Lasso is usually such a "fount of energy" who wakes up eager to face the day's challenges. After a red-eye flight, he and his colleague and best friend, Coach Beard, hurry from the airport to the soccer stadium. As they take a deep breath in the locker room, Lasso says, "I do love a locker room. Smells like potential" ("Pilot"). When questioned by Crimm about coaching a sport he doesn't know, Lasso responds: "Trent, what do you love? Is it writing? ... Me? I love coaching" ("Trent Crimm: The Independent"). He would not be able to serve as a spark plug for his players without believing in himself and pursuing what he loves.

Third, like Roark, Lasso has a "self-sufficient ego," which means that he "cannot be affected by the approval of others"[17] in any fundamental sense. When the first fan he meets tells him how stupid he is for taking the job of coaching AFC Richmond, Lasso responds, "Well, you know, I've heard that tune before. But here I am, still dancing" ("Pilot"). He sticks to his principles even when 50,000 angry fans chant, "You don't know what you're doing!" Lasso is certain about who and what he loves. *That* buck starts and stops with him. He encourages Welton to trust herself as well. When she asks Lasso for advice about whether to continue a romantic relationship with soccer player Sam Obisanya, he says, "Listen to me. *Don't* listen to me" ("Midnight Train to Royston"). Similarly, when Keating asks Roark whether he should accept an architecture job or a prestigious scholarship, Roark tells him, "If you want my advice, Peter ... you've made a mistake already. By asking me. By asking anyone. Never ask people. Not about your work."[18]

This might sound incompatible with Lasso taking advice, but it's not. Like any good leader, he gets input from those around him and then makes his own decision based on evidence. But he is sometimes wrong. For instance, when the team is on the verge of being relegated to a lower division, Lasso insists that he'll start aging soccer player and team captain Roy Kent in the next game to keep Kent from feeling humiliated on the bench because "this ain't about winning to me" ("All Apologies"). Beard pounds the table in frustration and corrects him by insisting that for these professional (as opposed to college) athletes, this time it *is* about winning: "Losing has repercussions. We lose, we get relegated. We get relegated, this is over, and we will have built nothing. And if you wanna pick a player's feelings over a coach's duty to make a point … I don't wanna drink with someone that self-ish" ("All Apologies"). That reminder of what he ultimately values gets Lasso's attention. Lasso realizes his error and reverses his judgment. The one thing that Beard doesn't get quite right is calling Lasso's short-sighted initial choice "selfish." If winning is an essential step for building and keeping a team, and having a team to coach and build is what Lasso loves, then it *would* be (properly) selfish for him to seek winning strategies.

Fourth, Lasso is a self-interested value-seeker. He seeks out the good in each person, providing a lifeline—you could say a lasso—to their best selves, should they choose the work of walking that path. He is famous for saying, "For me, success is not about the wins and losses. It's about helping these young fellas be the best versions of themselves on and off the field" ("Trent Crimm: The Independent"). He knows that bringing out that best is a win-win approach to sports *and* life. Lasso extends this approach even to Mannion. In a pivotal scene at the Crown & Anchor pub, Mannion reveals to Lasso and Welton that his new wife has bought ownership shares in AFC Richmond. He sadistically hints that he'll sit in the owner's box every week and criticize Welton's every move. Instead of letting things take a bad turn, Lasso gently lures Mannion into a game of darts. The wager is: if Mannion wins, he gets to pick AFC Richmond's lineup for the last two games, but if Lasso wins, Mannion is barred from the owner's box as long as Welton's in charge. Just when it looks like cocky Mannion will win, Lasso comes back to win with a bullseye and reveals his (ostensibly) Walt Whitman-inspired philosophy: "Be curious, not judgmental" ("The Diamond Dogs"). Lasso treats Mannion respectfully and *shows* him how egoistic self-development—not narcissism—is a winning strategy. Whether the furious Mannion will choose to learn from Lasso's moral high ground remains to be seen.

Value-seekers have a benevolent sense of life, which is perhaps Lasso's most winsome characteristic. He believes people are empowered to control their own lives by the choices they make. They are not doomed to failure. Rejecting the local saying that "it's the hope that kills you," Lasso insists, "I believe in hope." Even in defeat, Lasso teaches the team to take it as a life lesson: "Lift your heads up and be grateful that you're going through this sad moment together.... Nobody in this room is alone" ("The Hope that Kills You"). He keeps his positivity grounded in reality. Life (or football) isn't always roses and rainbows, but neither is the universe out to get you. The norm is that *mostly* life is about joy and achievement, as long as you don't forget that "the harder you work, the luckier you are" ("Pilot"). We learn that Lasso has retained his indomitable spirit in the crucible of his father's suicide and a dissolving marriage. A poignant parallel to Roark is that although it was agonizing for him to lose his beloved architecture job and go work in a quarry, he says, "I'm not capable of suffering completely.... It goes only down to a certain point and then it stops. As long as there is that untouched point, it's not really pain."[19] The "untouched point" in Lasso and Roark is their strong sense of self. They are confident about their inner resources to rebuild and to achieve again.

Value-seekers also think long-term. Since the ultimate value is having a happy life, which is a long-range project, then all of one's choices should serve that end. Lasso seeks long-term success over short-term gains—and gets a bit of help from his friends (like Beard) now and again to keep him on that straight and narrow path. This might sound like it doesn't fit with Lasso's advice to Obisanya to "be like a gold-fish" because goldfish have no long-term memory. Lasso's point, though, is that a player should not dwell on a bad play during the course of a game. Learn from it, move on, and play better. This will help him in the future. Lasso's goal is to point him toward self-development and enable him to deal with life's obstacles.

Time to Face the Press

These seem like good reasons for thinking that Lasso is an egoist. But now it's time to call on all those journalists waving their hands with objections they have for us. Let's start with one from the fella over there in the tweed jacket.

One objection is that Lasso is not consistently egoistic, since he sometimes supports sacrifice. First, he sacrifices his marriage for his wife's sake. Second, he asks his players to sacrifice something they value in the "curse reverse" ceremony. We would submit that these, however, are only apparent sacrifices. A closer look reveals Lasso's potentially egoistic reasoning.

Lasso accepted Welton's coaching offer and moved 4,438 miles from home mostly to give his wife Michelle space to sort out her feelings for him. He is hopeful for reconciliation when she and their son visit. But Michelle makes it clear that she is no longer in love with him, assuring him that he's "not quitting" but "letting her go." Lasso realizes that Michelle would have to sacrifice her happiness to stay married to him. He tells her, "Michelle, if there was something I could do, something I could say that would make you happy, just being with me, I'd do it in a nanosecond. But I ain't got no control over any of that. You don't have to keep trying anymore. It's okay. I'm gonna be okay" ("Tan Lines"). A one-sided marriage is no marriage. It's a bitter recipe for misery, like mixing up the salt and sugar in Ted's biscuits. Lasso knows that his life and happiness are his responsibility, and he refuses to bring down others in their pursuit.

Let's recall the context of the "curse reverse" ceremony. The soccer players superstitiously believe that Dani Rojas's mysterious injury is caused by a cursed training room that once was used to recruit unsuspecting doomed soldiers. Lasso facilitates the "curse reverse" to deal with his team's various psychological blocks that impede their ability to work together. He asks the players and staff to honor the ghosts of the past by bringing to the ceremony a valued item to burn. Each does so in turn, vulnerably revealing to one another who they are and what they care about ("Two Aces"). This psychological visibility brings the team together, which is the long-range goal Lasso sought. Team building is of greater value than any of the material possessions they incinerated.

Another objection (thanks, Trent Crimm!) is that Lasso's self is not really the sturdy, serene, integrated egoist we've made him out to be. Underneath the smile, he's falling apart. It takes repeated panic attacks to get Lasso on Dr. Fieldstone's couch. This is how we eventually find out that his father committed suicide when Ted was sixteen, which led him to blame his father for quitting on life and his family and to vow never to be a quitter ("No Weddings and a Funeral").

Contrary to this showing Lasso to be a disintegrated mess, his choosing psychological self-care arguably reveals his egoism. Humans are not *born* complete. They have the potential *to become* so through the constant hard work of achieving ever-greater wholeness. Lasso admits, "Life is hard. It's real hard," but he is not a quitter. He courageously journeys the bumpy road and navigates its twists and turns. Fieldstone asks Lasso what he loved about his father ("No Weddings and a Funeral"). This helps him work through his anger and sadness to reconnect with the motive power of love—love of his life and all those who have made it richly stocked with value.

Ted Lasso invites its audience to be more curious and less judgmental. That includes wondering whether the concepts and labels we use to describe things and people get at what and who they really are. If that means Lasso—like Roark—is an egoist, then so be it. The "Lasso Way" egoistically lifts up all boats with his inspiring wit and wisdom to create "The Richmond Way" and a world worth living in.[20]

Notes

1 Ayn Rand, *The Fountainhead*, 25th anniversary ed. (New York: New American Library, 1971 [1943]), 583.

2 Ibid.

3 Aristotle, *Nicomachean Ethics*, 2nd ed., trans. Terence Irwin (Indianapolis, IN: Hackett Publishing, 1999), 1097a35–1097b21; Ayn Rand, "The Objectivist Ethics," in Ayn Rand, *The Virtue of Selfishness* (New York: New American Library, 1964), 25.

4 Nate violates Coach Lasso's "No schadenfreude zone" rule a few times ("Two Aces").

5 Aristotle, 1100b18–1101a22; Rand (1964), 28–29.

6 Thomas Hobbes, *Leviathan*, ed. Edwin Curley (Indianapolis, IN: Hackett Publishing, 1994).

7 Gregory Salmieri, "Egoism and Altruism," in *A Companion to Ayn Rand*, ed. Allan Gotthelf and Gregory Salmieri (Malden, MA: Wiley-Blackwell, 2016), 132–33.

8 Francis Hutcheson, *An Inquiry into the Original of Our Ideas of Beauty and Virtue in Two Treatises*, rev. ed. (Indianapolis, IN: Liberty Fund, 2004 [1726]), Treatise II; Joseph Butler, *Fifteen Sermons and Other Writings on Ethics*, ed. David McNaughton (Oxford: Oxford University Press, 2017 [1726]), Sermon 11.

9 Rand (1943), 609; see also Aristotle's discussion, at 1169a19–29, of the courageous solider who "awards himself the greater good" by risking death to protect others.

10 For a fuller discussion of sacrifice, see Ayn Rand, "The Ethics of Emergencies," in Rand (1964), 43–49.

11 Aristotle distinguishes character friends, who are people of good moral character loved for their own sake, from use friends and pleasure friends, who are loved instrumentally for only the sake of the use or pleasure that can be gotten from them. See Aristotle, 1156a8–1157b5 and 1166a1–1168b12.

12 Aristotle, 1168b17–1169a8 and 1166a14–24.

13 Rand, "The Objectivist Ethics," in Rand (1964), 31.

14 Season 1 Tartt doesn't realize how psychologically healthy this is. It takes losing some major values—like his romantic relationship with

Keeley and a place on a soccer team—before Season 2 Tartt appreciates Lasso's insight.

15 Rand (1943), 522, 604.
16 Ibid., 680.
17 Ibid., 609, 607.
18 Ibid., 33.
19 Ibid., 344.
20 We are grateful to be surrounded by family and friends who adore *Ted Lasso* as much as we do, as we have benefited from countless conversations that enriched our understanding of the series. We also are grateful to be the loves of one another's lives, which has allowed us to pursue this shared passion. We would be remiss not to note how the writing of this essay was fueled by lots of Yorkshire Tea. (This is not a paid advertisement.) Unlike Lasso and Fieldstone, we do not think that tea tastes like "garbage water" ("Biscuits") or "a wet paper bag" ("No Weddings and a Funeral").

Part II

THE BEST VERSIONS OF OURSELVES

5
Fear's a Lot Like Underwear

Corey Latta

From *A Wrinkle in Time* to *Sense and Sensibility*, books play a central role in *Ted Lasso*. They highlight themes, chart character progression, and enrich the plot. Some do all three.

In "Man City," Ted finds himself in Dr. Sharon Fieldstone's flat after she suffers a scary bicycle accident. Seeing an opportunity to learn more about the typically guarded therapist, Ted scans the mostly bare corporate rental until he comes across yet another book. This one belongs to the good doctor. In a brief but revealing moment, Ted flips it over just long enough for us to see the cover: James Hollis's *The Middle Passage: From Misery to Meaning in Midlife*.

Most people don't know who James Hollis is or what *The Middle Passage* is about, but that's changing. While not yet altogether famous, or even famous for being almost famous, *The Middle Passage* has its share of groupies that would make Nate envious. Hollis's popularity has grown in recent years, due, at least in part, to his ability to diagnose and deal with the complexities of the human condition. Hollis is a Jungian psychologist who writes like a philosophical existentialist, and *The Middle Passage* confronts readers with the need to reorient life around meaning of their own making.

Like Riding a Horse

According to Hollis, the first half of life burdens us with ideas and complexes handed down by society, our family, or the church. Rather than continuing to shoulder those burdens, we must choose those identities we want to leave behind and those we want to take up in the second half. The Middle Passage is the period between those halves,[1]

Ted Lasso and Philosophy: No Question Is Into Touch, First Edition.
Edited by Marybeth Baggett and David Baggett.
© 2024 John Wiley & Sons, Inc. Published 2024 by John Wiley & Sons, Inc.

when we painfully realize that many of the plays we ran in the first half leave us facing the drop in the second.

We are down on the scoreboard. Do we stick with Nate's false nine or park the bus? Too often we stand on the sidelines riddled with anxiety that hurts rather than helps, and our habits and practices hold us back from our best. We need a transformative pep talk, perhaps one that makes us mad. Moving forward through the Middle Passage requires undoing psychological and philosophical assumptions and promised safeguards, separation from those systems and structures that may have served us well before, but now impede our flourishing. How we play the second half, and whether we get over life's yips, is up to us.

The Middle Passage encourages readers to consider the ways our lives have previously carried the weight of our unconscious and unhelpful beliefs:

> One of the most powerful shocks of the Middle Passage is the collapse of our tacit contract with the universe—the assumption that if we act correctly, if we are of good heart and good intentions, things will work out. We assume a reciprocity with the universe. If we do our part, the universe will comply. Many ancient stories, including the Book of Job, painfully reveal the fact that there is no such contract, and everyone who goes through the Middle Passage is made aware of it.[2]

Life is hard, Ted admits to Dr. Sharon in a moment of transparent candor. As he learns, seeing it through a faulty lens can make it even harder. Ted's a delightful character, but there's more to him than meets the eye. Beneath his positivity and optimism lurk deep hurts and damage from a traumatic past that stays with him. He's skeptical of counseling and self-care, directing his focus more outward than inward. But as Plato (428–347 BC) recognized, we contribute best to the communities we're a part of when we are inwardly healthy. Ted needs to realize it's okay to admit his fears and come to terms with his past. He doesn't hesitate to offer others the help they need, but he also needs to learn to do the harder thing of accepting the helping hand that he needs.

What most concerns Hollis is that existential half-time between the two halves of the game of life. We must brave the Middle Passage of interrogating, maybe even abandoning, the unspoken contracts imposed on and appropriated by us in our first half of life. Then we can free ourselves to write an honest script by which we will live the second half with authenticity, courage, and ownership.

We don't choose to adopt a new philosophy of life for that second half out of whole cloth. Crisis or confrontation thrusts us into that stage. Without ever being asked if we want to play, we're thrown into the game with relegation on the line. Tragedy strikes. Relationships fail. We don't choose to leave Kansas City for Richmond. We're exiled there.

But along the road we find helpers and guardians.

Let's Get Started, Shall We?

Enter Dr. Sharon Fieldstone. From the moment she arrives at Richmond, Ted's discomfort is palpable. In a metaphor worthy of Beard, she interrupts their paper-passing game. Every initial encounter with her proves a bumbling failure on Ted's part to win yet another pessimistic soul over by his disarming personality. She shuts down his ice-breakers, rejects his biscuits, and chills any attempts at humor. He gradually realizes he might have to set his charm and charisma aside to be known, and to come to know himself.[3]

Lasso's awkwardness around Fieldstone makes more sense as Season 2 continues. He just doesn't trust therapists. He's got a general apprehension and modest Midwest skepticism of their practice. His failing marriage brought him to a therapist who piled shame on top the powerless grief of losing someone he thought he'd finish the game of life with. To make matters more unsettling, Fieldstone's confrontational style disillusions and disarms Ted by separating who he is from what he does. She can't be his mentor, recall, without occasionally being his tormentor.

Fieldstone represents, at least initially, all that Ted doesn't. She's the individuated self, and has seemingly come through her own Middle Passage. Lasso represents the emerging self, just entering his own time of transition. Fieldstone and Lasso stand as different answers to the existential question of what it means to play this game of life. But she can't help him settle into an answer that will serve him well until he sees just how the first half trick plays won't do.

Consider the contrasts. Fieldstone has boundaries. Ted doesn't. Ted barges into people's spaces. She reprimands him for it. She calls out his way of trying to connect with people, even resisting his nickname for her. Together they make up mismatching experiences. Ted brings life, unbridled, spontaneous, anxious. Fieldstone holds space for that sort of energy while bringing stoic calm. They clash. At least until they complement. By the time we get to "Man City," their relationship has improved slightly but still carries the tension of unspoken burdens.

Dr. Fieldstone is on a call with her own therapist, Bridget, who tells her that her frustration with Ted might have something to do not with their differences, but with their similarities. Where Ted uses humor, she uses intelligence to disarm others. If she wants Ted to be more transparent, she will have to model it herself. If she's going to help Ted into that second half of life, she will need to walk with him onto the pitch.

As Dr. Sharon heads into work that day on her transformer of a bicycle, she's hit by a car. She's okay, though concussed. Much to her annoyance, Ted steps up to help. Now in a vulnerable state, her humanity starts to show. The empty liquor bottles in her apartment clue Ted in to just how human she is. She's now able and willing to let Ted in a bit more, which allows Ted to do the same. That's when Ted takes her home, finds himself in her flat, and sees Hollis's book lying on the table.

With Dr. Sharon as his guide, Ted must now muster the courage to take a hard look at the assumptions he has lived by. He has to subject to critical scrutiny his tendency to evade, his use of humor to deflect, his winsome personality to avoid introspection. He needs to become painfully aware of the performative persona he's cultivated and worn like a uniform, in order to choose a philosophy of authentic participation going forward. He must don a jersey with the sponsorship of his own conscience instead of one of the many "Dubai Airs" that life—especially a tragic teenage experience—has cruelly foisted on him.

They Really Should Write Songs About It

Ted finally sees Fieldstone as a teammate, not an opponent, particularly after she admits her own fears. In this non-competitive, non-performative space, Ted sets the provisional personality of coach aside. We find out that his father committed suicide when Ted was only 16. In the aftermath of an emotionally charged scene with Jamie and his abusive father, Roy steps into a kind of fatherly role of his own with his heartwarming hug of a shattered Jamie. That hauntingly beautiful episode spurs Ted on to finally come clean to Dr. Fieldstone.

The significance of father figures in Hollis's framework can't be overstated. Parents, the arbiters of our first half experience, build the stage on which we play out the early decades of our lives. The beauty and the burden of being parented is living under the authority of someone else's ideas about how life should go. Our childhood years can be our best, or they can be predicated on covert emotional abuse or a philosophy of life marked by fear and scarcity. In Ted's case, his early years were formed around and defined by unspeakable trauma.

Ted's response was to refuse to let anyone else get by him without understanding they might be hurting inside. He would externalize his internal world by tending to others, often at his own expense. As Beard tells Ted, "You keep trying to hold all this in, I'm afraid your mustache is gonna pop off" ("Inverting the Pyramid of Success"). If there's a gateway into the Middle Passage, it's the awareness that we are more concerned with how others find meaning and purpose than we are with ourselves.

Of course, this is partly what makes Ted such a great coach and appealing figure. His attention is always pointed outward. This attentiveness to everyone else has allowed him to spend the first half of life avoiding those existential questions we must all answer. The question that comes to the fore is who Ted is. In the face of his father's suicide, who is he as a man and as a dad?

A later scene in Ted's apartment explores this further. As he gets ready for the funeral of Rebecca's father, Ted once again is overcome by panic. He calls on Sharon for help. In their poignant conversation, Ted confesses his core conviction, the belief that has kept him stuck in place. If his father only knew, Ted imagines, that he was a good dad, then maybe he wouldn't have taken his own life. Ted's great regret is that he never told him how good a dad he was. Who we are is inextricably tied to who we come from. Much of what it means to work meaning out for ourselves is a matter of working out what meaning our parents left us with.

In another book, *Living an Examined Life*, Hollis writes about the enduring importance of parenting:

> The one thing parents can do for their children is live their lives as fully as they can, for this will open the children's imagination, grant permission to them to have their own journey, and open the doors of possibility for them. Wherever we are stuck, they will have a tendency to be stuck also or will spend their life trying to overcompensate. Living our own journey as fully as possible is not only a gift to our soul, it also frees up the generation behind us to live theirs as well. The very freedom to live our lives that we wished from our parents, we thereby grant to our children to live theirs.[4]

In Ted's case, his journey has been pulled into the black hole of his father's suicide. Despite Ted's inviting personality and seemingly care-free attitude and his daring and willingness to venture into the unknown, his life remains a reaction to the burden his dad placed on him. Though he's gone to London, he remains within the orbit of his trauma.

A Longer Run Than He Thinks

This brings us to Ted's son Henry. Careful viewers will note one glaring point of confusion. Ted is a winning character. What's not to love? His personal appeal is a major reason for the success of the show. We've noted the charm, but let's not stop there. He's hilarious. He's kind. He's thoughtful. Infectiously gregarious. Optimistic. Encouraging. He brings out the best in others. A faithful friend. A conscientious spouse who cares enough to work on the relationship even when it is undoubtedly over. A master of semantic satiation with a rhyme for every occasion.

Yet there's a major problem, and it's located in the same place as his philosophical and psychological wound: his parenting. Despite all his virtues, Ted seems to have decided that the best way to be a parent is to move to another country, settling for an on-screen relationship with a son in the middle of his formative years. That Ted, of all peo-ple, would do anything less than stay as close as possible to his son is confounding. What parent who has endured Ted's loss and abandon-ment moves 4,438 miles away?

It makes sense only if we understand it as an essential feature of Ted's personal Middle Passage. The narrative of Ted's childhood fills one of the show's greatest character holes. Like a vocation, romantic relationship, or religious commitment, parenting is a new height to which the self can rise. Only when we realize we have most certainly failed to reach those heights do we position ourselves to ascend.

It's safe to say that Henry gives Ted a chance to look more closely at himself. In so doing, he can choose who he wants to be, apart from what his trauma says he must hide. But first he has to confront those wounds that his charm has concealed. If Hollis is right, Ted's choice to move to London might have chosen him:

> If we realize that the assumptions by which the person has lived his or
> her life are collapsing, that the assembled strategies of the provisional
> personality are decompensating, that a world-view is falling apart, then

the thrashing about is understandable. In fact, one might even conclude that there is no such thing as a crazy act if one understands the emotional context. Emotions are not chosen; they choose us and have a logic of their own.[5]

Richmond isn't so illogical when we consider all Ted might be running from. Perhaps England is the best path to return home as a better man and father. It's from the pained center of the Middle Passage that we choose which direction to go.

Season 3 offers something of a hero's return home. From the initial episode, Ted and Henry's relationship takes center field. Henry returns to the States after a quick visit, setting in motion Ted's own eventual return home. His emotional detachment from life in Richmond, his acknowledgement of what's really going on inside him, and his desire to go back home to his son: all these pieces work in concert, like well-coordinated players in Total Football, to direct Ted into an adulthood of his choosing.

Just as Ted is about to make the most significant second-half decision of his life, his mother suddenly appears. As an archetypical stand-in for Ted's late father, she gently pressures Ted: "Your son misses you" ("Mom City"). In this crucial conversation, Ted tells his mother the difficult truth. He finally faces his inner-child fear of abandonment. And in doing so he achieves the resolution needed for a second adulthood.

By the season finale, Ted is home, geographically, emotionally, relationally. He's brought some of his journey back to Kansas. He is still Coach Lasso, but only by choice, not avoidant compulsion. No longer running, he is now returning.

Onward, Forward

Here's where Hollis meets Lasso meets ... Søren Kierkegaard (1813–1855). Like Hollis's project of personal responsibility in *The Middle Passage*, existential philosophy is about the discovery of and adherence to personal meaning. Orienting around a purpose one can live for is how the second half of life is won. In a diary entry, the Kierkegaard captured it like this:

What I really need is to get clear about what I must do, not what I must know, except insofar as knowledge must precede every act. What matters is to find a purpose, to see what it really is that God wills that I shall do; the crucial thing is to find a truth which is truth for me, to find the idea for which I am willing to live and die.... I certainly do not deny that I still accept an imperative of knowledge and that through it men may be influenced, but then it must come alive in me, and this is what I now recognize as the most important of all.[6]

The heart of Ted's struggle is finding what truth he's willing to live and die for. His Middle Passage is converting what happened *to* him into something happening *for* him, getting clear on what purpose emerges in that conversion. The events of Ted's life—his failed marriage, isolation from his son, immersion into a world about which he's almost entirely ignorant and ill-equipped—all conspire to move Ted from the life he's known to something better. Ted's vulnerability with Fieldstone proved to be the prelude to a life of greater purpose, that of fatherhood.

Besides Ted's mustache, one of the best aspects of the show is how each character seems to stand midfield between the pain of who they've been and the gift of who they are becoming. We first meet Rebecca betrayed, broken, and bitter. Later, because of newfound relationships and a reinvigorated team, she can look toward a hopeful horizon.

Past his professional prime and thrust into a very different life, Roy embraces a new career and a new identity. When Jamie looks into the abyss of his own ego, he finds the face of an abusive father. One of the most rewarding storylines of the series turns out to be Jamie's transformation into the man his father never chose to be. Nate's own painful relationship with his dad and resulting insecurity and betrayal of Ted could precipitated a crisis of Middle Passage proportions. It's love and Ted's unrelenting grace that guide him through into his own story of return. Even Trent's quest for something deeper initiates a passage of his own, journeying from skeptic to believer, outsider to teammate, cynical journalist to good faith storyteller.

Every principal character enacts the existential choice the Middle Passage offers. And each, led by Ted, will have to trade philosophies of performance for philosophies of authenticity. In the first half, Ted could get by on charm, high energy, and Biz Markie-style beatboxing. But the second half requires that he up his game. It comes down to honesty and choice, action and belief, the rules of the game of Middle Passage. In the end, Ted avoids relegating himself from his own life. He plays with heart and achieves the only promotion that matters.

Notes

1 The book title calls to mind the gruesome Middle Passage of the Transatlantic Slave Trade of the 16th through 19th centuries. This was an intentional connection by Hollis, who depicts this process as one of suffering that stems from confronting a huge, powerful other. It perhaps also invokes the specter of shackles that hold us in bondage and vitiate our freedom.
2 James Hollis, *The Middle Passage* (Toronto: Inner City Books, 1993), 41.
3 Rest in peace, Socrates (469–399 BC).
4 James Hollis, *Living an Examined Life* (Boulder, CO: Sounds True, 2018), 32.
5 Hollis, *Middle Passage*, 35.
6 Søren Kierkegaard, *Søren Kierkegaard's Journals and Papers* (Bloomington, IN: Indiana University Press, 1978), 34.

Lassoing Aristotle

Joseph Forte

"Know thyself. Rest in peace, Socrates."

So Ted responds to Roy's comical claim that he's usually better at holding in his anger ("All Apologies"). Ted surely knows Roy and, as his coach, helps the soccer legend increase in self-awareness. In turn, Roy draws out the best in his fellow Greyhounds when he becomes a coach himself. Socrates (469–399 BC) also had a famous protégé: Plato (428–347 BC). The most famous student of Plato's Academy was Aristotle (384–322 BC), "the Stagirite," also known simply as "The Philosopher." Aristotle then tutored Alexander the Great (356–323 BC)—not to be confused with Nate—who ended up doing more conquering than philosophizing, winning more battles than arguments.

Of all the riches to be mined from this impressive list of Greek first teamers, Aristotle's virtue ethics is a gem that's stood the test of time. This chapter examines *Ted Lasso* through an Aristotelian lens and argues that The Philosopher's approach to character development dovetails with a modern "strengths-focused" approach. Quite the combo.

A Bad Start for Rebecca, Nate, Roy, and Jamie

Is it possible for someone to be incurably, hopelessly bad? Aristotle thinks so. Although rare, such vicious people think their evil ways are actually good. And they feel good doing them.[1] Gangsters like Al Capone or Jimmy Conway come to mind.[2] And some of the

Ted Lasso and Philosophy: No Question Is Into Touch, First Edition.
Edited by Marybeth Baggett and David Baggett.
© 2024 John Wiley & Sons, Inc. Published 2024 by John Wiley & Sons, Inc.

characters in *Ted Lasso* seem to fit this description, at least when we first meet them.

Take Rebecca. Her rash, vengeful spitefulness extends as far as bringing two unwitting American football coaches across the Atlantic to destroy the soccer team she got from divorcing her philandering husband. Rebecca doesn't seem to care that she might be harming innocent people. She even gets some satisfaction from it. On first glance, Rebecca certainly seems vicious. Knowing who she becomes, though, we suspect that deep down Rebecca is pained by her decisions and regrets them. If so, and time would tell, then she was never truly vicious.

Aristotle has another term for people like that, ones who make poor choices but feel bad about them and want to become better. They are "incontinent." By that, he's not referring to what happened to Roy after too much ice cream, or to being sick at both ends, as Sam would say, reminding us the body is a miracle. Aristotle means they're "morally weak."[3]

Nate, Roy, and Jamie start off in a lousy place, each falling somewhere between vicious and morally weak in Aristotelian terms. Nate is initially sheepish, painfully shy, and indecisive. It's not clear what motivates his timidity—lack of confidence or actual cowardice. It likely owes, to some extent, to his dysfunctional relationship with his dad, which perhaps makes him vulnerable to overcorrection later. But assuming something like cowardice is part of Nate's personality or character, it's clear he isn't happy to be this way. He is probably, in fact, disgusted by it. How else should we take his spitting at his reflection in the mirror? So Nate's initial cowardice seems more incontinent than vicious.

Roy is Nate's polar opposite. Roy is excessively bold, as well as harsh, brash, and rash. He mocks Ted incessantly, employing the worst stereotypes of the artless American. If he really enjoys being this way, he is vicious, but we eventually see another side of him. His relationships with Keeley and his niece show a softness and highlight his vulnerabilities. Roy is dissatisfied, going through a life crisis, and open to correction, suggesting he is simply incontinent at worst.

Courage, or bravery, is a significant moral virtue for Aristotle. He defines it as a mean or sweet spot between excessive fear and caution on the one hand, and excessive boldness, or even rage, on the other. For Aristotle, these excesses are the vices that are properly opposed to courage: cowardice on the one hand (Nate) and rashness on the other (Roy).[4]

Then there's Jamie. He contrasts with Nate as well, arrogant where Nate is timid. Jamie thinks the world revolves around him, like Narcissus in love with his own image. Early on Jamie cruelly makes fun of Sam and ridicules Roy for being old and hairy. "Mate, if you're gonna go to the shower, you should take your sweater off first, pal" ("Biscuits"). Roy doesn't laugh, though viewers probably do.

Roy later asks Jamie if he realizes his influence on the team, and Jamie responds, "I'm the shit, yeah." As to why Jamie finds the bullying funny, "Cause Nate's a weak baby and he can't do anything about it" ("Trent Crimm: The Independent"). Jamie is either unaware of or indifferent to how disagreeable he is.

Wit is a minor moral virtue according to Aristotle. Jamie fits the description of its opposite: the vice of being annoying.[5] It's an obstacle to being just, a virtue that Aristotle thinks develops through friendship.[6] Jamie is notably unjust in his treatment of others, especially Nate, and seems to revel in it, putting him on the verge of viciousness, at least at first.

Immorality ➡ Loneliness ➡ Misery

Not only are our four Greyhounds morally deficient when we first meet them. For related reasons, they are lacking real friends too, making them pretty miserable.

Aristotle wrote that friendship is necessary for happiness.[7] We need it as much as food, clothing, and shelter. As an early biologist, Aristotle knew a great deal about animals. He argued that we are not only rational, but political animals, meaning that we thrive most when living in a *polis*—a community. The only ones who can live a solitary life well are either beasts or gods, according to Aristotle.[8] Most of us flourish when living in community with others, and friendship is the best way to do this.[9] In *Nicomachean Ethics*, his most authoritative and famous book on ethics, Aristotle lays out three kinds of friendship: utility, pleasure, and complete.

A friendship of utility involves two parties exchanging beneficial goods or services. The friendship lasts only as long as the benefits. One party preying on another falls short of a true friendship of utility, which is based on equality and mutual benefit.[10] In the beginning, Rebecca's only relationships are with people she treats as pawns, like Higgins. Rebecca uses people, and Nate allows people to use him in a harmful way. None of these meet Aristotle's criteria for even this lowest form of friendship.

The second type Aristotle identifies is a friendship of pleasure. This occurs when the parties involved take pleasure in each other's company, perhaps through shared activities. As with friendships of utility, friendships of pleasure must be reciprocal. Both parties must benefit by enjoying each other in order for the friendship to be true. It's only really friendship when it's good for those involved. Nothing less deserves to be called friendship.[11]

In the sense that Roy and Jamie enjoy playing soccer, and do so together, one might think they have a friendship of pleasure. But it's clear that Roy doesn't enjoy playing with Jamie, and Jamie is none too fond of Roy early on. One might consider Jamie's romantic relationship with Keeley a friendship of pleasure, but it doesn't fulfill Aristotle's criteria either, because it's mainly about sex, which Aristotle doesn't consider to be a true friendship of pleasure. Whether Aristotle was right about that or not, their relationship does not do them much enduring good, at least not until after they break up. It doesn't lead to their development or flourishing—admittedly Jamie did later claim that Keeley had cultured him a bit—and their trouble comes to a head at the charity auction when Keeley gives Jamie the boot.

In each instance, these characters lack friends, primarily because of their moral flaws. Rebecca, Nate, Roy, and Jamie are lonely and somewhat miserable. They need help to be better fit for society and to become the best versions of themselves. None of them is yet even close to a complete friendship, which will be discussed shortly. This is where virtue ethics and strengths-based self-improvement come in.

Best Version of Ourselves

Virtue ethics dominated ethical theory in Western philosophy through the early modern period. The goal of virtue ethics is the improvement of one's character (*ethos* in ancient Greek) for the sake of deep and persisting happiness. This approach developed through the work of such luminaries as Socrates, Plato, Aristotle, Epicurus (341–270 BC), the Stoics, and Thomas Aquinas (1225–1274).

Aristotle is virtue theory's most famous advocate, forging a tight bridge between virtue and happiness. His conception of happiness (*eudaimonia* in Greek) should not be confused with what we call happiness today. Eudaimonia is best translated as "flourishing." Because of its intense focus on character development, virtue ethics has a great deal to say about human flourishing. Many of its insights can also be applied to performance enhancement, like honing specific skills or attaining certain career goals. Unlike performance-enhancing drugs, though, it won't shrink parts of the male anatomy or cause unpredictable fits of rage.

A strengths-focused approach to character development is fairly new. It emerged from the modern positive psychology movement and is now widely practiced in education and corporate settings. Two notable identification tools are CliftonStrengths by Gallup and the Character Strengths Profile by the VIA Institute on Character. According to Gallup, strengths, like virtues, develop through habits, particularly those that involve the repeated application of talents.[12] Character strengths such as adaptability, empathy, and focus are essentially inborn, vary from person to person, and are able to grow through habit.[13] A strengths-based approach to improving performance, achieving goals, and attaining well-being shifts the emphasis from the traditional vice-aversive fixation on weaknesses or deficiencies. One should mainly direct one's gaze to the positive—one's strengths—when figuring out how to improve.

Princess and Dragon

An extreme form of the traditional approach might involve channeling our inner Led Tasso, shaming incontinent characters, and making them run a thousand laps until they're as dehydrated as the trees in *Dumbo*. A less extreme and more reasonable approach would involve identifying the players' weaknesses and eliminating them.

Aristotle would fit into this camp, in his own unique way. He'd first want to make sure the players know why their tendencies are wrong. He would then make sure they know that the goal of their improvement is virtue. He'd finally recommend that they shoot for the mean—the sweet spot between excess and deficiency—by habitually counteracting their vices. In other words, compensate for their excess or deficiency.

Roy tends toward rashness, but one corrective is his relationship with his niece Phoebe. She helps him improve by encouraging him to be softer, meeker, and gentler. He plays Princess and Dragon with her and shows patience and understanding when she makes mistakes. The result is that Roy becomes less harsh overall. He's also supposed to clean up his language, though with little success. Because his relationship with Phoebe is ongoing, it's not just once that Roy has to act contrary to his natural tendency, but many times. Again, habits are central to this approach. Aristotelian virtues of character such as moderation (temperance), courage, and generosity develop through habits and practice. Training.

You Complete Our Team

Ted's approach, though consistent with Aristotle's, features a strengths-focused angle as well. His coaching style is subtle, never hitting you over the head, as Trent writes. Ted often elicits people's strengths just by being himself, rather than through explicit coaching efforts. He aims at developing the well-being of the whole person, as opposed to simply optimal performance in soccer and the victory that results.

Roy's self-improvement is due not only to Phoebe's influence, but to Ted's as well. A key part of Roy's success is that he taps into his natural strengths, representing a synthesis between virtue ethics and a strengths-centric strategy. A good coach, like Ted, helps people identify their strengths and use them to attain specific life goals.[14] Even if that involves encouraging Roy to assume the mantle of leadership, like the little girl from *A Wrinkle in Time*. Roy clearly has this character trait, which corresponds with justice, and Ted sees that with clarity and prescience right off the bat. "He's the one. If we're gonna make an impact here," he tells Beard, "the first domino that needs to fall is right inside that man's heart" ("Trent Crimm: The Independent").

Roy is gifted in judgment, too, especially when it comes to spotting errors, Jamie's for example. Roy is unflinchingly honest, a quality that corresponds with the virtue of courage. And Roy at his best seems to display exceptional focus. Consider the intensity that he devotes to any task at hand. Ted excels at spotting talent, and he takes notice of Roy's good judgment on the field, his brutal honesty, his leadership, and his focus.[15] The mustachioed surprise thus ambushes Roy at his favorite kebab shop and attempts to persuade Roy, after he retires, to join the coaching staff and employ his considerable gifts, talents, and strengths for the betterment of the team.

It's not only Ted who helps Roy discover his strengths and develop them. Nate, too, draws out Roy's strengths in his challenging pregame talk before their Everton contest. It's a confrontation that humbles the soccer legend, a much-needed move in Roy's character development. Despite his timidity, Nate deftly challenges Roy to regain his focus and direct his rage to compensate for the toll aging has taken on him and face this new stage of his career with courage. Roy had to run like he was angry at the grass one more time.

Even Jamie, surprisingly enough, gives Roy a chance to show his kinder, gentler side. When Roy sees Jamie's mistreatment by his father, Roy's sense of justice and leadership kick in. It all culminates in a poignant hug that showcases the gentleness Roy has cultivated in his other relationships, a touching moment that would prove a harbinger of things to come. After their previous tensions and altercations, this moment of reconciliation and tenderness is deeply moving indeed, a signature *Lasso* moment.

These strengths also manifest in Roy's relationship with Keeley. In some ways, theirs is an Aristotelian friendship of pleasure in Season 2. Roy and Keeley's enjoyment of one another's company is obvious, enhanced by Roy harnessing his judgment and tempering his anger with meekness and humility. By Season 3 it was hoped that their relationship may even fit the description of a complete friendship, a friendship of virtue as Aristotle conceives it.[16]

Jamie Less Tart

Jamie also taps into his own natural strengths while developing habits that guide him toward the mean between deficiency and excess. His most obvious talent is his athletic ability. Roy remarks that his "right foot was kissed by God" ("Trent Crimm: The Independent"). Jamie's arrogance, rendering his behavior appalling and his personality grating, begins to erode. His pride leads to a fall. He's kicked off *Lust Conquers All*, not invited back to Manchester City, and shunned by his teammates on his return to Richmond. He's a battler with the strengths of hope[17] and self-assurance[18] for his own success, but he needs to follow Keeley's advice and stop battling those who only want to help him. Jamie knows he can be great, but he's been channeling this self-assurance the wrong way. By finding some humility, he starts to be more intentional in treating others better, as justice dictates.

Ted and the other coaches leverage Jamie's natural tendency for competition,[19] and help him develop this potential virtue by encouraging him to become more of a team player. In his zeal to curb Jamie's selfishness, Ted actually does this so much that the team misses out on goals that they might otherwise have had. With their permission, Jamie takes the occasional salty cue—colorful sign language—to get under the opposing team's skin and score more goals, while remaining a Jamie his mom can be proud of—an even greater Jamie inside an already great Jamie. In this way Jamie undergoes a significant transformation, both by avoiding vices and by cultivating strengths and virtues.

Self-Love and Self-Loathing in Richmond

Though Rebecca deserves most of the credit for her own self-improvement, Ted and Keeley play vital roles. They both counsel Rebecca, empathically listen to her, and encourage her to use her natural leadership abilities to navigate her painful situation.[20] They recognize and encourage her innate ability to command.[21] All of this, plus Ted's kindness, helps Rebecca become a better person.

The result? Rebecca resumes doing good for those around her. She had simply lost her way for a minute, but then rediscovers her better, truer, sillier self. She is on the road back. Ted and Keeley also help Rebecca love herself more, which is crucial to friendships and flourishing, according to Aristotle.[22]

By blending virtue ethics and strengths-based approaches, Roy and Jamie, Ted and Sam and Rebecca all become happier, develop healthy self-love as the seasons progress, and form genuine friendships.

What about Nate? He's a perplexing case because of his devolution even after Ted's exceptional efforts to help him cultivate his strengths to become more virtuous. Ted, Keeley, and Rebecca all mentor and empower Nate to help him become more confident and courageous. But something goes wrong. Missing the right note makes potential strengths into weaknesses. Nate's ill-fated attempt to kiss Keeley brings shame and self-loathing.

At the end of Season 2, Nate is so critical of Ted that he leaves Richmond to coach West Ham, participating in Rupert's scheme to exact revenge on Rebecca. He had yet to develop proper self-love in the Aristotelian sense. Missing Aristotle's mean makes him mean. But he remained a work in progress. We found ourselves hoping for the best, and the question of Nate's possible redemption loomed at the end of the second season.

A Work in Progmess

Whether people can change is a central question come the close of Season 3. The Diamond Dogs agree that we should aim for progress over perfection. To many philosophers, including Aristotle, happiness can only be fully realized once our lives are complete. In this life, Higgins asserts, "The best we can do is to keep asking for help and accepting it when you can. And if you keep on doing that, you'll always be moving towards better" (So Long, Farewell"). In this way, Rebecca, Jamie, and Roy are no different from Nate the Great.

Jade motivates Nate's improvement over the course of Season 3. She sees Nate's goodness in spite of his initial timidity and his eventual arrogance. In order to earn and maintain Jade's respect, Nate has to hit the mean between cowardice and overconfidence. He does this when he drums up the courage to ask her out, and he continues to do so as he honorably excuses himself from the double date Rupert sets up.

As he escapes Rupert's influence and finally apologizes to the Greyhounds and rejoins them, Nate is humbled in the process, taking the role of assistant to the kit man before being later promoted to his old job as assistant coach. To navigate this process, Nate taps into his strengths of taking responsibility, strategizing, and believing in himself and others.

Roy, Jamie, and Rebecca also remain in process in Season 3. Roy becomes a full-fledged Diamond Dog. Jamie remembers that on the pitch, he's just one of eleven. Rebecca relinquishes her desire for revenge against Rupert and finally lives for her own life goals—*teloi* according to Aristotle. In the process, all of these characters achieve stronger friendships. For Aristotle, creating and nourishing a thriving community conducive to human flourishing is the ultimate goal of ethics and politics.

Beard's slide show brings the larger Lasso community of friends into clear and heartwarming focus, including team victory celebrations, one of many locker room haircut sessions, the amusement park trip, and Christmas dinner at the Higgins home ("So Long, Farewell"). It illustrates the power of friendships, a team united, and a mission accomplished. Through thousands of imperceptible moments, Ted has enabled them to find, at long last, the Richmond Way.

Notes

1 Aristotle. *Nicomachean Ethics*, trans. W. D. Ross, available at http://classics. mit.edu/Aristotle/nicomachaen.html, bk. 7, chs. 7–13. The *Nicomachean Ethics* is widely regarded as Aristotle's most complete and authoritative work on ethics, the study of the good life. It's divided into books, which are further subdivided into chapters.
2 I'm thinking of *The Untouchables* for the former and *Goodfellas* for the latter.
3 Aristotle discusses this throughout a great deal of *Nicomachean Ethics* (henceforth "NE") bk. 7.
4 Ibid., bk. 3, chs. 6–7.

5   Ibid., bk. 4, ch. 8.

6   Ibid., bk. 8, ch. 1.

7   Ibid., bk. 8, ch. 1.

8   Aristotle, *Politics*, trans Benjamin Jowett, available at http://classics.mit.edu/Aristotle/politics.html, bk. 1, ch. 2.

9   Aristotle argues for this throughout much of NE bks. 8 and 9.

10 NE, bk. 8, chs. 2–3.

11 NE, bk. 8, ch. 2.

12 *Clifton StrengthsFinder Resource Guide for Coaches*, Gallup, Inc., 2000, 2012.

13 *What Are the 34 CliftonStrengths Themes?*, https://www.gallup.com/cliftonstrengths/en/253715/34-cliftonstrengths-themes.aspx (accessed July 20, 2022).

14 This is the language Gallup uses in training its strengths coaches.

15 https://www.viacharacter.org/character-strengths.

16 NE bk. 8, ch. 2.

17 https://www.viacharacter.org/character-strengths.

18 https://www.gallup.com/cliftonstrengths/en/253715/34-cliftonstrengths-themes.aspx.

19 Ibid.

20 https://www.viacharacter.org/character-strengths.

21 https://www.gallup.com/cliftonstrengths/en/253715/34-cliftonstrengths-themes.aspx.

22 NE bk. 9, ch. 4.

Ted Lasso's Personal Dilemma Squad

R. Keith Loftin

> Perfect friendship is the friendship of men who are good, and alike in excellence; for these wish well alike to each other *qua* good, and they are good in themselves.[1]
>
> — Aristotle

> [The Diamond Dogs are] just a group of people who care, Roy. Not unlike folks at a hip-hop concert whose hands are *not* in the air.
>
> — Ted Lasso

Who wouldn't want to be friends with Ted Lasso? Like some preternatural, irresistible force, he draws people into friendship. Or at least into desiring his sort of friendship. From those like Trent Crimm, who is indifferent about Ted's success, to Rebecca Welton, who actively undermines and pursues ill for him, most everyone eventually falls under Ted's spell. And if the show's popular reception is any indication, that attraction is felt well beyond the screen. We not only like Ted, we admire him. We long to enjoy the more satisfying, more *substantive* friendship he offers. The best of us hope to offer such friendship to others.

Ted is following an ancient playbook: true friendship requires genuinely desiring and pursuing another's highest good. And like Jamie Tartt when it comes to passing the ball, we need to rethink the concepts foundational to friendship: *happiness*, *selves*, and *human flourishing*.

Ted Lasso and Philosophy: No Question Is Into Touch, First Edition.
Edited by Marybeth Baggett and David Baggett.
© 2024 John Wiley & Sons, Inc. Published 2024 by John Wiley & Sons, Inc.

Personal Metaphorical Saint Bernard

"Success," Ted says to Trent over lunch, "is not about the wins and losses. It's about helping these young fellows be the best versions of themselves" ("Trent Crimm: The Independent"). Through the prism of Ted's philosophy of coaching, we glimpse a central theme: the beauty and challenge of helping one another flourish. Trent initially perceives Ted's outlook as practically incomprehensible. That's how it must seem to those intent on using others "for the sake of utility" (such as cannon fodder in a sports column) or "for the sake of what is pleasant to themselves" (as a pawn in one's revenge scheme). In both cases it is *oneself* that is loved (however poorly), not the other. "[S]uch friendships ... are easily dissolved" because they are not genuine.[2] Abuses of others begin with a misconception of what is "good," as Ted suggests.

Misunderstanding the good can ruin friendship quicker than a fish pie can ruin an afternoon. Take Jamie. We meet Jamie as the self-centered, arrogant star striker for AFC Richmond. He's a fan-favorite, but Jamie is nowhere more beloved than in his own mind. Having crowned himself the highest good, Jamie has neither companion nor friend. At best, others have value only in support of Jamie's self-satisfaction. In this early state Jamie seems incapable even of affection, a rather low bar.

As C. S. Lewis (1898–1963) explains, "[T]he especial glory of Affection is that it can unite those who most emphatically, even comically, are not [friends or lovers]; people who, if they had not found themselves put down by fate in the same household or community, would have had nothing to do with each other."[3] Affection requires, minimally, seeing and appreciating others with whom one is familiar. It requires at least acknowledging the good in and for others.[4] If failure here prohibits affection, then it rules out friendship.

Although Rebecca Welton does display affection, we nevertheless meet her in a friendless state. In fact, she has been estranged from her best friend for six years ("Make Rebecca Great Again"). Having been hurt deeply by the betrayal of her husband, Rupert, Rebecca has reoriented her every action and relationship toward exacting revenge. She has, in effect, set up the self-satisfaction of realizing this revenge as her "good," ruinous consequences for others be damned. Like Jamie, she is initially consumed with the solitary pursuit of harmful self-satisfaction.

"Friendship," Lewis explains, "must be *about* something, even if it were only an enthusiasm for dominoes."[5] The pursuit of your harmful self-satisfaction is an endeavor into which no one else can plausibly enter. The idea is that, fundamentally, two people cannot pursue the *same* (ultimate) thing when they are each pursuing self-satisfaction. If Edwin Akufo is pursuing, as his ultimate purpose, *his* own self-satisfaction in purchasing Raja Casablanca, and Sam *his* own self-satisfaction in deciding whether or not to join the team, then Edwin is not pursuing Sam's ultimate purpose and vice versa. The pursuit of Sam's satisfaction would not be Edwin's ultimate purpose. The pursuit of Sam's satisfaction could be, at best, only useful to Edwin in pursuing Edwin's own self-satisfaction. With nothing in common, Edwin and Sam will not be friends. (Edwin's temper tantrum when Sam rejects his offer suggests this is probably a good thing.) Likewise, Jamie and Rebecca have nothing to *share* with others. In this state, they are closed off to friendships.

Jamie and Rebecca share the same fundamental problem: misconceiving the good as self-gratification. "Lovers of self," like Jamie and Rebecca, "who are grasping with regard to these things gratify their appetites and in general their feelings and the irrational element of the soul."[6] They are justly reproached as real stinkers and (at this point) definitely not real friends.

But what about the claim that, at root, humans only (can) ever pursue their own happiness? This is a multiply flawed idea, and humans have known so for some time. As Joel Feinberg notes:

> Astute observers of human affairs from the time of the ancient Greeks have often noticed that pleasure, happiness, and satisfaction are states of mind which stand in a very peculiar relation to desire. An exclusive desire for happiness is the surest way to prevent happiness from coming into being. Happiness has a way of "sneaking up" on persons when they are preoccupied with other things; but when persons deliberately and single-mindedly set off in pursuit of happiness, it vanishes utterly from sight and cannot be captured.[7]

Beyond desiring one's own good (which of course we all do), a true friend, at least according to Ted, desires and even pursues the good of a friend—for the sake of the friend. "If you remove good will from friendship," as Cicero reminds us, then "the very name of friendship is gone."[8]

The Lasso Way

What, then, is this "good" that is essential to friendship? The answer has a lot to do with one's happiness. But in a plot twist equally surprising but far less psychologically damaging than finding out your boss wants you to fail, that happiness is not really a matter of one's feelings. It is a matter of one's *kind*: humankind.

As Philippa Foot (1920–2010) puts it, "[W]hen we talk about a happiness that is supposed to be humanity's good we cannot intend pleasure or contentment alone."[9] This much is evident from considering the (early) situation of both Jamie and Rebecca. What we need—and what Ted seems to grasp instinctively—is a notion of good that goes beyond our individual self-satisfaction but that takes seriously the (human) kind of thing we are. The "evaluation of human action depends," that is, "on essential features of specifically human life."[10]

Even if precisely defining "human being" can be difficult, like the offsides rule in soccer, we surely know one when we see it. A human being is a member of the human kind, a bearer of human nature. This matters to our discussion of friendship because we ground moral evaluations of human action and claims about the good for human beings in facts about human nature. The way to think about "nature" here is in terms of natural kinds: groups of things that are similar to one another in virtue of the kind of thing they are (horses or radishes, for example).[11] So, the good that is essential to friendship is going to be specific to the human natural kind. It is good for oak trees to have strong and deep roots: lacking these, an oak tree will be defective. Strong and deep roots are good not merely for a particular tree. They are good for oak trees as such. It is similarly good for human beings to have, among other things, friends.

It may be helpful to clarify two different senses of "good." Aristotle (384–322 BC) distinguishes between "goods in their own right" and merely "useful goods."[12] The latter are often termed "instrumental goods" because they are good only insofar as they help you achieve something deemed to have greater value. Why toil all week? To earn a paycheck. Why bother about a paycheck? To purchase tickets to see AFC Richmond. Thinking again of our oak tree, its instrumental goods would include, say, sunlight and access to water (as these things are useful to its growing strong and deep roots).

What Aristotle calls "goods in their own right," on the other hand, are commonly termed "intrinsic goods" because their value is inherent and not in relation to anything else. These have value, not because they can be traded up for something else, but in themselves. Intrinsic good is not derived. The good that friendship is to human beings is of this intrinsic sort. Friendship is not primarily a matter of what instrumental use someone may be—although friends are certainly useful when planning a choreographed goodbye for Dr. Sharon—but rather they contribute to being a human properly.

Friendship is a good of human beings, both instrumentally and intrinsically, given the kind of things human beings are. The problem is that, much like Ted's grasp of the rules of soccer, we often fail to achieve the clarity we need on this score. Life is messy, and people are flawed to be sure. Things are not the way they are supposed to be. These conditions all but encourage us to treat others as instruments for personal gain or the satisfaction of personal appetites. But in Ted we find someone whose vision of humanity makes sense of life and, importantly, makes it possible to help others become the best versions of themselves.

Best Versions of What?

An old adage reminds us that, like fire and water, feelings make good servants but ruinous masters. One's feelings do not determine one's good. We can easily imagine having feelings of pain in connection to something that is good for us. To be clear, it is perfectly appropriate to recognize that the capacity for feelings is natural for human beings. It is *good for* us that our mental life includes feelings. But if we've learned anything from Liam and Noel, it's that a soul controlled by feelings will slide away, until it can only look back in anger.

Having said that feelings neither determine nor constitute the good for human beings, it may seem odd now to claim that the human good is happiness. The catch is that "happiness" admits of several meanings, and here happiness does not refer to ongoing enjoyment or self-satisfaction. Like contestants on *Lust Conquers All*, a life aimed at perpetual amusement "appears stupid and excessively childish."[13]

What we have in mind is rather the mode of existence called *flourishing*. Imagine an orange tree. An orange tree flourishes when, in keeping with its natural kind, it produces juicy oranges. That is the best version of an orange tree. Similarly, a human being flourishes when it pursues a life of activity in accord with virtue.[14] Human beings pursuing such a life—for its own sake, not for the sake of "getting ahead"—will be the best version of themselves. Encouraging others, for their own sake, toward this happiness and the meaningfulness it contains is the Lasso way of friendship. Even when this demands making sacrifices. "If the Lasso way is wrong," writes Trent, "it's hard to imagine being right" ("Trent Crimm: The Independent").

The Knights of Support

As will be obvious to anyone making effort toward virtue, one does not become a virtuoso overnight. *Gradarius firmus victoria.*[15] Or, as Beard and Ted say, bird by bird. Not to go all Bill Withers on you, but it also does not happen alone.[16] We need friends to help us, and whether we realize it or not, we need to offer friendship to others.[17]

When AFC Richmond returns from Liverpool, it is evident that Ted is emotionally out of sorts and in need of support. Coach Beard, of course, is there for him. What is surprising, perhaps, is Ted's willingness to be vulnerable in front of Nate and Higgins, as well. Is he naïve? Reckless? Quite the contrary. As a person of good will, Ted has vulnerability as a superpower.

As John Cooper explains, enjoying the flourishing life involves friendships where we can be vulnerable with others. This is because, in order to engage in the sort of activities proper to a virtuous life, we "must come to know, and be known by, the other party or parties quite intimately."[18] Needless to say, relationships of this stripe demand a certain character of participants. For this reason, Cooper concludes,

> a human being cannot have a flourishing life except by having intimate friends to whom he is attached precisely on account of their good qualities of character, and who are similarly attached to him: it is only with such persons that he can share the moral activities that are most central to his life.[19]

Whereas to date Ted repeatedly demonstrates his good will toward the others, in making himself vulnerable before Beard, Nate, and Higgins, he takes a step further, inviting them into virtuous activity—into friendship.

As if to accentuate the moment of this scene, we shortly thereafter see a redemptive moment in Higgins. At the first gathering of the Diamond Dogs, Ted's concern for transparency and honesty in his relationship with Rebecca causes Higgins to literally choke on his words. At the time, Higgins was in collusion with Rebecca to hurt Rupert by sabotaging Ted. Awakened through Ted's friendship to a dignity and meaningfulness beyond being Rebecca's lackey, Higgins soon apologizes to Rebecca for past injuries and refuses to participate further in her scheme of ill will. The striking contrast of a relationship sustained by virtue and a relationship fueled by hurt and hate is hard to miss.

A Team United

As David McPherson helpfully clarifies, humans are "fundamentally and distinctively the *meaning–seeking* animal."[20] Although we are rational, human beings also seek a meaningful life. But we often fail to observe the strong goods in our lives that define for us the good—that is, the meaningful life. McPherson calls these "constitutive goods" because they constitute what is for us the good life, beyond any of our personal desires or aims.[21]

When Rebecca makes her full confession to Ted ("All Apologies"), she recognizes that Higgins is correct: "You won't take away your pain by constantly punishing Rupert" ("The Diamond Dogs"). Her pain does not magically vanish, of course, but Rebecca realizes that friendship can fulfill the promise falsely made by self-satisfaction. In friendship she finds redemption and meaning.

Jamie's redemption is similar, as he recognizes the truth in Keeley's admonition: "Jamie, not everyone in your life is out to get you" ("The Hope That Kills You"). Having long sought them through self-centeredness, Jamie ultimately discovers a sense of dignity and belonging through opening himself to the friendship Ted offers. As McPherson makes clear, this vision of happiness does not exclude pain, but it is "a normatively higher, nobler, more meaningful mode of life."[22]

And then there is Nate, who seems initially to believe his life lacks meaning. Beyond awkward, he experiences terrible social anxiety. He's bullied and lacks confidence. Nate seems to believe meaning in life comes from social acceptance and indeed status, which he seems increasingly willing to lord over others. While Ted and Beard treat Nate with dignity, Nate treats Will (the club's new kit man) with condescension and harshness.

Ted invites Nate into friendship, which Nate seems to accept. But in his brokenness, Nate does not recognize true friendship, so he does not respond in true friendship. He *thinks* he is responding in friendship, no doubt. What becomes clear is that Nate's grasp of friendship is even more tenuous than Beard and Jane's relationship.

"The Hope that Kills You" features Nate's promotion to the coaching staff. He seems to believe that his good has been achieved and that his life now has meaning. But perceived threats and slights are interpreted as jeopardizing his "good." The realization that others enjoy greater social status breeds resentment. When Nate cannot reserve the window table at A Taste of Athens ("you know, just to impress my dad"), his instinct is to assert his status, such as it is. Nate informs the hostess that he knows Roy Kent, but he is crushed by the reply: "Please let us know if Mr. Kent ever wants the window table" ("Rainbow"). Given his misperception of the good, Nate can hear this only as a challenge to his sense of self.

Later that same day the coaches are discussing Isaac's yips, and Ted notes his desire to find someone of gravitas to speak with Isaac. "Isaac is a big dog," Ted remarks, "so he's only going to respond to a big dog" ("Rainbow"). With genuine resolve Nate replies, "I'll do it." This moment offers the most overt attempt by Nate to find value in his status. Then comes the genesis of Nate's betrayal of Ted's friendship. Ted, who incorrectly assumes Nate is kidding, responds to Nate's offer with a laughing dismissal. Realizing his insensitivity, Ted apologizes, but nevertheless goes on to cement Nate's perception that Ted does not genuinely value him by saying, "I just think we've got to get [Isaac] a *real* big dog" ("Rainbow").

Instead of the vulnerability that makes way for reconciliation, Nate becomes increasingly embittered. The end of Season 2 stuns viewers. The normally soft-spoken Nate, newly emboldened, with a shock of gray hair reflective of his inner transformation, lashes out at Ted. In the process it's almost as if Ted's the proxy receiving the brunt of all of Nate's frustrations with his own father. Although Nate rips Ted's motivation sign "BELIEVE" asunder and leaves to become the boss at West Ham, perhaps achieving the status and meaning he has yearned for, he's obviously in a bad way.

In a resolution less surprising than Shandy's meltdown, Nate ultimately finds neither happiness nor friendship in his new position. Rupert lavishes Nate with all the status and accompanying swag he has sought, but throughout Season 3 he begins quietly to doubt that the god of status is worth worshipping. Rupert, ever manipulative, grants to his coach irregular personal access, which Nate for a time (mis)interprets as overtures of friendship. He happily accepts Rupert's invitation to post-match drinks ("just the two of us, a guy's night"), where he realizes that Rupert is neither good in himself nor does he truly wish for Nate's good.

Disillusioned (at last) with Rupert, Nate now must enter the darkness of realizing he has misidentified the good, sought meaning in life where it cannot be found, and generally been a dummy head, poo-poo face. As Roy observes to the press, "None of us know what is going on in each other's lives" ("La Locker Room Aux Folles"). Still, it seems apparent that many of Nate's missteps are consequences of a strained relationship with his demanding father. Might we find here the source of Nate's belief that his worth as a person is defined by achievement?

"I pushed you to be the best at everything," his father tearfully admits, "and I thought that's what I had to do.... Be successful, don't be successful—I never cared about any of that. I just want my son to be happy" ("International Break"). What's certain is that these words are a revelation to Nate, a revelation that his father (as well as Ted[23]) desires for Nate a life of activity in accord with virtue: a truly flourishing life, regardless of status. That's the basis for friendship. That's the Lasso Way. After all, what would it profit anyone to gain the whole world and yet forfeit their soul?

Notes

1   Aristotle, *Nicomachean Ethics*, in *The Collected Works of Aristotle: The Revised Oxford Translation*, vol. 2, ed. Jonathan Barnes (Princeton, NJ: Princeton University Press, 1984), 1156b7–10.
2   Ibid., 1156a15–1156b5.
3   C. S. Lewis, *The Four Loves* (New York: Harcourt, Inc., 1988), 36.
4   Fortunately for Jamie "almost anyone can become an object of Affection," including "the exasperating" and "the unattractive." Lewis, *Four Loves*, 32, 37. So Jamie can, despite himself, become a recipient of Ted's affection and friendship.
5   Lewis, *Four Loves*, 66–67.
6   Aristotle, *Nicomachean Ethics*, 1168b15–22.
7   Joel Feinberg, "Psychological Egoism," in Russ Shafer Landau ed., *Ethical Theory: An Anthology* (Malden, MA: Blackwell, 2007), 187.
8   Cicero, "Laelius on Friendship," in *Cicero*, vol. XX, ed. and trans. by William Armistead Falconer (Cambridge, MA: Harvard University Press, 1923), 129.
9   Philippa Foot, *Natural Goodness* (Oxford: Clarendon Press, 2001), 86.
10 Ibid., 14.
11 E. J. Lowe, *The Possibility of Metaphysics: Substance, Identity, and Time* (Oxford: Oxford University Press, 1998), 174–185.
12 Aristotle, *Nicomachean Ethics*, 1096b13–15.
13 Ibid., 1176b33.
14 Ibid., 1098a16–20.
15 This is the Latin motto of the Richmond Greyhounds, translated to "slow and steady wins the race."
16 Aristotle offers additional reasons why attempting to live in isolation is not conducive to human flourishing. See John M. Cooper, *Reason and Emotion: Essays on Ancient Moral Psychology and Ethical Theory* (Princeton, NJ: Princeton University Press, 1999), 345ff.
17 This lends poignancy to recent research conducted by the American Enterprise Institute's Survey Center on American Life indicating that, in

the United States, the percentage of people who report having zero close friends has *quadrupled* since 1990. The study can be found at https://www.americansurveycenter.org/research/the-state-of-american-friendship-change-challenges-and-loss.

18 Cooper, *Reason and Emotion*, 351.

19 Ibid., 351.

20 David McPherson, *Virtue and Meaning: A Neo–Aristotelian Perspective* (New York: Cambridge University Press, 2020), 2. Emphasis mine.

21 Ibid., 32.

22 Ibid., 63.

23 The blocking in this scene matches that of Nate's confrontation with Ted at the end of Season 2, highlighting that Nate had projected onto Ted his complex feelings about his father.

8
The Affable Gaffer

Andy Wible

Ted Lasso is darn right friendly. No doubt about it. That's why people love him. He's like an adult puppy dog mixed with the wit and wisdom of Calvin and Hobbes. Winter, spring, summer or fall, with Ted, you've got a friend. Players, staff, fans, and even the team owner can't help but be Ted's friend. He's irresistible. Yet, as Bill Clinton taught us, not all close relationships with subordinates are appropriate. Is Ted's friendly relationship with his players and staff moral?

Some might criticize the show by saying it is like the summer between my seventh and eighth grades: too campy. But behind that folksy veneer is a needed conversation about the nature and meaning of friendship. Ted's virtues of care, optimism, and loyalty are heartwarming, and as a coach he values personal development over wins. This is not to say Ted is perfect. He doesn't know the rules of the game he coaches, is culturally incompetent, and is fighting personal demons, but we appreciate how his love and loyalty shine through these deficits. He's not preachy, he's friendly. Does this friendliness translate to being actual friends with his players and staff?

Seems Mighty Fragile

To answer this question, we first need to look at what it takes to be a friend. As the philosopher Bennett Helm points out, three characteristics are needed to make a friendship: shared activity, intimacy, and mutual care.[1] The first of these obviously exists for players, coaches, and staff. They are all working towards the goal of having a successful team. Some aim to win, and Ted strives to bring out the best in each player. They are pursuing these goals together, which

Ted Lasso and Philosophy: No Question Is Into Touch, First Edition.
Edited by Marybeth Baggett and David Baggett.
© 2024 John Wiley & Sons, Inc. Published 2024 by John Wiley & Sons, Inc.

brings them closer and gives them a shared history. When shared goals are missing, the friendship seems to be missing. In the first season when Rebecca wanted the team to fail, it was hard for the others to be her friend.

The second characteristic of friendship is intimacy. Friends know us and have spent time with us. The coaches and players practice, travel, and play together. They dine, volunteer, and converse. Friendships take time, as Ted seems to recognize from the start. Working and playing together certainly gives people the opportunity for intimacy. We often reveal more of ourselves through this time together. Roy becomes more of a friend when he tells the team about his blankie (sorry, blanket) he has had since age nine ("Two Aces"), and the team bonds more with Colin when he comes out.

If intimacy is lacking, friendship is missing. Many teammates and even Ted have trouble early on being friends with Jamie because he is guarded. Worse, he doesn't participate in team activities, insults fellow players, and picks on the weakest link, Nate, to show his strength. We don't know the real Jamie. As with a shared activity, intimacy alone isn't enough for a friendship. Players share their intimacies with Dr. Fieldstone in therapy, but they are not her friend. A shared goal and intimacy are both needed for a friendship, but individually neither is enough.

Are intimacy and shared goals together sufficient for friendship? It doesn't seem so. We might know someone intimately and work with them, but not be their friend. A teammate or coworker who hates me is not my friend no matter what we do together or what we know about each other. In Season 1, Roy can't be friends with Jamie. He hates his narcissism and the way he treats Keeley and fellow teammates. Friends care about each other. When friends do well, we cheer, and when they hurt, we cry. Roy is able to become friends with Jamie after his return to Richmond because he is now more open about his feelings and mistakes, and remarkably seems to care about other people and the good of the team.

Rebecca found herself liking and caring about Ted because he cared about her. Despite her best efforts to resist, she found herself becoming his friend. The care must be genuine too. Trent Crimm noticed this about Ted after Ted said he enjoyed spending time with him. Trent replies, "You actually mean that, don't you?" ("Trent Crimm: The Independent"). Ted reminded the team about the importance of care when Colin came out as gay to the team. Some of the players reacted to the news with "Big whoop," "We don't care," and "It's all good." Ted replies, "No, we do care." After fumbling with a comparison between being gay and being a Denver Bronco's fan, he continues, "We care very much. We care about who you are and what you must have been going through" ("La Locker Room Aux Folles"). Friends should care about and, he asserts, support something so important in Colin's life.

Like a shared goal and intimacy, care is not a sufficient condition by itself. Dani has long cared about Zava. The star was crucial to his coming of age, but that does not make Zava his friend. Intimacy must be present and the care must be mutual for a real friendship to exist.

If we enjoy shared activity, intimacy, and mutual care, is that sufficient for friendship? We certainly seem closer to what friendships are. Yet parents and younger children have all three of these and don't seem to be friends. Another requirement is needed for friendship. There must be relatively equal power. If one person can't consent and be themselves due to a power difference in the relationship, then a genuine friendship cannot form. Inequality can make friendships difficult. Coaches, like employers and managers, have power over the other person in the relationship. The player can be fired, traded, or benched based on decisions made by a coach. They are in a vulnerable position and often not as free to speak as friends should be.

The Power of Friendship

Why are friendships important? Most philosophical discussions on this question begin by examining the first Western authority on friendship: Aristotle (384–322 BC). Aristotle thought that friendships are central to eudaimonia.[2] Eudaimonia may sound like figurines sold on the Home Shopping Network, but for Aristotle it meant flourishing. Humans are rational and social creatures. We enjoy other people and are made better by engaging with society. We can expand ourselves with friends. We treat friends like we treat ourselves because we care about them like we care about ourselves. A Greek Proverb appropriately says, "Show me your friends, and I'll show you yourself."

Vacations, work, and football victories are better when they are experienced with friends. Not only do we enjoy the victory, but we are also happy that our friends get to enjoy the victory as well. David Hume (1711–1776) wrote, "A perfect solitude is, perhaps, the greatest punishment we can suffer. Every pleasure languishes when enjoyed apart from society."[3] Even our darker moments are eased with friends. Death, injury, and losses are made tolerable due to friends, making the team's appearance at the funeral of Rebecca's dad so meaningful.

Ted said after relegation, "I promise you that there is something worse out there than being sad, and that is being alone and sad. Ain't no one in this room alone" ("The Hope that Kills You").

The importance of friendships is also shown when we lose one. When a friend dies, moves away, or stops caring about you, it can be devastating. We find solace from the death of friends through funerals that bring mutual friends together. We regret when friends are not able to be present for important events in our lives. A father or friend not in attendance can make a victory feel hollow. Nate the Great's betrayal of Richmond, the Diamond Dogs, and Ted for West Ham United left his friends disappointed and bewildered. By contrast, Jamie's departure for Manchester City left most Greyhounds unfazed because he wasn't a close friend.

Three Amigos

Aristotle thought that friendships are relationships based on care and that we can care about one another for three different kinds of reasons: pleasure, utility, or virtue. The first type of friendship comes from taking pleasure in the other person's company. People enjoy being around Ted because he is funny, and they like being around Keeley because she is fun and beautiful. The second type of friendship comes from one or both parties benefiting in some way. Coaches and players certainly can be friends in this way. The coach benefits from good players and the players benefit from the coaching. We want to help and do good for friends. As Ted says, "We can't really be good partners unless we get to know each other, right?" ("Biscuits"). This approach comes to fruition with Total Football. It requires players to trust and care about each other due to constant interchangeability and dependency on teammates. The strategy succeeds because they are friends. "It's putting aside personal glory for the good of the team" ("The Strings that Bind Us").

The final type of friendship is a virtue friendship, which comes from caring about the other person due to their good character. The shared goal of such relationships is excellence. Virtuous friends and relationships make us better persons. Perhaps that is why so many people delight in Ted: he is a good person. In fact, his virtuous character makes it hard not to like him. As even Trent wrote, "I can't help but root for him" ("Trent Crimm: The Independent").

The first two types of friendships are less noble than the third, according to Aristotle. Immanuel Kant (1724–1804) can help us see why these types of friendships may be deficient. Kant believed that we are all rational beings who deserve to be treated with respect. Using a person for some end is wrong.

In coaching, friendliness doesn't always get results, so yelling might sometimes be necessary. Led Tasso, Ted's alter ego, came out when the team's hatred of Jamie was harming them. The coach was using any trick he had to motivate the players to succeed. So there may be a challenge to coaches being friends with players in more than the pleasure and utility senses. Coaches' friendships are likely to be fragile and end when players don't perform, are traded, or retire. Can a virtuous type of friendship exist between Ted and his players?

Hire Your Best Friend?

There are moral limits to what a coach can do to benefit the team. An opposing coach shouldn't weaken the leash to kill Richmond's Greyhound Mascot (RIP Earl) and Coach Cartrick would be nuts to take out Jamie to help West Ham win as Rupert desires. Coaches should play within the rules of the sport and morality. Giving banned performance-enhancing drugs, or stealing the signals of the opposing team *à la* the Houston Astros go against the rules and moral spirit of the game.

Friendships similarly have moral boundaries. Friendships delight, but they can also cause pain and result in conflicts of interest. The philosopher Alexander Nehamas writes, "Friendship begets joy and contentment, but also leads to affliction and misery—the dull aches of abandonment, the sharp stabs of betrayal, and the agonizing dilemmas of loyalty."[4]

A paradigm conflict of interest is when one's professional obligations conflict with one's personal obligations. We benefit from friendships, and so we have obligations of gratitude to friends that we don't have to others. Coaches have professional obligations to do what's best for the team, and these professional obligations can conflict with their personal responsibilities. An owner or coach might say to a traded player that it was "just business," a move for the good of the franchise. But as friends they may have an obligation of loyalty to keep the player if they want to stay. That is what friends do. Should the coach follow the personal obligation to the friend or do what is best for the team? The answer may be unclear. Rebecca and Ted become good friends over time. Then there were legitimate calls for her to fire Ted and she refused. Did their friendship cause too much loyalty to Ted?

Common conflicts of interest in coaching and business include when sexual harassment occurs or a sexual relationship develops. Ted evidently saw this type of conflict first-hand as a kid: "I haven't seen a pass that soft, since my high school drama teacher asked me to mow his lawn" ("Do the Right-est Thing"). These precariously close relationships are routinely prohibited in employment contracts and codes of ethics for coaches.

The reason is twofold: The intensity of these relationships does not allow for good judgment and impartiality. Parents should not be their child's surgeon, and coaches shouldn't date their players. And the power imbalance between coach and player or boss and employee undermines the possibility of genuine consent. As intense and luxurious as their relationship was, Keeley found out that she never should have dated Jack. When people in these different power relationships are too close, it is morally wrong. Which brings us to Rebecca and Sam.

Friendly Bantr

Like many parts of *Ted Lasso*, the relationship between these two is heartening. They are smitten with each other mentally and sexually, and they provide the companionship and happiness both desperately need. But there is a clear conflict between professional duties as player and owner and their personal interests in developing the relationship. This is particularly true for Rebecca. Owners have even greater power than coaches do over their players. Rebecca can trade and fire without even Ted's consent, making Sam quite vulnerable.

We might wonder if Rebecca and Sam's relationship is wholesome enough to override the apparent conflict. Their relationship does bring them both joy, and clearly there is consent on both sides. Sam seems to play better because he is so happy. Rebecca makes him realize his worth as a player and person. Rebecca wouldn't want to trade him. They are both good persons, and we want to see two good people be together. The show tries to present their relationship as the exception to the rule of not allowing superiors to date subordinates. True love can't be wrong.

Still, the risks that the relationship involves are prohibitively high, even if bad consequences don't occur. Like the time I made my way to the front of a Bad Company concert, it's just too close. Professionalism concerning the overall good of the team and fairness to the other players is in jeopardy. Rebecca fights the desire, but has trouble overriding her passion for Sam. The intensity of the relationship keeps it going and is the biggest reason for conflict. Romantic love can cloud our moral senses. Rebecca eventually does realize the mistake and cuts it off with Sam. She loves him but realizes her love of AFC Richmond is more important.

The Lasso Way

Should Coach Lasso be less of a friend to players and staff to avoid a conflict of interest and possible harm? Sheryle Bergmann Drewe holds that coaches like Ted should have only a limited utility friendship with players.[5] A romantic or virtuous friendship is too close, but a lesser utility friendship is allowed and even recommended. A utility relationship exists only when the person is useful. So the relationship can end when the athlete is no longer performing or injured, as with Roy. These types of relationships allow players to be close and benefit from that friendship without being so close as to cause vexing conflicts of interest.

It is better in life for people to be friendly in interactions. Players get mucho, mucho joy playing for Ted Lasso. Not so much for Led Tasso. The criticism of Drewe's position is Eddie Haskell-style brown nosing.[6] Fake friendliness to get the desired effect. Aristotle pointed out that such friendships often seem hollow because true care is missing.

For example, it would seem wrong for Ted to jettison any care for Roy after he was injured or Jamie after he was traded. He would be like a friendly salesperson who sells you a defective 2010 brown Chevy Malibu and doesn't seem to know you after the sale (still bitter). The appropriate disappointed reply would be "I thought you were my friend." It may even seem a little worse when a person is used in a friendly way—looking at you, Rebecca, when Ted arrived! There is an added sense of deception. True friendships continue even when the person is not useful, making Ted's fatherly gesture of kindness to Jamie at the end of Season 1 so poignant.

The question now is whether there can be a genuine friendship without conflict and harm. Aristotle may have provided the answer with virtue friendships. In these relationships, the two people are friends regardless of benefit and pleasure. They remain friends even when playing for an opposing team, and do so because of each other's virtuous character. The best of sports comes out when we see opposing players hug, congratulate, and console rivals after a competition. They play hard against each other but remain loyal friends throughout. The competition matters, but the people matter more. As both Ted and Pep agree, "For me, success is not about wins and losses. It is about helping these fellas be the best versions of themselves on and off the field" ("Mom City").

Ted brings out the best in his staff and players. He helped Jamie be less obnoxious and care about the good of the team with comments such as "I think you might be so sure that you are one in million, that you forget that you are just one in 11" ("Biscuits"). Roy swears a little less and is more caring due to the team's new camaraderie, and Rebecca is less devious after Ted's biscuits with the boss. The team is at their moral best when they help Sam clean up Ola's after it was ransacked, bringing a gratifying tear to every fan's eye. Ted's virtuous friendships are infectious. If you focus on the person, the wins will likely follow. Spoiler: AFC Richmond almost won it all. And if the wins don't come, you still have each other and can feel good knowing you did the right thing. As Rebecca learned from Nora, "Sometimes you have to do the right thing, even if you lose" ("Do the Right-est Thing").

Such relationships raise concerns about conflicts of interest. A virtuous person can best mediate conflicts between the good of the team versus the good of the individual. The virtuous coach knows when to prioritize the team over the players, and in other instances when to prioritize the players over the team. Prioritizing the players over the wins and losses is important. At other times, Ted prioritizes the team over the individual. He benched Jamie to improve the team. Jamie was livid, but it helped the other players stop relying so much on him and work better together.

Virtuous persons also know when more care is needed and when not to get too close. Ted befriended Sam when he was homesick and Nate when he was ignored and abused. But Ted also avoided the team Christmas party at a time of intense personal loneliness. Ted even knew to liberate his most loyal friend Coach Beard so he could follow his heart and be with Jane. He's constantly trying to know when to hold 'em and when to fold 'em.

Judgment is vital for virtues because they strike the balance between extremes, according to Aristotle. Virtuous persons, for example, are honest with each other, but honest to the right degree. On occasion they should probably refrain from painfully brutal honesty, at least so think the Diamond Dogs. But at other times they should tell truth even when it hurts, such as when coaches tell players they are not NSYNC. "You may hate me, but it ain't no lie" ("Midnight Train to Royston").

Virtuous persons and friendships are not perfect. Doing the right thing isn't easy. Ted is not perfect. He admitted he got it wrong when he failed to tell the team about his panic attack. The players shouldn't have learned about it through the tabloids. The secrecy threatened to result in less trust from the players ("Inverting the Pyramid of Success"). Ted is slowly working on being more culturally competent to boot, and at long last, he finally understands the offsides rule. Virtuous persons know to introspect for faults and identify where they are susceptible to error. Virtuous friends then help each other understand why and when they screw up or "put the game before the dame" ("For the Children").

Virtue friendships between coaches and players are possible, and as Ted has shown, they are preferable. Ted's friendships make the players and himself better persons. These friendships bring joy, meaning, and excellence on and off the pitch. Like many goods, they involve potential pitfalls that need constant attention. Big mistakes should be avoided, and little ones corrected. Eudaimonia is a process as much as an end. These friendships should be a part of coaching as much as friendships should be a part of life. As Ted said, "I think that if you care about someone and you got a little love in your heart, there ain't nothing you can't achieve together" ("For the Children").

Notes

1 Bennett Helm, "Friendship," *Stanford Encyclopedia of Philosophy*, available at https://plato.stanford.edu/entries/friendship/.
2 Aristotle, *Nicomachean Ethics*, trans. W. D. Ross, available at http://classics.mit.edu/Aristotle/nicomachaen.html.
3 David Hume, *A Treatise on Human Nature (1739)*, available at https://oll.libertyfund.org/title/bigge-a-treatise-of-human-nature.
4 Alexander Nehamas, *On Friendship* (New York: Basic Books, 2016), 187.
5 Sheryle Bergmann Drewe, "The Coach Athlete Relationship: How Close is Too Close?" *Journal of the Philosophy of Sport* 24 (2002), 174–181.
6 Psychologists now even have a condition called the Eddie Haskell Syndrome for people who have dual personalities. They ingratiate superiors, as Eddie did with June and Ward, and then abuse subordinates, as Eddie did to Beaver.

Part III
MAN CITY

9

Poop in the Punchbowl

Caleb McGee Husmann and Elizabeth Kusko

Around the same time Ted Lasso was learning not to trust candy bars from Ronnie Fouch "on the rough and tumble playgrounds of Brookridge Elementary School," philosopher Harry Frankfurt was also having a poop-related epiphany: "One of the most salient features of our culture is that there is so much bullshit."[1]

These words were true in 1986, but unfortunately, they're even more true today. BS is everywhere. It pervades our institutions from left to right, top to bottom. It's in our politics, of course, but also in our news, entertainment, social networks, and workplaces. There's nary a realm untainted by its stench.

As a consequence of this reality, one would think that those looking to reverse this scatological scourge would be legion, that proponents of truth would be champing at the bit to extirpate the excrement. This is not the case, however. When most people identify BS generated in service of something that they *don't* agree with, they counter by proffering BS in service of something that they *do* agree with. Bullshit is winning and few seem to care. People are either embracing the stink or snapping a clothespin on their nostrils, content to soldier on as best they can amidst the growing turd-mounds.

Or at least this used to be the case. Then came *Ted Lasso*, a show so earnest and committed to the truth that one can't help but feel that it was written with the singular goal of turning back the tide, or, at the very least, to serve as a life raft for those drowning in the droppings.

Ted Lasso and Philosophy: No Question Is Into Touch, First Edition.
Edited by Marybeth Baggett and David Baggett.

The Anatomy of BS

More is needed to distinguish BS from lying. According to Frankfurt, BS is fundamentally different from lying, and in some ways, more dangerous.

Lying, according to Frankfurt, "is an act with a sharp focus. It is designed to insert a particular falsehood at a specific point in a set or system of beliefs, in order to avoid the consequences of having that point occupied by the truth."[2] Liars know what the truth is, but intentionally replace it with a falsehood when they find it necessary. BS-ers on the other hand, are completely unconcerned with the truth. Their goal is not to strategically insert a lie among a set of true beliefs. Their goal is simply to get away with whatever they're trying to get away with. The truth is of little interest to the BS-er. Words and facts matter only insofar as they either inhibit or assist them in achieving their aim. In short, liars are concerned with the truth, BS-ers are not.

That key difference shows why the latter can be more problematic than the former. Liars, after all, care about the truth, which means they are engaged in the same game as truthful people. The BS-ers, on the other hand, are not. When an honest person like Coach Beard sits down to play chess against a liar, they both acknowledge the same rules. If a cheat is perpetrated, it is carefully crafted not to stick out. The cheat is conceived of and executed with the rules of the game in mind. An unauthorized computer-assisted move, for instance, might be something a liar would try to get away with.

In contrast, when a truthful person plays chess with a BS-er, there is no telling what might happen. Maybe the BS-er agrees to let white open, maybe he turns over the board, maybe he convinces onlookers that the deep state has rigged the game, maybe he claims that his opponent has ruined the pieces by misgendering the queen. Or maybe he replaces his rooks with Sour Patch Kids, calls them Lobsterguns, and claims they're invincible. Nothing is off the table. The truth is irrelevant. All that matters to the BS-er is that they are successfully manipulating the situation in their desired direction. If people are buying Lobsterguns, then the BS-er will sell Lobsterguns, rules and facts be damned.

This cavalier disregard for the truth is one of the hallmarks of BS and it is what makes the phenomenon so troubling. Quite simply, BS destabilizes life in a way that a lie cannot. Take the chess example again. If the liar gets away with his cheat, he might obtain an undeserved victory. This is bad. But it pales in comparison to what might happen if the BS-er is successful. The BS-er can ruin the game forever.

This is not an exaggeration. Chess is, after all, governed by a set of rules. If those rules are successfully smudged, painted over, or erased by such an artist, then the game is effectively destroyed. Such an outcome could never stem from the liar's cheat. It is for this reason that Frankfurt concludes that "bullshitting constitutes a more insidious threat than lying does to the conduct of civilized life."[3]

So, what is the remedy to BS? Is it sincerity? Although Frankfurt finds this approach valuable, he proposes that sincerity alone is too fixated on honestly representing oneself. Instead, the antidote to BS is not sincerity, but correctness, where the primary focus lies in seeking accurate representations of a common world.[4] This, the pursuit of correctness *first* followed *then* by sincerity, is what makes *Ted Lasso* stand out in its unrivaled repudiation of BS. *The Office, Parks and Rec, Schitt's Creek*, all of these *Ted Lasso*-predecessors make good faith efforts to counter the cynicism and ironic detachment that has come to dominate in these times of growing BS. But all of these shows attempt to do so exclusively via sincerity. *Ted Lasso* may be the only comedy in the streaming era to seek both correctness and sincerity, perhaps the best solution to combat BS effectively.

In order to demonstrate this claim, the rest of this chapter will be devoted to detailing three specific ways in which *Ted Lasso* is a clear renunciation of BS. First, the importance of integrity and how various characters accept truth, even when that truth is not what was desired. When Ted realizes that Michelle is indeed asking for a divorce, it is truly heartbreaking and leads first to a panic attack during karaoke and then to lashing out at Nate in the hotel. But by correctly accepting the truth that his marriage is ending, Ted develops as an individual, friend, and coach. It also endears us to his goodness. This sort of ideal is a hallmark of the show's good guys. Second, BS is the main approach of the show's big bad guy Rupert Mannion. Lastly, characters who demonstrate personal growth over the course of the show do so by dialing back their BS and turning up their correctness followed by their sincerity.

Like Dani Rojas greeting the pitch, let's now happily attend to point number one.

The Good Guys of *Ted Lasso*

Good guys. There are a lot of them in *Ted Lasso*. They come in all shapes, sizes, and flavors. Introverted, extroverted, silly, serious, lively, gruff, there is no single specific disposition or demeanor shared by all of them. There is, however, one thing they all reject: bullshit.

Let's start with Ted Lasso himself, the title character who exemplifies the anti-BS message at the heart of the show. Ted is an American football coach managing a European soccer team. He knows next to nothing about the sport he is coaching, the country in which he is living, or the league in which he is participating. This is a situation ripe for BS. Indeed, it is hard to envision a scenario that would be more encouraging of the behavior, especially when one considers Frankfurt's insight that it is more prevalent when "a person's obligations or opportunities to speak about some topic exceed his knowledge of the facts that are relevant to that topic."[5] Despite spending all day every day in an environment that begs him to become a BS-artist, Ted never succumbs. Instead, he seeks to be correct and honest and sincere in all of his actions. Is he optimistic? Sure. Naive? Perhaps. But does he intentionally deceive himself or others about how the world actually is? Never.

Ted's truthful optimism is perhaps his most defining characteristic, and it is on display throughout the show. It is evident in how he coaches. He never feigns tactical knowledge of the game, but instead manages the team's cohesiveness and the players' mental hang-ups, things that are actually in his wheelhouse. It is evident in how he interacts with reporters. He never feeds them boilerplate answers he doesn't believe, nor does he lie about his goals or motives.

Instead, he's forthright and transparent even if that invites harsh criticism. It is evident in the way he responds to difficult truths. Ted doesn't pretend that it's easy for him to deal with his wife's feelings, or benching Roy, or accepting Dr. Fieldstone's help. But he does these things anyway because he accepts the reality of the matter and forces himself to respond appropriately. Quite simply, Ted doesn't BS. It is anathema to him. It is off limits because it's dishonest and because it's insincere, and, most importantly, it's incorrect. That's what *Ted Lasso* teaches us.

Sam, Roy, Trent, Keeley, Beard, and every other "good guy" reinforces Ted's anti-BS stance. Sam demonstrates this most clearly when he rejects a large amount of money and endangers his career to protest a company that's destroying the environment in his home country. Roy does so when he accepts his spot on the bench rather than engage in a fake-injury ruse to protect his transfer value. Trent does so by consistently living up to the journalistic ideal of following the evidence and shooting straight. Keeley does so by repeatedly addressing difficult truths head-on regardless of who she has to confront about them. The same is true of Beard's outburst at the pub when Ted announces he will not be benching Roy Kent, and even Sassy's gentle demand of Rebecca that she take responsibility for her abandonment of home, friends, and goddaughter Nora. And these are but a few examples. For each of these examples, many more anti-BS instances could be provided. The theme and examples are *that* prevalent. A repudiation of BS truly is a critical characteristic that defines and binds all of *Ted Lasso*'s good guys.

And just in case that wasn't enough to drive the point home, the show goes ahead and makes the clear-cut bad guy a big fan of BS.

Portrait of a BS Artist As an Old Man

Ted Lasso has few true villains. Sure, characters will do bad things, but they are rarely bad people. There is, however, one obvious exception: Rupert. He is awful. That fact is obvious from the moment he's introduced in Season 1 to the moment he purchases the West Ham United Football Club at the end of Season 2. And when it comes to being awful, Rupert has one medium that he prefers: bullshit. Rupert works with BS the way Van Gogh worked with yellows or Bernie Mac worked with cuss words. He is a master of the form, demonstrating his immense and terrible prowess every single time he steps on screen. This is not hyperbole. In the first two seasons, Rupert appears in only six episodes, but in each BS is his modus operandi from beginning to end. Correctness, honesty, reality: none of these concern Rupert. All that matters to him is hurting his ex-wife and helping himself. That's his purpose. If he can get away with something and it suits his purpose, then he will do it without a second thought. End of story.

Rupert's first appearance comes at Richmond FC's annual benefit gala ("For the Children"). Rebecca has already started her speech and is just hitting her stride when Rupert enters the room and interrupts with a cheeky comment. This is BS artistry at its finest. Rupert is getting away with a deception while simultaneously achieving his primary aims of hurting Rebecca and helping himself. He is hurting Rebecca by surprising her and making the event that *she* planned all about *him*. And he is helping himself by making it look as though the two of them set their differences aside for the sake of the gala.

But of course, the reality of the situation is that Rebecca is the only one rising above. She is the one putting her feelings aside for the sake of the charitable cause. Rupert is doing the opposite. He's sinking below. He's using the charitable cause as a venue to act out on his worst tendencies. He is rubbing salt in his ex-wife's wound while also rehabilitating his own reputation, making it seem as though the two of them have a more amicable relationship than they actually do. The fact that Rebecca can't do anything about it without ruining the event, and looking bad, makes it all the sweeter for him. It is a stroke of evil genius from a world class BS-er, and that is just the beginning.

After his initial interruption of Rebecca's speech, Rupert continues with his masterclass in BS. He offers to "solve" the live music problem that he secretly created and takes over the auctioneer's role "for the children." Ultimately, he usurps the entire event with a donation of a million pounds that "helps" in reaching Rebecca's more modest goal. The latter two BS maneuvers succeed with flying colors, and the former fails only because Ted manages to track down the greatest busker in London.

Over the course of his next five appearances Rupert manages to rub his new baby in Rebecca's face, degrade Ted in front of the fans, and crash the funeral for Rebecca's father. All these things are bad, clearly the actions of a villain, yet Rupert never does any of them in an overtly villainous way. He does them by deploying BS. He tells Rebecca about his new baby in order to "save" her from finding out via the tabloids. He insults Ted in front of the fans because he "cares" about the fans and is looking out for their team. He crashes Rebecca's father's funeral because the deceased was "family" and meant so much to him.

Every time Rupert carries out something heinous, he does so in a way that could lead someone to perceive it in the exact opposite way. Rebecca herself admits that she fell for it in the past. If Rebecca, who has repeatedly proven herself to be perceptive, can be fooled by such BS, then anyone can be. BS is a danger to all. It must be fought. That is what *Ted Lasso* teaches us.

A Yardstick for Growth

The good guys reject BS, the bad guys embrace it. *Ted Lasso* makes these points powerfully, but it doesn't stop there. The show rejects black-and-white thinking and instead grapples with the gray. This is important because the key to fighting BS is correctness, and the key to correctness is a desire to describe reality accurately, and an accurate description of reality has a whole bunch of gray.

That's not to say that BS itself is gray, but rather that people are. Good guys occasionally do bad things, and bad guys do good things. Just as Ted says, we all do both good and bad. Where someone falls on the spectrum of good to bad largely comes down to the frequency and magnitude of their bad actions. This means that for *Ted Lasso,* a show that uses BS as its main way to delineate between good guys and bad guys, there have to be characters that occupy the middle of the spectrum, people that slide up or down based on the frequency with which they deploy BS. And the show certainly features several such characters. Three stand out above the rest: Rebecca, Jamie, and Nate.

When we first meet Rebecca, she is spewing BS just as Ted spews sparkling water. Her primary purpose is to hurt her ex-husband by destroying his beloved soccer club, and that's all that matters to her. Anything and everything is on the table as long as it helps her achieve that aim. Correctness, honesty, sincerity: she engages in these only when it suits her purpose. She is a BS artist working with a full palette, eagerly deploying whatever hue of poo she needs in order to paint her masterpiece. She hires a coach she doesn't believe in, she sends the paparazzi to capture deceptive photos, she sets Ted up with a gotcha interview, she gets rid of the most talented player just when he starts to come around. Rebecca does terrible thing after terrible thing, and she is forthright about none of it. At least not at first.

But then Rebecca grows, and that growth is largely influenced by two things: an appreciation for the honesty and sincerity of both Ted and Keeley, and a disdain for the deceitfulness and disingenuousness of Rupert. Combined, these characters reveal to Rebecca the good and bad endpoints of the BS spectrum. This, in turn, allows her to realize that, although she wants to hurt Rupert, she doesn't want to slide down to his end of the spectrum in order to do so.

Jamie also grows a great deal over the course of the series. As with Rebecca, both Ted and Keeley play a large role in his growth. Jamie differs from Rebecca, however, in that his propensity for BS is not solely the product of anger toward another person. Sure, his father is a factor, but he is not *the* factor in the way that Rupert is for Rebecca. Instead, much of Jamie's BS is a product of his own shortcomings and insecurities. For instance, he intentionally underrates the skills of his teammates in order to make himself the sole star of the team. He gaslights Keeley about their relationship so that he can play the field. And he joins a reality television show—the most BS-y form of entertainment—in order to stroke his own ego. Time and again Jamie trashes others in order to inflate himself.

All of this means that in order to rebuff BS and grow as a person, Jamie needs to find much of the inspiration from within himself. Rebecca could look at Rupert, a man she already loathed, and realize that she wants to move away from his end of the BS spectrum. Jamie, on the other hand, can look only at himself. This means that his path away from BS is more difficult. So it is unsurprising that Jamie's personal growth takes longer than Rebecca's. It's worth the wait, though. Watching Jamie evolve, with the surprising help of Roy, is rewarding and instructive in a way that few television character arcs are. It is perhaps the most effective argument against BS in a show laden with effective arguments against BS.

Lastly, there is Nathan Shelley. Unlike Rebecca and Jamie, Nate's story is not one of steady growth in the right direction. Instead, he journeys up and down the BS spectrum. When we first meet Nate, he is painfully timid. He doesn't engage in BS or repudiate BS because he is too lacking in confidence to do either. Then Ted comes along and everything changes. Ted imbues Nate with confidence, and in response Nate becomes a competent truth-teller. This period in Nate's development is best exemplified by his harsh but hilarious locker-room speech that inspires AFC Richmond to victory over Everton ("Make Rebecca Great Again").

By all appearances Nate has found his voice and decided to use it to rebuff BS. Alas, this is not the case. Instead, when Nate's successes don't deliver all of the approval and acceptance he anticipated, the lure of BS gradually wins him over. Nate begins to spurn the people that helped him and instead embraces a brutal and condescending version of himself. Which is to say, a version of himself that isn't himself at all, a version of himself that is BS. Rupert, of course, loves it.

At this point it seems as though Nate's character arc might just be the reverse of Rebecca's and Jamie's. Indeed, when Season 2 ends, that is exactly what we expect. However, Nate's evolution continues in Season 3. As he spends more time with Rupert at West Ham, he realizes that BS isn't the path to approval and acceptance either, at least not *genuine* approval or acceptance. Instead, he's on a path to fame, women, and wealth of a thoroughly BS variety. We see Nate's dawning comprehension on this matter on his guys night out with Rupert, on his date with Anastasia, and during Ted's press conference. Nate finally sees the BS for what it is and that he doesn't want to be a part of it. His growth comes as he seeks a path away from it.

However, this transformation doesn't come easy. Nate tries to apologize to Ted numerous times: on the elevator, at the bus after the game, via text message. Yet he repeatedly fails. As these failures mount, it begins to look like he might never succeed, like he might give in to the BS. Then the moment comes when he is forced to decide who he wants to become, the moment when Rupert demands that Nate follow in his footsteps and become a philandering BS artist. Ultimately, Nate rejects Rupert's bidding.

That resistance has a price. It costs him his job, his prestige, and his reputation. While these losses take their toll on Nate, he knows he made the right decision. In the end, Nate gains a breakthrough in his relationship with his father, finds a supportive girlfriend in Jade, and recovers his true place back at FC Richmond with Ted and the team. He is yet another example of how *Ted Lasso* is a meaningful rebuff of bullshit.

Let's end this chapter on BS by calling out one of Ted and Michelle's "Oklahomas" and telling the God's honest truth. We didn't need nearly 4,000 words to get to the point of this chapter. Although we admit our case was brilliant and no doubt massively entertaining, all we needed were these nine simple words from Ted: "Doing the right thing is never the wrong thing."

Notes

1 Harry Frankfurt, *On Bullshit* (Princeton: Princeton UP, 2005), 1. Frankfurt's book developed from a 1986 essay of the same name published in *The Raritan Quarterly Review*.
2 Ibid., 51.
3 Harry Frankfurt, *On Truth* (New York: Alfred A. Knopf, 2006), 4–5.
4 Frankfurt, *On Bullshit*, 65.
5 Ibid., 63.

10
Doing Masculinity Better

Marcus Arvan

Ted Lasso begins with AFC Richmond's new owner, Rebecca Welton, hiring Ted Lasso to get revenge on her ex-husband, Rupert Mannion. Rupert, the club's former owner, cheated on Rebecca repeatedly before leaving her for a much younger woman, and Rebecca hopes that Ted's ignorance of football will bring Rupert the same misery and embarrassment he caused her. As Rebecca says to her assistant Higgins, "I hope [Ted] fails miserably. See, my ex-husband truly loved only one thing in his entire life—this club—and Ted Lasso is gonna help me burn it to the ground" ("Pilot").

Rebecca's plan perpetuates the harms of Rupert's toxic behavior and spreads them to everyone around her. There are many other cases of toxic masculinity in the series, yet *Ted Lasso* is not mainly about that. It is, among many other wonderful things, a touching and philosophically insightful story about *positive masculinity*—of what it is to be a *good* man. It's a comedy, not a tragedy, and reveals how better norms of masculinity can be beneficial for people regardless of gender and can help people heal from and overcome toxic masculinity.

I Want to Torture Rupert

Masculinity pertains to the "qualities or attributes regarded as characteristic of men,"[1] and "qualities traditionally ascribed to men, [such] as strength and boldness."[2] *Toxic* masculinity in contrast is "a set of attitudes and ways of behaving stereotypically associated with or expected of men, regarded as having a negative impact on men and on society as a whole."[3] This includes "expectations that boys and men must be active, aggressive, tough, daring, and dominant,"[4] and

Ted Lasso and Philosophy: No Question Is Into Touch, First Edition.
Edited by Marybeth Baggett and David Baggett.
© 2024 John Wiley & Sons, Inc. Published 2024 by John Wiley & Sons, Inc.

embody a "warrior ethic" that embraces anger, violence, and extreme self-reliance.[5] Toxic masculinity is also associated with male domination of women[6] and the repression and stigmatization of "girly" qualities such as crying or emotional vulnerability.[7]

Ted Lasso depicts several flavors of toxic masculinity. We see it most obviously in Rupert, who habitually aims to dominate and humiliate other people in stereotypically masculine ways. Crashing the charity auction, showing up uninvited to the funeral of Rebecca's father, purchasing the rival club West Ham United. Like a GIF, which some people pronounce JIF, Rupert's toxic masculinity is relentless.

In the series pilot alone, toxic masculinity is rather like tea in the UK. It's everywhere, and it's horrible—absolute garbage water. AFC Richmond players bully the team's equipment manager Nate, Trent Crimm belittles Ted in his first press conference, Jamie Tartt objectifies his girlfriend, Keeley, and Roy Kent tells Ted he hopes he chokes on a Big Mac.

The pattern persists. Jamie's father calls him soft when he doesn't dominate. Nate's hunger for approval and obsession with professional success transforms him from timid kitman to abusive coach. And Beard engages in risky and impulsive behavior—drinking too much, crashing an exclusive club, fighting with Jamie's father and his friends—as a way of handling the team's loss to Manchester United.

Even Ted, who otherwise embodies many features of positive masculinity, is not unaffected by toxic masculinity. In contrast to Rupert, Jamie, and Nate, Ted subtly illustrates the harmful *internal* psychological consequences of traditional societal expectations for men, including extreme self-reliance and suffering in silence rather than asking for help.[8] When he eventually opens up to Dr. Sharon Fieldstone, Ted's trauma is revealed as at least partially rooted in stereotypical male values. He decries his father as a quitter who abandoned his family and his obligations.

At the same time, toxic masculinity can be seductive. As Rebecca tells Keeley, Rupert was "charm personified." "He made me feel special" ("(I Don't Want to Go to) Chelsea"). Zava is the same as Rupert, but different. He is not malicious, but he upstages Ted in the locker room and encourages the other Greyhounds to idolize him as "an angel" or "a god." Only Jamie recognizes him as one of those "self-absorbed glory hunters who only care about themselves" ("4-5-1"). Of course, Jamie admits that he's being hypocritical, not ironic … which is actually ironic. But even after Zava quits the team during a losing streak to focus on his avocado farm, Dani Rojas breaks down weeping ("Signs"). The size of Zava's avocados might be as remarkable as the size of his ego, but like Rupert, Zava is toxic. There's a reason he was with fourteen teams in the last fifteen years.

Success Is Not About the Wins and Losses

In "Headspace," after witnessing Nate humiliate Colin, Beard calls him out, telling him to "do better." But how? One option might be to reject masculinity altogether, regarding it as inherently toxic, an approach not without precedent.[9] *Ted Lasso* instead promotes *positive* masculinity.

Aristotle (384–322 BC), who was twice the philosopher than Ted's a coach, defends a theory of morality known today as virtue ethics.[10] For Aristotle, each of us desires more than mere moments of "feeling happy." We want to live fulfilling, flourishing lives—what the Greeks called *eudaimonia*. Aristotle recognizes that, though much is up to chance in life, we can take specific steps that conduce to deep satisfaction and joy, especially by developing moral and intellectual virtues.

Aristotle thinks virtues in general are beneficial means between harmful extremes. Whereas cowards are unable to face danger, and reckless people rashly rush headlong into unwinnable battles, courageous people know when to stand up and fight and when to live to fight another day. Or consider honesty. Although it's possible to get away with lying, lies often backfire—hence, the common saying, "Honesty is the best policy." Yet most of us also recognize that it can also be bad to be *too* honest. Most of the Diamond Dogs think Higgins shouldn't share his reservations to Beard about his relationship with Jane, though, interestingly, Roy does think such transparency is called for when it comes to Rebecca's relationship. The arguable lesson is that a properly honest person knows not to be dishonest, nor too honest, but to display the right amount and kind of honesty in a given context.

Or consider intellectual virtues. We all know it's bad to be closed-minded. But as they say, if we're too open-minded, our brains will fall out. It's beneficial neither to be closed-minded nor to believe everything we hear. What's optimal is to "hit the bulls-eye," to find the right moderate view in between the extremes, what Aristotle dubbed the "golden mean." In this case, to be appropriately open-minded and responsive to good evidence.

Aristotle contends that the virtues are (i) settled dispositions, (ii) learned and lost through habitual practice, (iii) to think, feel and act, (iv) in beneficial ways, (v) relative to the person, (v) known through practical wisdom. This is a lot to unpack, but the basic ideas are simple, intuitive, and critical for understanding *Ted Lasso*'s lessons on toxic and positive masculinity.

By "settled dispositions" Aristotle means that honest people, for example, don't just tell the truth on occasion. They practice honesty as a matter of habit. Through practice they acquire particular thoughts, emotions, and desires. The honest person learns to want to tell the truth more than they want to lie; they learn to feel guilty for lying; and they learn ways of telling the truth beneficial in each situation.

Between the Goal Posts

Aristotle doesn't think the beneficial mean or "bulls-eye" for a given virtue is the same for everyone. We all have our own unique life circumstances and distinctive strengths and weaknesses. When Roy returns to AFC Richmond as a coach in "The Signal," the team's fans go wild over "the Roy Kent effect." Ted Lasso's official X account describes it "like having Chewbacca on your team. He may be loud and hairy, but he also knows how to steer the ship (and I assume gives incredible hugs)." When Roy acts tough and assertive, it's natural, effective, and endearing.

Yet things are very different for Nate, as we see in "Rainbow." Rebecca and Keeley try to teach him the right way to be assertive, but not too dominant, to get a window table for his father at A Taste of Athens. Nate's newfound assertiveness later morphs into something far uglier: a kind of smug and casual cruelty replete with insults that are personal. And weird. To ensure a flattering silhouette worthy of strutting, the kind of toughness, honesty, or courage that is beneficial needs, like Nate's suit, to be personally tailored.

For Sam Obisanya, courage involves risking his public persona and leveraging his celebrity as a professional athlete to protest the harmful actions of a team sponsor in Nigeria ("Do the Right-est Thing"). For Ted, courage demands telling Sharon about his father's suicide ("Man City"). For Roy, it requires embracing change and accepting that he is no longer a star player ("Tan Lines"). For Jamie, courage entails vulnerably admitting his father's cruelty and confessing that his mother wouldn't be proud of his behavior ("Two Aces"). Finding the right path of moderation is a personal journey of learning practical wisdom about what works well and what doesn't.

Missing the Mark

Toxic masculinity is the wrong path, clearly a moral vice. It encourages harmful behavior, such as sexual assault and domestic violence.[11] Toxic masculinity has been found to harm men, increasing rates of depression, stress, and substance abuse,[12] as well as alcoholism, cancer, and sexually transmitted infections.[13] Those who internalize traditional masculine attitudes are less likely to seek health care[14] or share their health issues with physicians,[15] which may partly explain men's shorter lifespans.[16]

Paradigms of such dysfunctia abound in *Ted Lasso*. Rupert is a psychologically abusive philanderer. Jamie's father is psychologically and physically abusive toward him. Ted fails for far too long to seek professional psychological help. And, as Ted insightfully implies to Rupert during their dart game in "The Diamond Dogs," toxic masculinity also involves *intellectual* vices:

> All them fellas that used to belittle me, not a single one of them were curious. You know, they thought they had everything all figured out, and so they judged everything, and they judged everyone. And I realized that their underestimating me? Who I was had nothin' to do with it. Because if they were curious, they would have asked questions—you know, questions like, "Have you played a lot of darts, Ted?" Which I would have answered, "Yes sir, every Sunday afternoon at a sports bar with my father, from age 10 till I was 16 when he passed away.... Barbeque sauce" [Ted hits the bullseye to win].

It's unclear whether Ted has toxic masculinity in mind here, but men have been found to be more overconfident than women.[17] Overconfidence may help men dominate the workplace,[18] but that doesn't make it any less toxic. "The mother of all biases," it tends to backfire, just as we see in Rupert's defeat.[19]

Toxic masculinity harmfully suggests that there is only one way to be "a real man." One must be aggressive, tough, and self-reliant, rather than gentle, vulnerable, or empathetic. Toxic masculinity, in other words, is extreme, not the kind of moderate mean between harmful extremes that Aristotle advocates.

Time to Woman Up

In contrast, *Ted Lasso* consistently depicts positive masculinity as balancing traditionally masculine and feminine traits. When Ted instructs Jamie to resolve his differences with Roy in "The Signal," he tells Jaime,

"You and Roy got to get together and woman up." Then, when Jamie responds, "I think you mean 'man up,'" Ted responds, "No, you all been manning up for a while and look where that's got ya."

Similarly, in "Goodbye Earl," Ted learns from Rebecca and Keeley "the two lessons of girl talk": listening and not trying to solve things. These examples pile up. In "Make Rebecca Great Again," when the team watches the animated film *The Iron Giant*, they cry in front of each other. Ted and the other coaches start the Diamond Dogs support group, which leads Nate to say, "Ever since I was little, I always used to dream of sittin' down with a bunch of mates talkin' 'bout the complex dynamics between men and women." In "Rainbow," Ted and the team openly discuss their love of romantic comedies.

Roy's response in "Man City" to the provocation of Jamie by his father draws on this same synthesis of masculine and feminine. In one of the show's most gripping and moving scenes, a devastating scenario that leaves Jamie on the verge of tears, Roy, of all people, is the one who gives Jamie a long hug in front of the team as Jamie breaks down weeping. Incidentally, this is just one of many intentional and poignant scenes in this series involving meaningful, protracted hugs, a stereotypically feminine gesture.

Ted Lasso applies Aristotle's practical wisdom to the question at hand, showing the right amount and kind of masculinity that works in a situation. Consider Ted's alter ego, Led Tasso. In "Do the Rightest Thing," to address the team's struggles, Ted adopts a hilariously exaggerated tough guy persona. Beard says to Nate, "The Ted you know is gone for now." Led's behavior is stereotypically masculine— competitive, dominant, and aggressive. Yet it is beneficial in the context, giving the team a common enemy besides Jamie and healing a rift that divides them.

Most of the male characters in *Ted Lasso* are striving to determine what positive masculinity requires for them. For example, after returning to the Greyhounds, Jamie experiences less success. He has become *too* unselfish, losing the pizzazz that made him an ace. In "The Signal," Roy tells Ted, "You've made him a team player ... and in doing so, you've made him average." Roy recognizes that Jamie's impudence is the key to his talent.

But that brashness needs to be modulated. As Roy explains: "[S]ometimes, *when it is appropriate* ... yes, be a prick." Being a good man need not involve abandoning traditionally masculine qualities or forms of behavior. *Ted Lasso* also shows that positive masculinity is not limited to men, as when Roy's niece, Phoebe, tells him (the series' paradigmatic "good tough guy"), "Because of you, I stand up to bullies."

Doing the Right Thing Is Never the Wrong Thing

But how can we know what kind of masculinity is actually beneficial? Aristotle offers no rule book for this, but instead provides several helpful guidelines. These include avoiding the worst excess, knowing our own excess tendencies, and being on guard against what gives us pleasure.

Roy especially exemplifies this process. At the beginning of the series, Roy starts off a bit toxic: relentlessly hard on himself and everyone around him. Over time, thanks in no small part to others holding him accountable, he grows into a far better man. For example, in "The Diamond Dogs," Ted criticizes Roy for having a double standard about Keeley's sex life. Roy concedes the point, and that the time for being a baby child is over. "I'm done being mad about Jamie. I'm a grown man." Although Roy doesn't always get things right, he strives to avoid the worst vices of toxic masculinity, knowing his own excess tendencies, and being on guard against the vices that may make him feel good in the moment but wouldn't end up for the best.

Ted Lasso also illustrates Aristotle's thesis that virtue requires the practical wisdom to know what is beneficial in different situations ("*phronesis*"). Aristotle thinks such wisdom can be learned only through experience or from those who already have it. For example, Beard teaches Nate about forgiveness and second chances by recounting his own experience of being forgiven by Ted. It takes a good man to learn wisdom from his mistakes, and an even better man to help other fellas be the best versions of themselves on and off the field.

Finally, the show's positive masculinity also illustrates Aristotle's "unity of the virtues." For Aristotle, virtues don't function in isolation. For example, proper honesty requires courage, kindness, and sensitivity. Such unity of virtues is also needed for being a good man, as *Ted Lasso* illustrates. In "All Apologies," when Rebecca finally comes clean to Ted, apologizing for her deception, Ted surprisingly responds, "I forgive you. Divorce is hard. Makes people do crazy things." In this deeply touching scene, Ted shows that to be a good man is to be honest, forgiving, courageous, temperate, and kind. Similarly, Sam shows us that part of what it is to be a good man is to stand up for justice.

What about Rupert? Doesn't he benefit from toxic masculinity? For most of *Ted Lasso*, Rupert seems to have everything he wants. He's fabulously rich; the public and tabloids seem to adore him; and he has a beautiful young wife and new child. Why should *he* be a good man? Well, in a particularly subtle moment in "The

Hope That Kills You," *Ted Lasso* shows us why. Just after AFC Richmond is defeated by Manchester City, Rupert sees Ted congratulate the other team on television. The look on Rupert's face, as he sits alone on his couch, is a strange mix of awe and sadness that Ted's team lost.

In that moment, arguably Rupert realizes what the rest of us already know. Ted is a far better man than he, someone who wins in life where it really counts. This recognition is fleeting, and Rupert quickly reverts to the toxic man he increasingly is. And when Rupert is accused of sexual misconduct and assaults West Ham's new coach on the field ("So Long, Farewell"), his toxic masculinity blows up in his face, just as Aristotle thinks vices tend to do. The truth holds: It's better to be like Ted, Roy, and Sam—good, honest, courageous, tough, sensitive, accountable men—than to fall prey to or be complicit with toxic masculinity.

Positive masculinity is kinda like seeing Billy Joel live. It never disappoints.

Notes

1   *Oxford Languages*, s.v. "masculinity (n.)," accessed July 19, 2022, https://www.google.com/search?q=Google+English+Dictionary&rlz=1C1VDKB_enUS990US990&oq=Google+English+Dictionary&aqs=chrome..69i57j6 9i64j69i60l2.4540j0j9&sourceid=chrome&ie=UTF-8#dobs=masculinity.
2   *Dictionary.com*, s.v. "masculine (adj.)," accessed July 19, 2022, https://www.dictionary.com/browse/masculine.
3   *Oxford Languages*, s.v. "toxic Masculinity (n.)," accessed July 19, 2022, https://www.google.com/search?q=toxic+masculinity+definition&rlz=1 C1VDKB_enUS990US990&oq=toxic+masculinity+definition&aqs=chro me..69i57.3255j0j4&sourceid=chrome&ie=UTF-8.
4   Michael Flood, "Toxic Masculinity: A Primer and Commentary," *XY Online*, June 7, 2018, at https://xyonline.net/content/toxic-masculinity-primer-and-commentary.
5   Steven Conway, "Poisonous Pantheons: God of War and Toxic Masculinity," *Games and Culture* 15 (2020), 943–961.
6   Debbie Ging, "Alphas, Betas, and Incels: Theorizing the Masculinities of the Manosphere," *Men and Masculinities* 22 (2019), 638–657.
7   William Ming Liu, "How Trump's 'Toxic Masculinity' Is Bad for Other Men," *TIME*, April 14, 2016, at https://time.com/4273865/donald-trump-toxic-masculinity/; and *Cambridge Dictionary*, s.v. "toxic masculinity (n.)," accessed July 14th, 2022, https://dictionary.cambridge.org/us/dictionary/english/toxic-masculinity.

8   Louise Leighton, "Why are Men Still Suffering in Silence?" *Counselling Directory*, April 23, 2021 at https://www.counselling-directory.org.uk/memberarticles/why-are-men-still-suffering-in-silence.

9   Sam de Boise, "Is Masculinity Toxic?" *Norma: International Journal for Masculinity Studies*, 14 (2019), 147–151.

10   Aristotle, *Nicomachean Ethics*, trans. W.D. Ross, available at http://classics.mit.edu/Aristotle/nicomachaen.html.

11   Ronald F. Levant, "The New Psychology of Men," *Professional Psychology: Research and Practice* 27 (1996), 259–265.

12   Y. Joel Wong, Moon-Ho Ringo Ho, Shu-Yi Wang, and I.S. Keino Miller, "Meta-Analyses of the Relationship Between Conformity to Masculine Norms and Mental Health-Related Outcomes," *Journal of Counseling Psychology* 64 (2016), 80–93.

13   Roger Kirby and Mike Kirby, "The Perils of Toxic Masculinity: Four Case Studies," *Trends in Urology & Men's Health* 10 (2019), 18–20.

14   Mary S. Himmelstein and Diana T. Sanchez, "Masculinity in the Doctor's Office: Masculinity, Gendered Doctor Preference and Doctor–Patient Communication," *Preventive Medicine* 84 (2016a), 34–40.

15   Mary S. Himmelstein and Diana T. Sanchez, "Masculinity Impediments: Internalized Masculinity Contributes to Healthcare Avoidance in Men and Women," *Journal of Health Psychology* 21 (2016b), 1283–1292.

16   Himmelstein and Sanchez (2016a).

17   Brad M. Barber and Terrance Odean, "Boys will be Boys: Gender, Overconfidence, and Common Stock Investment," *The Quarterly Journal of Economics* 116 (2001), 261–292.

18   Ernesto Reuben, Pedro Rey-Biel, Paola Sapienza, and Luigi Zingales, "The Emergence of Male Leadership in Competitive Environments," *Journal of Economic Behavior & Organization* 83 (2012), 111–117.

19   Don A. Moore, "Overconfidence," *Psychology Today*, January 22, 2018, at https://www.psychologytoday.com/us/blog/perfectly-confident/201801/overconfidence.

11

Inverting the Gender Pyramid

Willie Young

"It's kind of like being a dad," Ted Lasso tells his son, when describing the challenges of coaching soccer. You have to teach your players before the game, and once they're on the field you really can't do much. Like parenting, coaching has a lot to do with how games are played and the lives that players lead. Good coaching may help players to become their best selves, but coaches also shape what those "best selves" are.

Ted Lasso provides a window into athletics for thinking about masculinity, and the shape that it takes on and off the pitch. Along with those of other characters, Ted's journey offers a critique of the toxic masculinity that informs much of sport, including shouting, abuse, and aggressive dominance. To be sure, coaches themselves often exhibit precisely these qualities. Ted's alter ego "Led Tasso" is funny precisely because we have all known so many coaches like him. Or, in our lesser moments, we have been that coach. Still, as Dr. Sharon Fieldstone says, not all coaches are macho dickheads. Ted's players come to love him in large part because he rejects such behavior, and his coaching guides the team in both achieving excellence and dealing with failure.

Drawing from feminist philosophy, this chapter argues that the journey of Richmond's players and coaches critiques domineering masculinity and also creatively imagines masculinity in ways that transcend male dominance. Beyond patriarchy's toxic limits, "being a man" can mean being more fully human, not less. Even still, while offering an incisive critique of patriarchal masculinity, *Ted Lasso* also shows the difficulty of moving beyond it. Challenging gender

Ted Lasso and Philosophy: No Question Is Into Touch, First Edition.
Edited by Marybeth Baggett and David Baggett.
© 2024 John Wiley & Sons, Inc. Published 2024 by John Wiley & Sons, Inc.

oppression requires ongoing individual and collective struggle. However, when practiced as an act of love, coaching can create the bonds that help to make this transformation possible.

Playing a Man Down

For the most part, feminist philosophy has focused on the harms and injustices sexism has inflicted on women. Those harms are readily apparent, ranging from economic and political inequality to physical and sexual violence. All the same, some feminists have also recognized that this sexism has likewise harmed the very men who seem to benefit from their positions of privilege. One challenge feminism faces is to develop alternative models of masculinity that counter these harmful patterns of behavior.

One feminist thinker who focused intently on these patterns is bell hooks (1952–2021). In *The Will to Change: Men, Masculinity and Love*, hooks introduces the term *patriarchal masculinity*. For her, patriarchy is a political and cultural system that "insists that males are inherently dominating, superior to everything and everyone deemed weak, especially females, and endowed with the right to dominate and rule over the weak and to maintain that dominance through various forms of psychological terrorism and violence."[1] As a system of domination, patriarchy creates and enforces gender inequality, normalizing and perpetuating male dominance.

While patriarchy harms women through control and oppression, it likewise creates a kind of masculinity that encourages violence and refuses weakness from men, impairing their capacities for mutuality, affection, and love. As she writes, "No male successfully measures up to patriarchal standards without engaging in an ongoing practice of self-betrayal,"[2] suppressing or destroying emotional and ethical capacities in order to conform to society's norms.

hooks's distinction between patriarchal masculinity and men allows her to articulate how patriarchy is damaging to both men and women, even as both men and women can act as patriarchy's supporters. It also enables her to bracket sexist and patriarchal behavior as *one* form of masculinity, which opens the possibility for other types of masculinity to emerge.

For hooks, central elements of patriarchal masculinity include misogyny, abuse, sexual promiscuity, dishonesty, and the suppression of emotion. Early on, Jamie Tartt embodies many of these traits, and his character epitomizes its destructive power.

On loan from Manchester City, he treats his Richmond teammates with disdain. Abused by his father, who demands he score goals and pursue glory only for himself, Tartt treats others abusively, Sam and Nate especially. The abuse leads him to suppress any sense of softness or emotional connection. He lies to and cheats on Keeley and sees himself as better than everyone else. With his entrenched sense of impunity and lack of accountability, Tartt perfectly fits Aaron James's definition of an asshole, marked by deep-seated entitlement and immunity to others' complaints.[3] Tartt's identity is both an effect of patriarchal terror and its further enactment.

Perhaps Not an Oasis

Still, Jamie Tartt is just the tip of the iceberg. Let's examine how patriarchal masculinity shapes the show's characters and how *Ted Lasso* critiques this form of manhood. These depictions set the stage for the portrayal of a less toxic masculinity.

In the opening scene of *Ted Lasso*, Rebecca, the new owner of Richmond, brings Coach George Cartrick into her office. She calls him out for his casual misogyny and contempt, firing him on the spot and making his jaw drop even lower than Liam and Noel. George returns in Season 2 as a TV pundit, and he remains irredeemably misogynistic. He demeans players by challenging their manhood until Roy puts him in his place. George serves as a foil for Ted, whose self-deprecating humor and biscuit-baking charms disarm his skeptics. Still, misogyny in soccer is anything but a joke. As of this writing, at least five women's teams in the NWSL, the US women's soccer league, have recently fired coaches after years of tolerating abusive coaching practices. Abusive and misogynistic coaching runs through the college and youth ranks as well.[4]

As Rebecca says, misogyny is a "big word" for George. (Fortunately his daughters can explain it to him.) Feminist philosopher Kate Manne defines misogyny as those forms of hostility and violence that keep women down, often targeting especially women who challenge male entitlement.[5] In her words, misogyny acts as an "enforcement mechanism" for sexism through hostile speech and action toward women who claim equality and independence. Rupert epitomizes such action, as Rebecca lives with the terror of him and his media colleagues demeaning her in public. He threatens and diminishes her independence, and arguably her fear influences her decision to break up with Sam.

But *Ted Lasso* also highlights other dimensions of misogyny, as men assert their dominance with respect to other men *through* the denigration of women. Misogyny can involve hostility toward the display of non-patriarchal attributes by men—targeting men who challenge patriarchal standards. In Jamie's abuse of Sam and Nate, and Nate's later abuse of Colin and Will (the new kit man), one can see hostility toward emotional expression and "softness." In both cases, misogyny involves aggression toward the emotionally vulnerable aspects of one's own self, acted out through aggression toward, and subordination of, others. When he spits at himself in the mirror, Nate's hostility toward his own sense of weakness is palpable. Misogyny often inflicts on others the shame and fear that its perpetrator seeks to avoid for himself, leading its victims to dominate others as a form of self-protection.

hooks writes that our culture presumes that male sexuality is "addictive," and that being a man requires engaging in predatory sexual behavior. Such conceptions of sexuality center on "the need to constantly affirm and reaffirm one's selfhood" through sex, even if such affirmation is only temporary and always requires further enactment.[6] In such an understanding, promiscuity and sexual infidelity enhance one's selfhood rather than *undermining* it. In myriad ways our culture praises male promiscuity even while denigrating women's sexuality.

Sexual promiscuity combines multiple levels of license, from infidelity to dishonesty. Lying is fundamentally manipulative, denying others respect and agency, and promiscuity manifests a similar refusal of accountability. As hooks writes, "The very concept of 'being a man' and a 'real man' has always implied that when necessary men can take action that breaks the rules, that is above the law."[7] Rupert's rampant infidelity exemplifies this predatory sexuality. He would never grant Rebecca the right to cheat on him. His promiscuity and lying and her subjection to him are two sides of the same coin: male control. This impunity is also evident in Jamie's infidelity, which finally leads Keeley to break up with him and later gets him kicked off *Lust Conquers All*. Dominant patriarchal sexuality means never being accountable. It means manipulating and controlling others while being free of obligations to them.

Suffering Is Necessary

In (British) football as in life, men are taught to be callous or "hard," meaning indifferent to suffering and pain, able to set emotion aside, single-minded in commitment to winning, and reluctant to open up.

Among English footballers, the "hard men"—Roy Keane of Manchester United and Patrick Vieira of Arsenal, above all—hold a special pride of place. As Musa Okwonga writes, "The hard man is a feature of any successful football team: its guardian, its cornerstone, and its dark heart."[8] This privileged place is in part due to football's rivalry with rugby. Compared with the style of play in many other European nations, English football places far greater emphasis on physicality, strength, and hard-tackling aggressiveness. Until recently it dismissed the value of tactics and technical ability.[9]

In *Ted Lasso*, Roy Kent epitomizes the hard man. Lionized for his toughness on the field, he blows up opponents with tackles and his teammates with F-bombs, then takes a turn at punditry. As Nate says, Roy's anger is his superpower. His character and name directly send up ManU icon Roy Keane and lay the groundwork for his emotional and relational transformation with Keeley.

A hard man dominates opponents on the pitch, but hardness is also important in dealing with the pressures on players and the toxic culture of the locker room. Insults, shaming, and hazing from teammates and fans often demand emotional repression. Patriarchal masculinity is founded on the denial and shaming of vulnerability, often demanding that men ignore both others' suffering and their own. Before Ted's arrival, we see Roy and others shy away from addressing Jamie's humiliation of his teammates and Nate, allowing such toxicity to fester.[10] Higgins also owns up to Rebecca for his years of silently enabling Rupert's infidelity.

In its frequent acceptance of patriarchal masculinity, philosophy has often given a bro-hug to emotional hardness. Friedrich Nietzsche (1844–1900) embraces such hardness most explicitly. His "philosopher of the future" embraces cruelty and shows indifference to suffering as he strives to remake humanity.[11] For Nietzsche, like Diego Simeone (the coach of Atletico Madrid and a "hard man" if there ever was one), "suffering is necessary."[12]

While Nietzsche is a philosophical outlier, he continues a long tradition of philosophers suspicious of emotions. From Descartes through Spinoza and Kant and beyond, modern philosophy tends to view emotions as irrational obstacles to moral reasoning and behavior. Similar views exist in ancient Platonism and Stoicism as well.

Much as Higgins enabled Rupert, the widespread denial of emotion permits the hardness and cruelty of patriarchal masculinity to thrive. By acknowledging how patriarchal masculinity distorts our sense of virtue and feeling, feminist philosophy can help us to develop forms of virtue that speak to our full humanity and flourishing.

Be Curious, Not Judgmental

In Britain's stuffy world of soccer, Ted Lasso sticks out like a sore thumb—but it's more than his Marlboro-man mustache and distinctive drawl. As the Brits puzzle over him, they comment that "his players love him," cluing us in to his success as a coach. Arguably the players love him because he shows love *for them*, which allows them to flourish and bond in ways that patriarchy denies.

As hooks writes, "There is a creative, life-sustaining, life-enhancing place for the masculine in a nondominator culture. And those of us committed to ending patriarchy can touch the hearts of real men where they live, not by demanding that they give up manhood or maleness, but by asking that they allow its meaning to be transformed."[13] Through his practice of love, Ted both displays and cultivates just such a non-patriarchal masculinity in his players.

For all its importance in human life, love has often been overlooked within philosophy. Iris Murdoch (1919–1999) argued in *The Sovereignty of Good* that modern moral philosophy rarely considers love,[14] and hooks likewise sees it as marginalized by patriarchal culture. She insightfully defines love as "the will to nurture our own and others' spiritual growth."[15]

This will to nurture growth is manifest in a range of practices, including care, respect, integrity, and a will to cooperate. Ted not only practices these qualities toward his players and co-workers, but also instills them in the team. In a patriarchal culture of hostility, fear, and dominance, love stands as a radical form of resistance, enabling alternative modes of masculinity that patriarchy can see as only dangerous.

A crucial moment is when Ted gathers players and staff to exorcise the ghosts from the training room. Each participant sacrifices something of personal importance. The ritual enables the sharing of emotion and intimacy, allows players to care for each other, and engenders mutual respect. This moment of shared vulnerability makes them a team, bringing them closer to each other and building trust. It starts Roy's journey and hints that there is more to Jamie than we'd been led to believe. The exorcism sets their turnaround (and even their transformation) in motion, which continues after they suffer the failure of relegation.

Of course, there is vulnerability, and then there is *vulnerability*. In Season 2, we learn that Ted's constant quips and extroverted positivity conceal his own traumatic family history. While he has created a setting in which players can freely share feelings and flourish in their own ways, his defensiveness toward therapy highlights the limits of his willingness to address his own feelings and fears. Only by acknowledging and facing his fears can Ted become his best self, a move modeled by Dr. Sharon's vulnerability with Ted after her accident.

Roy's transformed masculinity rightly draws much of the attention, and other chapters in this book address it more extensively. But Sam Obisanya's character offers another hopeful trajectory. Like Nate, he was often demeaned by Jamie's behavior, and his game clearly suffered as a result. With Ted's nurture, Sam comes out of his shell and becomes one of Richmond's most valued players during their Season 2 promotion quest and FA Cup run.

His development off the field is even more striking. Sam frequently talks with his father, which spurs his protest against Richmond's airline sponsor. He takes to Bantr, the anti-Tinder social media app, conversing with women whose age and appearance he doesn't even know. He and Rebecca eventually find that they are a pair and strike up a romance. Sam's openness to emotion, conversation, and love sets him apart, and he develops the courage and passion to reject Edwin Akufo's invitation to star on the first powerhouse African football team. In contrast with Rupert's and Jamie's failure to keep Big Ben in their pants, Sam remains faithful to Rebecca and to Richmond, even when he is no longer with her. Being true to himself—and to his pursuit of his best self—helps him to be true to others as well.

Holding On to Your Manhood

Late in Season 2, Ted and Roy become concerned that Jamie has lost his edge. He has become too much of a team player, no longer the goal-scoring threat or agitator he once had been. Taking the lessons of love and bonding to heart, he no longer seems to have what it takes to win. As we often hear, the "new age" man seems too sensitive and "soft" to come out on top. Roy tells Jamie that sometimes he *needs* to be a bit of a jerk, for the sake of the team. Finding the balance between self-assertion and team play—winning the penalty and then letting Dani take it—Jamie helps the team win promotion and becomes a better Jamie in the process.

Likewise, as Richmond struggles in Season 1, Ted and Rebecca find themselves in a pub with Rupert, who challenges Ted to darts. Rupert presumes he will dominate the "hillbilly" American and further humiliate Rebecca in the process. Much to Rupert's surprise, Ted comments that he's noticed that men like Rupert often fail to be "curious"—to consider what those whom they judge to be inferior are capable of.

Ted then drives the point home. Recalling games of darts with his father, he nails the bullseye and triple-score and trounces Rupert. For all his kindness, Ted can be tough when he needs to, mostly in white-knighting on Rebecca's behalf. The spiritual growth of feminist masculinity need not suppress anger or strength, but requires knowing when and where to use them in the name of justice, to hold both ourselves and others accountable.

As Season 2 ends, numerous characters navigate their own independence and growth within relationships. Sam and Keeley in particular begin to chart their course, even while remaining within the relationships and team structures that have helped them develop into their best selves. If part of love is respect, then it requires creating the trust that helps those whom we love to go beyond our own demands and expectations.

Coaching, in this framework, becomes a form of mentoring. As Higgins tells Keeley, "A good mentor hopes you will move on; a great mentor knows you will" ("Inverting the Pyramid of Success"). Allowing others such freedom, however, is not possible within patriarchal masculinity. Finding the proper balance between connection to others and the cultivation of one's own independence is part of the growth that love encourages.

As hooks writes, the practices of dominance and violence at patriarchy's core prevent both women and men from discovering and expressing their full humanity. Patriarchy fears the possibility that non-patriarchal men and women might be *stronger* and *better* than patriarchal ones. *Ted Lasso* shows how breaking free from patriarchy's constraints is necessary for the spiritual growth of both men *and* women. Sometimes you can be the princess, and sometimes you're the dragon. At its best, coaching can be the act of love that makes our best selves possible.

Inverting the Pyramid the Richmond Way

The end of Season 2 brings to a head the conflict between Nate and Ted. Nate says that Ted had ignored him, was looking to blame him for their failure, and had belittled him since raising him up and "making him feel he was the most important person in the world" ("Inverting the Pyramid of Success"). We should take Nate's rant with a handful of salt. He is burning bridges to justify his betrayal (disclosing Ted's panic attack to the media), and thereby making way for his departure to West Ham. By this point, both Nate's tendency to deflect blame and his willingness to undermine others are readily apparent.

Still, the conflict runs deeper, pitting Nate's "brilliance" as a tactician against his misunderstanding of what coaching requires. The final game of Season 2 epitomizes the problem: playing Nate's false nine formation, the team lacks cohesion and energy. They are playing the right way. They agree it's the best setup. And they have the individual ability. As Jan Maas says, they *can* do it, but in order for the tactics to really work, they have to really play together. It requires *belief*: trust in one another, coordination, working together to create an organic, corporate sense of activity. Coaching can help players apply their individual skills toward these collective ends. For all of his tactical prowess, Nate is not a great coach.

What Nate wants is to stand out above others. He's clamoring for celebrity, fame, maybe a couple of groupies. Given how much he was belittled by British society, Jamie, and especially by his own father, his desires are understandable. Yet Nate remains trapped within a model of patriarchal masculinity, in which one can achieve one's best self only at the expense of others. It is no accident that Rupert, the poster child of patriarchy, hires him to coach his newly-acquired West Ham. As Season 3 begins, celebrity and power still enthrall Nate. He enjoys trashing Ted to the press and seeing his name online. Rupert buys him a fancy car and introduces him to fashion models.

Gradually, Nate realizes how much his desire for patriarchal affirmation has cost him, and begins to make amends. He still loves A Taste of Athens, and finds Jade far more enchanting than Anastasia's obsession with how photogenic her food is on social media. The Love Hounds, to put it mildly, are not the Diamond Dogs. Nate even finds it within himself to refuse Rupert's offer. He rejects not only a "boys' night out" that would be cheating on Jade, but quits West Ham to boot. The Wonder Kid becomes a man, in the best sense, by turning down the poisoned gifts of patriarchal manhood that Rupert offers him.

Great coaching is more than tactics. As Ted says in Season 1 to a disbelieving Trent Crimm (and Pep repeats in Season 3), the game isn't all about wins and losses. Rather, Ted's goal is to help the players and coaches become their best selves. He helps make Roy a leader and brings out Sam's joy, courage, and integrity. He helps Jamie and Nate find themselves, in building friendship and connections with others.

And he helps Rebecca find her place as a matriarchal figure at Richmond, a title that certainly has more gravitas than soccer mom.

Ted excels as a coach because of his care and respect for the players, and the way he helps them to bond with each other into a team. One of the radical arguments that *Ted Lasso* persuasively makes is that achieving real human excellence requires recognizing and breaking away from the patterns of patriarchal masculinity that dominate and constrain our sense of who we can become. As in soccer, this requires cooperation and mutual respect. Through becoming a team, we flourish most fully in our own respective ways.[16]

Notes

1   bell hooks, *The Will to Change: Men, Masculinity, and Love* (New York: Washington Square Press, 2004), 18.
2   hooks, *The Will to Change*, 12.
3   Aaron James, *Assholes: A Theory* (New York: Basic Books, 2013), 5–6.
4   Alex Azzi, "2021 Timeline: NWSL Abuse Allegations," https://onherturf. nbcsports.com/2021/11/23/2021-nwsl-timeline-five-male-coaches- ousted-allegations-of-abuse, Accessed June 23, 2022.
5   Kate Manne, *Down Girl: The Logic of Misogyny* (New York: Oxford University Press, 2018), 33.
6   hooks, *The Will to Change*, 82.
7   hooks, *all about love: new visions* (New York: William Morrow, 2001), 37–8.
8   Musa Okwonga, *A Cultured Left Foot: The Eleven Elements of Footballing Greatness* (London: Duckworth Overlook, 2008), 99.
9   Michael Cox, *Zonal Marking: From Ajax to Zidane, the Making of Modern Soccer* (New York: Bold Type Books, 2018), 390.
10 It goes beyond the bounds of this chapter, but what goes by the name of "locker room talk"—the term used to excuse Trump's misogynistic descriptions of sexual assault—is one of the central mechanisms by which patriarchal masculinity inculcates its culture of dominance and hostility in young boys, often enabling misogyny, homophobia, and racism. Too often, those in positions of authority willfully ignore and enable this. Recently, however, a hopeful sign emerges from Blackpool, England, where 17-year old midfielder Jake Daniels has come out as the first openly gay professional football player in England in 30 years, with the full support of his teammates.
11 Friedrich Nietzsche, *Beyond Good and Evil*, translated by Walter Kaufmann (New York: Vintage, 1966), 134–5, 137.
12 "Diego Simeone: Football Needs the Supporters," https://getfootball- newsspain.com/diego-simeone-football-needs-the-supporters/, May 13,

2021 accessed July 28, 2022. My thanks to the Stadio podcast for the reference.

13 hooks, *The Will to Change*, 115.

14 Iris Murdoch, *The Sovereignty of Good* (New York: Routledge: 2001), 46.

15 hooks, *all about love*, 8.

16 I dedicate this essay to all the players I have coached in youth soccer over the years, and especially to our two children, Madeleine and Sam. Being the coach's kid is not easy. Much of this essay was inspired by those I have coached with or admired as coaches: Brett Booth, Noah Quist, Lauren Sullivan, Chris Chirco, Dina Gentile, Doc Simpson, and above all, Scott Galbreath.

Who Is Right, Ted or Beard?

Michael W. Austin

In an early episode of *Ted Lasso*, AFC Richmond owner Rebecca Welton arranges for Trent Crimm to write a profile of the new coach Ted Lasso. *The Independent* journalist spends the day shadowing Ted, first during training, then during an event at a local elementary school. Early on he asks the coach a question:

TRENT CRIMM: After your resounding loss to Crystal Palace, one of your players said there was a party in the locker room. Do you feel it sends the right message having a party after a loss?

TED LASSO: Well, Trent, I've never really concerned myself too much with wins and losses.

TRENT CRIMM: Now that's a quote I'll probably use.

When the profile of Coach Lasso is published, it includes the following sentiments from Crimm: "If the Lasso Way is wrong, it's hard to imagine being right.... Though I believe that Ted Lasso will fail here ... I won't gloat when it happens, because I can't help but root for him" ("Trent Crimm: The Independent").

Winning Is the Only Thing

Trent Crimm may root for Ted and appreciate the Lasso Way, but most Richmond supporters aren't as enamored with it, which their fruity language regularly makes clear. They want their team to win. And there is nothing wrong with wanting to win. As NFL coach Herm Edwards once put it, when he was coaching the New York Jets, "You

Ted Lasso and Philosophy: No Question Is Into Touch, First Edition.
Edited by Marybeth Baggett and David Baggett.
© 2024 John Wiley & Sons, Inc. Published 2024 by John Wiley & Sons, Inc.

play to win the game! You don't play to just play it. That's the great thing about sports. You play to win."[1] Legendary Green Bay Packers coach Vince Lombardi famously took the idea much further: "Winning isn't everything, it's the only thing."

The words of Edwards and especially Lombardi reflect the way many people think of sports these days. Sport philosophers Mark Holowchak and Heather Reid discuss this conception of sports as war.[2] On this view, when Richmond plays Brentford it is not just a match, but something more. It is a kind of war. Competition is seen as a battle. Opponents are enemies. Winning is *the* goal of sports on this way of thinking. Only by winning is one able to gain status, fame, and wealth. According to Reid and Holowchak, the fundamental problem with competitive sports today is "an attitude that views sport as serious business—a form of war or commerce rather than recreation or even education."[3] They don't have a problem with winning, or even with the professionalization of sports. Rather, it is winning on steroids, so to speak, that is the problem, sports as war.

Take the infamous Lombardi quote. Is it really the case that winning is the *only* thing that matters in sports? We philosophers are notoriously picky about language, hopefully because this aids us in the quest for truth and wisdom. It's clear that winning isn't the only thing, that winning isn't all that matters. If it were, then teams should fill their schedules with vastly inferior opponents, maximizing their chances of winning most or all of their games. But they don't, and shouldn't. If winning really is the only thing, Richmond should try to get relegated so they can be in a league with inferior competition and have a better shot at winning more games. But they don't do that, and rightly so. As another cliché has it, to be the best you have to beat the best. Part of the value of sports is being tested, being stretched to play better than you ever have before, even if you end up losing.

Another problem with the "winning is the only thing" view of sports is that if it is literally and consistently applied, all kinds of cheating and dirty play would be justified. Again, if winning is the *only* thing, then it wouldn't matter *how* you win, just *that* you win. This is the approach Rupert takes, when he instructs George to have one of his West Ham players intentionally injure Jamie Tartt: "Take him out.... Get rid of him." To his credit George refuses: "I'm not playing the game like that" ("So Long, Farewell"). Those who, like Rupert, would cheat their way to victory have made a mistake. They have had a moral lapse. There are other ways of approaching sports, and one of them is the Lasso Way.

The Lasso Way

Ted cares about winning, as we see in the video of him dancing in celebration after his Wichita State Shockers win their first college football championship ("Pilot"). He repeats this exuberant dance after AFC Richmond keeps their title hopes alive, briefly, with a victory over West Ham on the last day of the season ("So Long, Farewell"). But winning is not how he measures success as a coach, as he explains to Trent:

> Now, I'm gonna say this again, just so you didn't think it was a mistake the first time I said it. For me, success is not about the wins and the losses. It's about helping these young fellas be the best versions of themselves on and off the field. And it ain't always easy, Trent, but neither is growing up without someone believing in you. ("Trent Crimm: The Independent")

Ted's thoughts resonate with another truism: It's not whether you win or lose, it's how you play the game. This cliché can be traced back in time at least as far as 1926, when the Sportsmanship Brotherhood formed. Here is their code of 8 rules:

1. Keep the rule.
2. Keep faith with your comrades.
3. Keep yourself fit.
4. Keep your temper.
5. Keep your play free from brutality.
6. Keep pride under in victory.
7. Keep heart stout in defeat.
8. Keep a sound soul and a clean mind in a healthy body.

Their slogan was "Not that you won or lost—but how you played the game." But their code and the accompanying slogan reflect a wider view of sportsmanship, one that includes but goes beyond what happens on the playing field. The purpose of this group was "spreading the gospel of sportsmanship throughout all aspects of life, from childhood games to international events."[4] The values of sportsmanship were thought to be important for all of life.

This is what Ted champions, what he values. Many of these eight rules in the Sportsmanship Brotherhood code of conduct would fit under the Lasso Way. Ted wants a team that keeps faith with each other, putting the team first. We see this in the first season when they decide to use Jamie as a decoy so that Sam is freed up to shoot, though Jamie bristles at it and falls short of the ideal ("Trent Crimm: The Independent"). Physical fitness is obviously important to Ted, as we see the team doing cardio and strength training (and ice bath recoveries) several times over the course of the show. Richmond does not play dirty. The team plays in a physical way, but the players don't cross the line into brutality. Richmond is not Stoke, after all. And Ted exemplifies keeping a stout heart in defeat, while encouraging his team to do the same when they are relegated by Man City: "We may not have won, but you all definitely succeeded. I mean you gave the champs 90 minutes of hell" ("The Hope That Kills You").

Ted wants a team of good human beings who care for one another. He wants to help them become the best people they can be. For Coach Lasso, that is more important than winning, and it's how he measures success. Many coaches think that the best way to get wins is by focusing on something other than winning. I think this is right. A focus on the process, on the values of the team culture, on developing excellence, on reaching one's potential, is the best way to get more wins. But Ted is clear here. He measures success, not by wins and losses, but by helping his players be better players and better people.

There is something to the notion that how you play matters more than winning. In my own experience as a high school soccer coach, I consistently tell players that I want their experience on our team to help them become better people, to help them grow as human beings, including growth in their character. We talk about the importance of respect, for oneself, teammates, coaches, referees, opponents, and fans. None of us is perfect, but we do value these things. I emphasize becoming better people because this will help them in other parts of their lives both now and in the future. I once heard a retired coach answer the question, "Where are your trophies?" by pointing to his players, to the people they had become. That was what he had to show for his years of coaching. His contribution to the persons they had become mattered more than any hardware. That is what mattered to him, and it matters to me. It also matters to Ted.

But isn't there a difference between youth sports and elite sports? Surely victory matters, especially at the professional level when people's livelihoods are on the line? And more philosophically, isn't winning at least part of the point of sports, after all? If you don't care at all about winning, why play? There is something to this, too. It's not about being better players *or* better people, it's not about seeking victory *or* virtue. This is a case where you really can have your cake (or biscuit) and eat it too, as Ted comes to see with the help of his best friend and assistant coach.

The New Lasso Way

The Lasso Way ends up causing a rift between Ted and Beard. In the days leading up to the last game of the season, when Richmond faces Manchester City and needs a good result to avoid relegation, the question of how to define success in sports comes up once again. Veteran midfielder Roy Kent has made serious mistakes in several games, and Beard thinks it best to bench him. Ted wants to keep Roy in the lineup because he believes taking him out would humiliate him. He defends Roy, and says that he's the backbone of the team when questioned about Kent's performances at a press conference. Beard and Nate confront Ted afterwards, telling him that he shouldn't start Roy. Ted refuses, and, after relenting, when he tries to tell Roy he's benched, he can't do it. Later, while Ted and Beard share pints at the local pub, the issue comes up again. Ted confesses that he couldn't tell Roy (though Roy figured it out), and that he plans to start Roy to spare him humiliation and loss of livelihood. The following argument ensues:

TED: Now you know better than anyone that all this ain't about win-
          ning to me cuz that ain't how we measure success, right?
BEARD: Dammit it is!
TED: Who put a firecracker up your butt and lit it?
BEARD: You did! I'm sick of it. I understood this mission when we were
          in Kansas but those were kids and these are professionals and
          winning does matter to them. And it matters to me. And that's
          okay…. How do you not get it, losing has repercussions. We
          lose we get relegated. We get relegated, this is over, and we both
          built nothing. And if you want to pick a player's feelings over a
          coach's duty to make a point, I don't want to drink with some-
          one that selfish. ("All Apologies")

During the match, Roy comes on at halftime with the score nil-nil. He chases down Jamie Tartt, preventing a goal. But in the process he sustains a career-ending knee injury. Richmond scores a late goal, thinking they are on the verge of tying and avoiding the drop. Joy is everywhere, but City gets a last-minute goal and Richmond is relegated. Players, coaches, and supporters are devastated ("The Hope That Kills You"). Winning matters and the loss hurts. Badly.

But Ted still values his players as people. Some coaches would let their team have it, out of disappointment, embarrassment, or a wounded ego. But in his locker room talk after the game, Ted uses the loss as a way to encourage them to appreciate what they have, rather than become bitter:

> We may not have won, but you all definitely succeeded. I mean you gave the champs 90 minutes of hell.... This is a sad moment right here. For all of us. There ain't nothing I can say, standing in front of you right now, that can take that away. But please do me this favor, will you? Lift your heads up and look around this locker room. Yeah. Look at everybody else in here. And I want you to be grateful that you're going through this sad moment with all these other folks. Because I promise you, there is something worse out there than being sad, and that is being alone and being sad. Ain't nobody in this room alone.... Let's be sad now. Let's be sad together. And then we can be a gosh-darn goldfish. Onward. Forward. ("The Hope That Kills You")

People matter, and they matter more, at the end of the day, than winning. But winning matters, too. Even Ted ends up believing that victory has value, that it is at least part of what it means to be successful in sports. Later, when Ted is in Rebecca's office, looking toward the future, he says, "So then next year we get ourselves a promotion ... then we come back to this league and do something that no one believes we could ever do. Win the whole fucking thing" ("The Hope That Kills You").

This New Lasso Way represents another contemporary view of sports, one that has much to offer. It comes from philosopher of sport Robert Simon.[5] He argues that sports are best thought of as a cooperative activity, rather than a combative one. We ought to think of sport as "a mutual quest for excellence through challenge."[6] For Simon, sport does not need to be a zero-sum game where the winner takes all and the loser is left with nothing. Rather, while sport is competitive and winning matters, it is not all that matters. Sport is a cooperative activity, one in which there is respect for persons. One way that such respect is shown is by seeking to do one's best to win, but also in part to bring out the best in one's opponent. Both teams are pursuing victory, but they want victory on the condition that both teams perform at their highest level within the rules of the game. Approaching competition as a cooperative endeavor keeps a focus on winning, but it also includes the values of seeking excellence as an athlete, as a team, and as human beings, win or lose.

Some are skeptical of this. For instance, Alfie Kohn, a well-known critic of competition, contends that competition is harmful to the self-esteem of individuals, because it leads us to define ourselves by our competitive successes and failures, and memorably puts it this way, "Competition is to self-esteem as sugar is to teeth."[7] On Kohn's view, we are harmed if we define ourselves by our wins and losses in the competitive contexts of life, including not only sports, but also school and work. When we approach education, sports, and our careers as competition, Kohn believes that we learn to see others as obstacles to our success in these realms. The result of this is hostility.

While competition *can* do this, it *need not* do so. Competition can include cooperation. It can bring out the best in us, not only as players, but also as people. We have to be intentional, no doubt, as it all too easily can devolve into a cauldron of disrespect and enmity. But if we enter competition wanting to produce excellence, both in ourselves and in our opponents, by giving them the best game we can, then competition need not be a force for decay, as Kohn believes. It can be a catalyst for good, for respecting and valuing other human beings as we pursue excellence together in sports, school, work, and all of life.

This is also consistent with the New Lasso Way. After the defeat to Man City, which relegated Richmond, Ted sends a note to his former player, Jamie Tartt, who provided the assist for City's game-winning goal against Richmond ("The Hope That Kills You"). The handwritten note, delivered by Beard to Jamie as he gets on the bus, said, "Way to make the extra pass." That extra pass sealed defeat for Richmond, but Ted still congratulated a former player who had used his own advice to defeat Ted's team. He didn't see Jamie as an enemy, but as another human being worth not only encouraging, but worth, dare I say, loving, regardless of the outcome of a game. And his self-esteem did not suffer, either. Even Pep Guardiola appears to agree with the New Lasso Way. After Richmond defeats Man City in Season 3, Pep tells Ted, "Don't worry about the wins and losses. Just help these guys be the best version of themselves on and off the field. This at the end is the most important thing" ("Mom City").

The Answer

At the end of Season 2, AFC Richmond earns promotion back into the Premier League. There is pure joy in the stands as supporters chant "We are going up! Yes we are going up!" ("Inverting the Pyramid of Success"). There is bedlam in the Richmond locker room. This same joy shines forth when Richmond defeats West

Ham and the fans storm the pitch, celebrating with each other and the players ("So Long, Farewell"). Big wins bring a lot of joy, at every level of sports.

As a coach, some of my favorite memories include big wins our team has had, including a district championship. That team was a special one, full of grit and heart. It included several players I'd coached since they were in 5th and 6th grade. Achieving that goal with my assistant coach Ed and all of our players meant a lot. We are a small high school, with about 240 students. We are in the same district with schools that have 5–10 times as many students as us. That win still brings a smile to my face, and a satisfaction that comes from setting, working hard towards, and then achieving a challenging competitive goal on the field together. But a lot of what makes coaching meaningful to me has more to do with my relationships with the players than the results on the pitch. I'm competitive and I want to win. But more than that, I want my players to have a positive experience, to become better players and better people. So I guess I'm a believer in the New Lasso Way, too. Winning matters. It is part of what it means to be successful in sports. But people matter more.

Another important takeaway from *Ted Lasso* involves what it means to be not only a good coach or player, but a good human being—namely, humility. After reading Trent Crimm's manuscript, *The Lasso Way*, Ted writes, "Great job Trent, I loved it!" He adds, "One small suggestion… I'd change the title. It's not about me. It never was" ("So Long, Farewell"). This is arguably related to why winning is not Ted's ultimate priority. His humility frees him to care about others, setting his ego aside for their sake.

The title of this chapter asks a question. Who is right, Ted or Beard? In the end, as we've seen, both of them are. The Lasso Way is about people. The New Lasso Way—The Richmond Way—holds on to that value, but it makes room for victory to have significant value, too. You can have both. We don't have to choose between winning or people, victory or virtue. People matter more than winning, but you can rightly value the people you work with while you work to win, together. You can build virtue while in pursuit of victory. Indeed, if pursued rightly, the quest for victory can deeply enhance the cultivation of character. Sometimes the results will bring joy, sometimes pain. But either way, we go through it *together*. When we approach sports this way, when we care about victory and virtue, winning and people, we see the best in sports, and the best in ourselves. And this is one reason so many people love *Ted Lasso*. It reminds us who we can be, when we're at our best.[8]

Notes

1 "Herm Edwards You Play to Win," https://youtu.be/b5-iJUuPWis.
2 M. Andrew Holowchak and Heather L. Reid, *Aretism: An Ancient Sports Philosophy for the Modern Sports World* (Lanham, MD: Lexington Books, 2011). They actually call it the Martial/Commercial Model, but our focus here is not on the financial aspect, since one can still have a winner take all attitude in amateur sports.
3 Holowchak and Reid, 53.
4 James Keating, "Sportsmanship as a Moral Category," *Ethics* 75 (1964), 28.
5 Robert L. Simon, "Good Competition and Drug-Enhanced Performance," in Jan Boxill ed., *Sports Ethics* (Malden, MA: Blackwell, 2003), 175–81. For more on this, see Simon's *Fair Play: The Ethics of Sport*, 3rd edition (Boulder, CO: Westview Press, 2010).
6 Ibid., 179.
7 Alfie Kohn, "The Case Against Competition," http://www.alfiekohn.org/article/case-competition; accessed June 20, 2022. See also Alfie Kohn, *No Contest: The Case Against Competition* (Boston, MA: Houghton Mifflin, 1986).
8 I dedicate this chapter to the 2020 Model Patriots, champions on and off the field: my good friend and assistant coach Ed Anania, and our players Maiya Bhandari, Anniston Bray, Maria Carey, Selise Forsythe, Claire Garner, Lily Halcomb, Keaton Hall, Brynna Lowery, Julia Luxon, Ciah Marks, Tatum Nelson, Rebecca Otieno, Rianna Pais, Madelynn Petrey, Holly Rice, Payton Sparks, Mary Alex Taylor, McKenna Tuttle, Analyce Valencia, and Jenna Wells.

Part IV

MOSTLY FOOTBALL IS LIFE

13

Amplifying Emotion and Warmth at Richmond

Lance Belluomini

One of the most memorable *Ted Lasso* scenes features Ted and Rupert playing a game of darts. A number of aspects make this scene aesthetically pleasing. First, there's the phenomenal acting by Jason Sudeikis: the way he expresses anger in his eyes with a smile on his face is terrific. There's also the brilliant writing of Ted's monologue. But what drives the emotion and warmth of this scene is the music by the show's composers Marcus Mumford and Tom Howe.

This "Dad & Darts" track is a heartwarming piece, the melody carried by an acoustic guitar and a Felt piano. Feelings of warmth and authenticity shine through with these instruments that nicely map onto Ted's story. The track delicately expresses empathy, connecting well with Ted's feeling of being underestimated. Yet the piece also elicits optimism. It starts with a sorrowful guitar melody, then evolves into hopeful energetic rhythms consisting of guitar, piano, and soft percussion chords—evoking joyful feelings.

Ted Lasso is one of the best written and funniest shows streaming today. It perfectly balances comedic beats with meaningful character moments. But many of us don't reflect enough on the aesthetic value of the show's music—the emotional impact of both the score and the soundtrack. The music expresses and arouses emotions, and a great deal more. This chapter reflects on these intricate musical achievements and how the music of *Ted Lasso* enhances our aesthetic appreciation of the series.

Ted Lasso and Philosophy: No Question Is Into Touch, First Edition.
Edited by Marybeth Baggett and David Baggett.

"Strange" by Celeste

We all have emotions that control our words and actions. And one trigger of those emotions is music that often influences our moods, feelings, and thoughts. The ancient Greeks knew this. In fact, Aristotle (384–322 BC) discusses the benefits of music in the eighth book of *Politics*, mentioning that music imitates emotions, thereby affecting our emotional behavior, allowing us to govern our emotions, and thus perfect our nature.[1]

Like the ancient Greeks, the music supervisors of *Ted Lasso*, Christa Miller and Tony Von Pervieux, are aware of music's benefits. The pop-culture songs that surface in the show are not only well-placed, carrying multiple layers of meaning. They also imitate the appropriate emotions that the characters are experiencing.

The show's best placed song is the smash hit "Strange" by Celeste. The song plays during the memorable ending scene from the episode "Make Rebecca Great Again." Ted has just recovered from his panic attack outside the Liverpool karaoke club where Rebecca comforts him. It's a sweet and tender moment. Right as Ted begins walking back to his hotel, "Strange" begins to play. We hear the lyrics, "I tried for you ... Tried to see through all the smoke and dirt" while the scene jumps to Ted signing his divorce papers in his hotel room. When he sends them off, he gets teary-eyed as we hear the lyrics, "Say isn't it strange? ... Isn't it strange? ... I am still me ... You are still you ... In the same place."

The song carries on as the scene flashes to outside the karaoke club where Keeley lets Rebecca know she's going on a walk with Roy while we hear the lyrics, "Isn't it strange? ... How people can change ... From strangers to friends." The scene then cuts to Keeley and Roy arriving outside the hotel room where the song continues, "Friends into Lovers ... And strangers again ... Back to this room." Roy passionately kisses Keeley but their romantic encounter ends awkwardly when he walks away from her and wishes her good night.

The song lingers as the scene shifts to Rebecca in the restaurant where she flirtingly nods to the waiter she's about to have a romantic encounter with. Yet the song doesn't stop as the scene cuts to Ted in his room where he receives a knock at the door. As he opens it and Sassy enters his room for a romantic encounter of their own, we hear the chorus again, "Isn't it strange? ... How people can change ... From strangers to friends ... Friends into lovers ... And strangers again."

Miller and Von Pervieux skillfully deploy this song to narrate the entire sequence. Everything fits—from the arrangement and harmony of the song to the resonating lyrics which describe lost friendships and broken relationships.[2] It's as if the song was written for the show. The silky strings and delicate piano melody that slowly builds lend a beautiful cinematic quality to the song. What's most striking, though, is how the song imitates sadness and joy. The melody and harmony capture the sadness and emotional turmoil that Ted is experiencing with closing out his relationship with his wife.

Yet, in certain sections, the song also elicits joyful feelings. While Ted is suffering from the pain of having to let his wife go, he's simultaneously opening a new "relationship" with Sassy (as the lyrics suggest—changing from strangers to friends ... friends into lovers). Additionally, the song's expression of joy speaks to the happiness that Keeley and Roy are experiencing together (changing from friends into lovers) as well as accentuating the newfound joy Rebecca is feeling in the restaurant—moving on from Rupert, bravely allowing herself to be vulnerable and open to new romantic relationships.[3]

In fact, the harmonic structure of the song captures the show's joy *and* sorrow. The song starts with a comforting "D chord," followed by piano chords that gives us this discomforting feeling of being uncertain and lost just like all the characters in the show are feeling. The song eventually descends back to joyful feelings of comfort. Because the song imitates emotions that move us, it plays a part in elevating the power of this scene and our admiration for the show. Aristotle would rightly say that the song also allows us to better govern the sadness and joy in our own lives.

"Wise Up" by Aimee Mann

Bravery is a prominent theme in *Ted Lasso*. In the episode titled "Goodbye Earl," Roy gives Rebecca his honest feelings about the man she's dating—her fine suitor John Wingsnight. Roy tells her that she shouldn't settle for someone just "fine." She deserves a better man, someone who makes her feel like she's been struck by lightning. Roy's opinion provides Rebecca with the bravery she needs to let someone wonderful into her life.

During her subsequent lunch date with John where he's talking, she realizes that he isn't right for her, that what Roy said was right. The song that softly plays here is "Wise Up" by Aimee Mann. The song gets louder (and John's voice fades out) as Rebecca's eyes drift off, gazing at the other happy couples in the cafe. We hear the lyrics, "It's not going to stop ... It's not ... going to stop ... It's not going to stop … until you wise up." When John asks her whether there's something wrong, the song fades. But it continues and gets louder as Rebecca mentions that her best friend Flo had once told her "that intimacy was all about leaving yourself open to being attacked … allowing yourself to be intimate again. I mean, you really do have to be brave. And that's it right there, isn't it? I need to be brave enough to let someone wonderful love me without fear of being hurt and without fear of being safe." The song fades again when John realizes that Rebecca is breaking up with him.

Beyond the pleasure we experience from enjoying the comforting and emotional movements of this song, Aristotle would mention that the song delivers another kind of pleasure: intellectual enjoyment. We find delight in reflecting on the appropriateness of the emotions imitated by the song. Aristotle says that our delight in sensing aesthetic order (between music's imitation of the feeling and the feeling itself) is driven by our natural desire to know.[4] We sense how both the song's instrumentation and Aimee Mann's voice appropriately imitate feelings of being lost and brave. These feelings are expressed in the strength of Mann's firm chest voice and her airy falsetto. The song's melody carried by solo piano elicits fragility, certainty, and authenticity, which matches what's happening in the scene for Rebecca—her emotionally bittersweet realization that John's not the right person.

We also experience intellectual pleasure through being moved by the lyrics in a way that aligns with Rebecca's brave assertions. She recognizes that she needs to wise up, give up on this desire to be with a safe person, and instead be vulnerable and brave in order to grow. The lyrics capture her self-realization, functioning to transmit important narrative information to us.[5] They not only resonate in this scene, but with the entire show as everyone is stuck in a rut and going through some kind of reckoning and inner turmoil.[6] We're constantly rooting for them. We want them to make the right decisions. The song's lyrics arouse our emotions by evoking this idea that "it's not going to stop until they wise up."

But the song also arouses our emotions in another way. According to the philosopher Jenefer Robinson, "People respond emotionally to music because of the associations they have to it … different sorts of music have associations that are widespread in the culture."[7] During this cafe scene, the song brings to mind the film *Magnolia*. This is because the song serves as the basis for that film, capturing the pain and tragic suffering the characters face while conveying feelings of loneliness, sadness, vulnerability, and confusion. Rebecca is in a similar predicament, especially in her struggles with loneliness and emotional vulnerability. This is why the song resonates with us and works so well here.

Earlier, Ted foreshadows the song's pop-cultural association when he comforts Dani Rojas over what happened between him and Earl. "You suffered an unlikely and tragic coincidence. Not too dissimilar from those seen throughout Paul Thomas Anderson's 1999 opus, *Magnolia*." This speaks to the consideration for music in *Ted Lasso*. Because music is intertwined with the writing, allowing certain pop-culture references to resonate in later scenes, it augments our emotional engagement and aesthetic appreciation of the show. Through excellent planning, the writers prime us for this associated reference which we get eleven minutes later during the cafe scene where we hear "Wise Up" from *Magnolia*.

"Piano Joint" by Michael Kiwanuka

Another well-placed song occurs in the episode "All Apologies" where Rebecca realizes that she needs to tell Ted the truth about everything. After Rebecca procrastinates and fails to follow through, Rupert pays her a surprise visit. He reveals that he and Bex are having a baby and that he didn't want a child with the wrong person. Adding insult to injury, he mentions, "In the end, it's just about being with the right person, isn't it?"

This is when the song "Piano Joint" by Michael Kiwanuka softly begins to play. Rupert's cruel remarks strike an emotional chord with Rebecca, prompting her to walk down to Ted's office and tell him the truth. The opening piano chords capture Rebecca's sadness and pain. The lyrics are also fitting. We hear, "Walking down the avenue" while Rebecca heads to the locker room. We then get the lyrics, "It's the right time to give in. The right time to lose. To begin again. Maybe win again" which is reflected in Rebecca's actions. She's giving in to being honest and truthful (important messages of the show). Further, it's the right time for her to lose—which Rebecca's goddaughter Nora under-scores later, "Sometimes you have to do the right thing even if you lose" ("Do the Right-est Thing"). Rebecca realizes that telling Ted the truth is more important than succeeding in her vengeful scheme against Rupert.

Right when she enters Ted's office, the lyric reveals what she's feeling, "All I want is to talk to you." The song delicately continues, playing instrumentally, as Rebecca says, "I have something I need to tell you. Ted, I lied to you. I hired you because I wanted this team to lose. I wanted you to fail and I sabotaged you every chance I've had." She confesses that she hired the photographer, set up the interview with Trent Crimm, and instigated the transfer of Jamie Tartt—all to destroy what Rupert cared for the most: the AFC Richmond club. The song faintly continues, capturing Rebecca's sorrowful feelings as she reveals that she wanted to cause Rupert as much pain and suffering as he caused her. She breaks down, "All you good people just trying to make a difference. Ted, I'm so sorry." The song fades as Ted forgives her, reassuring her that divorce is tough. Instead of shaking his hand, Rebecca hugs him.

We certainly enjoy listening to "Piano Joint" in this scene. There's a warmth that comes through in the song's instrumentation, a transcendent feeling in Kiwanuka's voice, and we appreciate how the lyrics map to the scene's dialogue. After all, it's a song about a healing love Rebecca is seeking that can deliver one from a life of "sadness and fury."

But beyond these delights, Aristotle would mention another benefit of music: influencing our moral character and disposing us towards moral virtue. For Aristotle, the movement of music arouses positive emotional movements in us due to its melody and rhythm. Because music at its best imitates positive emotions that stir us emotionally, he thinks it steers us towards being virtuous.[8]

Notice that "Piano Joint" contains a melody and rhythm that familiarizes us with positive emotions. Sure, the opening piano melody and soft-pitched vocal of Kiwanuka imitates Rebecca's shameful and regretful feelings. But the song quickly evolves, consisting of uplifting climbing piano chords, the soothing hums of a choir, and a soft drum beat that imitates feelings of hope, compassion, and forgiveness. The song's instrumentation, vocals, and lyrics also deliver this feeling of authenticity—another running theme in *Ted Lasso*. While the music doesn't give us virtue directly, it does dispose us towards being virtuous. The song certainly familiarizes us with positive emotions, such as hope and compassion, which can steer us towards making right choices in our own lives.[9] Because the song accomplishes this, it certainly enhances our aesthetic appreciation for the show.

"She's a Rainbow" by The Rolling Stones

Yet another appropriately-placed song, one that gets woven into the show's narrative, is the psychedelic rock song "She's a Rainbow" by The Rolling Stones. In the episode "Rainbow" Rebecca discovers that the song is Higgins's ringtone for his wife, Julie. Higgins explains that it's their song, that it was playing the moment he and his wife met, endearingly adding, "She really is my rainbow." When Rebecca asks Higgins what his brand was, how he first put himself across to Julie, he describes the night they met. He was trying to be a brooding punk and "She's a Rainbow" came on. He then started playing upright air bass but ended up spilling beer on his head. The only one who didn't laugh was Julie, who handed him a bar towel. Higgins then offers his opinion to Rebecca, "I suppose the best brand is just being yourself."

This conversation places "She's a Rainbow" in a specific context within the show, allowing the song to take on new meanings. It's about a beautiful lady who comes in different colors. But it now has another layer of meaning: "being yourself," something that many of the characters are struggling to do—living authentically as opposed to artificially pretending to be something they're not. Higgins didn't connect with Julie by pretending to be something he wasn't. Rather, he sparked a connection with her by just being himself.

"She's a Rainbow" also becomes associated with Roy Kent's character arc. In Season 2, Keeley coaxes him into being a football pundit for SkySports, a job that proves to be unfulfilling. What he does enjoy, however, is coaching his niece's West London under-nine team. We also witness his knack for coaching when he instructs Isaac McAdoo on how to rediscover the fun in football. But Roy is in denial that being a coach is his calling. At Roy's kebab place, Ted asks him what he thinks about joining the AFC Richmond coaching staff. Roy makes it clear he doesn't want to coach, that he likes his pundit gig, and that he's good at it. This is when the kebab shop owner tells Roy and Ted the story about how he left medical school, how he would have made a great doctor because he was really good at it, but realized what he was meant to do—make doner kebabs. We immediately make the connection: Roy needs to give in to what he was meant to do.

Roy reaches this understanding in the SkySports studio when he views a clip of Isaac smiling and warming up his old team for the big match against Sheffield Wednesday. Roy notices the effects he's had on Isaac and when asked whether he misses the cold, Roy says, "I miss all of it." Then "She's a Rainbow" starts to play. Roy leaves the studio and makes a run to Nelson Road Stadium. We're next treated to one of the best action sequences while the entirety of "She's a Rainbow" accompanies Roy's journey.

Structurally, the song is driven by catchy vocals and a delicate repeating mellotron motif, starkly contrasting with Roy's outer gruff and masculine behavior. But it all works. The soft instrumentation represents Roy's inner feelings, the vulnerable side he's struggling to express to others. The music keeps starting and stopping—the rousing chorus instrumentation led by celesta and strings evoking energetic feelings. Rhythmically, the song perfectly corresponds with the pacing of Roy's journey, contributing to the aesthetics of the scene.

There's also the clever visual details such as the rainbow streamers on the pedicab Roy rides as well as a brief appearance of Higgins's wife Julie[10] (his rainbow) who we see in the stadium hall dressed in blue as we get the lyric, "Have you seen her dressed in blue?" The visual of Julie reveals why there's so much emotional depth in Roy's journey. We're moved by the relationship between Higgins and his wife from earlier in the episode, how it's built on "being yourself." This is something Roy finally embraces, recognizing what he was meant to do and who he is. He's a coach. He's a Greyhound. He's Richmond 'til he dies.

Lyrically, "She's a Rainbow" takes on new meaning.[11] The lady referenced in the song's lyrics is now AFC Richmond, a team that comes in different colors (personalities). The team represents Roy's rainbow. And here he does everything he can to reach it. He runs despite his bad knee, gives all his money to the cab driver, and sacrifices his gold watch for a pedicab ride. But there's another rainbow in Roy's life who's encouraged him to be authentic: Keeley. It's not a coincidence that when he enters the stadium the camera focuses on Keeley in the crowd who's dressed in a gold jacket right as we hear the fitting lyric, "Have you seen her all in gold?"

The entire "Rainbow" episode is built on intertwining this moment of Roy's return with the song. By incorporating it into storyline, layers of meaning are established within the context of the show, thus making the song mean different things for us and deepening our respect for the artistry of *Ted Lasso*.[12]

Brilliantly, the scene even incorporates the scratchy cello and fuzzy electric guitar spurts at the end of the song. This is timed perfectly to the visual of Nate observing Roy pass him on the sideline. The music's dissonance and discordance reinforce Nate's dark turn and look of disapproval over Roy joining the coaching staff. In doing so, the music provides accurate commentary over these final moments, further enhancing our aesthetic appreciation of *Ted Lasso*. Philosopher Arthur Schopenhauer (1788–1860) underscores this point, "When music suitable to any scene, action, event, or environment is played, it seems to disclose to us its most secret meaning and appears to be the most accurate and distinct commentary on it."[13]

"Roy Walk Off" by Marcus Mumford and Tom Howe

The music in *Ted Lasso* also functions in other creative ways. There's a memorable piece with a unique function: signaling the presence of an emotional scene. The track is entitled "Roy Walk Off" by Mumford and Howe. It's an enchanting composition that plays in multiple scenes, tapping into the emotional moments shared by different characters. It consists of a repeating soft piano note, beautiful piano chords, and an ascending melody and harmony led by delicate piano and guitar. The piece functions in a similar way to John Williams's iconic shark motif in *Jaws*. In that motif, the repeating low staccato notes reliably signal the presence of the shark. But with "Roy Walk Off," the opening piano notes reliably signal the presence of a sentimental *Ted Lasso* scene. The melody and soft acoustic instrumentation evoke the feelings of warmth and authenticity reflecting in the on-screen acting. All of this contributes to the show's artistry and our emotional experience, something we aesthetically appreciate.

The track memorably surfaces in the episode "For the Children" when Ted comforts Rebecca after she thanks Rupert for his unbelievable donation. "What a charmer, huh? You may think that you're the only one that can see who he really is, but you're not." Ted's heartwarming lines here capture the care he has for Rebecca. But the opening piano notes prepare us for this emotional scene, capturing Ted's compassion and Rebecca's feeling of being cared for—all of which enhances the scene and our emotional experience.

The "Roy Walk Off" track intensifies plenty of other sentimental scenes as well. It strengthens the feeling of togetherness that Sam is experiencing when he asks Rebecca to participate in the team's "treatment room" ceremony ("Two Aces"). The piece adds poignancy to Ted's mournful feelings in the press room where he relates Earl's passing to his heartbreaking story about his childhood dog Hank ("Goodbye Earl"). Yet the track also magnifies Ted's feelings of remorse during his speech to the players where he confesses he made a bad choice in not telling them the truth—that he had a panic attack during their game against Tottenham Hotspur ("Inverting the Pyramid of Success").

What especially stands out is the heartfelt locker room scene featuring Roy and Keeley ("The Hope That Kills You"). After suffering a knee injury in the Manchester City match, a dejected Roy walks off the field and enters the locker room. The "Roy Walk Off" track then begins (indicating a sentimental scene) when the announcer Chris Powell mentions, "This may be the last time we ever see the great Roy Kent lace up his boots." Keeley then enters the locker room as Roy says, "You're not allowed back here during a game." Instead of leaving, Keeley sits next to Roy and gives him a supportive embrace. It's the melody and organic instrumentation, however, that amplify the emotional warmth and authenticity in the scene. By performing these functions, this piece therefore deepens our aesthetic respect for the series.

"Spiegel im Spiegel"[14] (Arvo Pärt) by Nick and Becka Mohammed

Many of the musical compositions from *Ted Lasso* arouse our emotions through the beauty of their melodies, rhythms, and harmonies, encouraging what Peter Kivy calls "emotions of appreciation."[15] A memorable instance occurs during Rebecca's heartwarming speech to the football owners in response to Edwin Akufo's Super League proposal ("International Break"), which is accompanied by Nate playing Arvo Pärt's famous violin and piano composition "Spiegel im Spiegel" on his childhood violin. Most impressive is that Nick Mohammed, the actor playing Nate, performs the piece himself. What's more, Nick's wife Becka joins him on the piano. Their breathtaking rendition complements and elevates Rebecca's courageous speech, adding a layer of AFC Richmond warmth to it.

However, the beauty of the music itself impacts us the most, arousing sadness, hope, and love. The sorrowful and sweet-sounding music is rather simple. Written in F major, the song creates a melodic voice as fragments of sound recur. The humbling and calming melody gently floats upward and downward as Rebecca explains that "football isn't just a game." It's an amazing thing in life that can make you feel down about yourself in one moment "and then, like it's Christmas morning the next."

The rising arpeggios and chords that Becka plays on piano, as well as her unchanging emphasis on each note, captivate us. We're amazed by Nick's long unwavering tones over simple sustained musical phrases on the violin, which also ascend and descend, perfectly complementing the piano line. And the subtle shifts of key and harmony in their rendition capture the scene's sad and loving atmosphere. The piece ends with the violin notes playing faster, climbing to a higher key, eventually reaching a crescendo when Rebecca poignantly says: "Just because we own these teams doesn't mean they belong to us. And I don't want to be part of something that could possibly destroy this beautiful game. Because I would hate for all those little kids and grown-ups out there to ever lose access to that beautiful passionate part of themselves."

We're emotionally moved by the beauty of Nick and Becka's elegant and delightful rendition. No doubt it's the well-crafted music that aesthetically amplifies the warmth in this scene, arousing "emotions of appreciation"—awe and amazement.

The "*Ted Lasso* Theme" by Marcus Mumford and Tom Howe

At times, the music of *Ted Lasso* also places us in certain moods. But in what way do moods differ from emotions? According to Robinson, "Moods differ from emotions in that they are not directed at anything in particular but pervade experience as a whole."[16] Recall the symphonic track titled "Wembley Arrival" by Mumford and Howe that soars when the team enters Wembley stadium ("Man City"). We're immediately placed into this triumphant and cheerful mood that fits with this cinematic moment. Or consider the upbeat song "Lovely Day / Good as Hell Mashup" by Pomplamoose in the opening KJPR scene featuring Keeley and Barbara in "(I Don't Want to Go to) Chelsea." The song's catchy bassline places us in a joyful and optimistic mood (matching Keeley's) with its mixture of soothing background vocals and backup singers.

Of course, the "*Ted Lasso* Theme" by Mumford and Howe that plays at the start of each episode places us in an uplifting mood, mapping well with the show's themes of believing and remaining hopeful. But it's not just the organic instrumentation that creates this mood. It's also the lyrics, "Yeah, it might be all that you get. Yeah, I guess this might well be it. But heaven knows I've tried." These lyrics characterize Ted who's been put into an impossible position but is doing everything he can to make it work. He's clinging to hope and giving his best efforts in bringing the team together. And yeah, it's all AFC Richmond gets.

Music is vitally important to *Ted Lasso*. Without it, the scenes wouldn't be as powerful. We wouldn't feel as much joy and sorrow. What's more, the music itself is a character on the show to such an extent that we feel *Ted Lasso* because of it. Unfortunately, there isn't enough room to cover all the impactful music. But we get it. The way that the music amplifies the emotion and warmth in the on-screen acting is nothing short of amazing. Every television series should aspire to this way of doing things. As Rebecca coined it, "That way is the 'Lasso Way'" ("Pilot"). And we would all agree with what Trent wrote in his article from the episode "Trent Crimm: The Independent," "But if the Lasso Way is wrong, it's hard to imagine being right."

Notes

1   Aristotle, *Politics*, trans. C.D.C. Reeve (Cambridge, MA: Hackett, 2017), ch. 5, 1340a23; b18–19.
2   The lyrics of "Three Little Birds" by Bob Marley also resonate ("Sunflowers"). Rebecca shifts from calling the message depressing to wholeheartedly embracing it, suggesting everything will in fact "be alright" for AFC Richmond.
3   "All That You Are" by Ben's Den in "La Locker Room Aux Folles" also touches on multiple storylines, adding a layer of beauty to the sequence it plays over, expressing unconditional love between Roy and Isaac, Jade and Nate, and Isaac and Colin.
4   Aristotle, *Metaphysics*, trans. Richard Hope (Ann Arbor, MI: University of Michigan Press, 1952), ch. 1, 980a21; ch. 2, 982a19.
5   Lyrics often amplify narrative themes. In "4-5-1," for example, the repeating lyric from "Out of My Head" by Fastball emphasizes Ted's, Jamie's, and Rebecca's unsettled minds.
6   Ted's inner turmoil is not something we immediately grasp. Ted is endlessly optimistic. But we later learn that his endless optimism comes from a dark place, something we learn when he opens up to Doctor Sharon about the guilt he still struggles with over his father's suicide ("No Weddings and a Funeral").
7   Jenefer Robinson, "Emotional Responses to Music: What Are They? How Do They Work? And Are They Relevant to Aesthetic Appreciation?" in Peter Goldie ed., *The Oxford Handbook of Philosophy of Emotion* (Oxford: Oxford University Press, 2010), 654–655.
8   Ibid., 1339 a 21–24.
9   "Fought & Lost" by Sam Ryder, which plays at the end of "Mom City," also familiarizes us with positive emotions, steering us towards being virtuous.
10   The marriage between Leslie and Julie Higgins is one of the most positive relationships featured in *Ted Lasso*. They clearly enjoy one another's company and bring out the best in each other. Interestingly, the actors (Jeremy Swift and Mary Roscoe) are married in real life.
11   In "We'll Never Have Paris," Coach Beard ingeniously repurposes the meaning and backstory of "Hey Jude" by the Beatles to reference Ted's divorce, Coach Beard's worries, and Henry's sad feelings.

12 One more song that achieves this is "Never Gonna Give You Up" by Rick Astley. The song's lyrics take on new meaning within the context of the show when Rebecca heartwarmingly sings it *a cappella* during her tribute eulogy at her father's memorial service ("No Weddings and a Funeral").

13 Arthur Schopenhauer, *The World as Will and Representation*, vol. 1, trans. Judith Norman and Alistair Welchman (Cambridge: Cambridge University Press, 2011), 262.

14 The title translates to "mirror in the mirror," underscoring the importance of self-reflection and identity in both Rebecca's and Nate's character arcs.

15 Peter Kivy, *Music Alone: Philosophical Reflections on the Purely Musical Experience* (Ithaca, NY: Cornell University Press, 1990).

16 Robinson (2010), 661.

14

Is This Indeed All a Simulation?

Andrew Zimmerman Jones

As the introduction to a drinking binge and a surreal night, a Richmond fan named Paul asks Coach Beard, "How do you cope knowing the universe is infinite, but your consciousness can end in a second?" Somewhere in responding to this question about the "fragility of life," Beard muses about simulated realities and concludes, "If this is all indeed a simulation, which everything in my experience suggests it is, then all we can do is tip our caps to the rascal pulling the strings" ("Beard After Hours").

Though it may just be the alcohol talking, let's take the observation seriously, and consider the implications of Beard's acceptance of a simulated existence at face value. He thinks not only that he is a simulation, but the three chaps sharing pints with him are likely also simulations, so they should all tip their caps to the unknown "rascal pulling the strings." By endorsing the idea that "this is all indeed a simulation," Coach Beard is embracing a thought experiment philosophers call "the simulation hypothesis."

It's a long-standing question in philosophy, well before the idea of computer simulations came into the picture: How do we know the world we experience is real? How do we know we aren't experiencing a dream, living within a seemingly realistic fantasy world within our mind?

With the advent of the modern world, and the wild growth and success of simulated computer worlds, the natural metaphor has moved from dream worlds to computer simulations. Beard doesn't specify that he means a "computer simulation," but let's assume he means some sort of technologically-driven simulated world.

Ted Lasso and Philosophy: No Question Is Into Touch, First Edition.
Edited by Marybeth Baggett and David Baggett.
© 2024 John Wiley & Sons, Inc. Published 2024 by John Wiley & Sons, Inc.

Could This All Be a Simulation?

For most people, the default evidence of their senses pushes strongly against intuitions that we are living in a simulation. We live in a rich, vibrant world. However well-developed our various digital simulations have become, they are far from replicating the full sensory richness of even our most humdrum day-to-day existence. It's hard to believe a simulation could generate Ted Lasso's delectable biscuits, after all. Or, for fans watching the show, that it could generate the warm feelings and sense of amusement we get from tuning in.

However, this is really begging the question. If we are living in a simulation, then our existence *is* evidence that we can simulate the full sensory richness of our world. The fact that we cannot currently create simulations at this level of detail doesn't prove that such simulations aren't possible, nor that we don't exist within one.

It's worth noting that the warm feelings and sense of amusement we get from the show *are* actually being generated, in a very real sense, by technology providing us with a simulated virtual world. Is it really too much to believe that more advanced forms of technology could generate those same feelings in a more direct way, perhaps even giving a means for the simulation itself to experience it?

So, the first point of consideration when thinking about Coach Beard's observation is that he must believe such a simulation is possible. We don't know exactly what transpired over the course of those many, many, empty pints of beer. Beard may or may not have addressed this point with the Richmond fans. Whatever the case, consideration of whether it's possible to make a simulation is the first step toward taking it seriously.

Here we don't mean the logistics of how one would go about creating a simulation or calculating the processing power required. No, instead the starting point for this consideration is more basic: Do you believe that it would ever be possible for a sufficiently advanced level of technology to exist that would allow humanity to run complex simulations? Ones so real that the people within them wouldn't recognize they were simulations.

Bostrom's Simulation Questions

Being able to create these simulations would be no simple feat. Even without diving into the logistics of what it would take to create many such complex simulations, it would need to be technology far beyond our own. After all, these people would need to be able to simulate all the details that we experience in the world, for every consciousness being simulated. Considering the current energy requirements to mine bitcoin and run video game simulations, the computing capacity and energy requirements would be immense, requiring resources orders of magnitude beyond our current limitations. The simulation creators would be descendants whose technology is incredibly advanced in comparison to us today. This isn't something that some lone coder just comes up with in their basement.

In considering the probability that the descendants might someday exist and create simulations of the type Beard is talking about, it is useful to consider two distinct questions:

1. How likely is it that the human species would go extinct before reaching this advanced technological stage?
2. How likely is it that any advanced technological civilization would run a significant number of simulations of their evolutionary history?

Humans have to survive long enough to get to the point where they develop the technology to create simulations. This is the starting point used by Oxford philosopher Nick Bostrom in his 2003 paper presenting a rigorous argument in favor of taking the simulation hypothesis seriously.[1] We won't get into the equations that Bostrom uses, but there's some probability that the human species will last long enough to get there.

We obviously can't determine this probability empirically. And Bostrom doesn't claim to. We have only the one human species as a data point, after all, and that species hasn't yet driven itself extinct nor reached this advanced technological status. The empirical argument from this one data point could be that this probability would be either 0 (none that we know about have yet reached this technological stage) or 1 (all that we know about have avoided becoming extinct, so far).

When Ted leaves his first press conference, one of the reporters says, "I give him two weeks" ("Pilot"). Like that reporter, we make predictions about the probability of future unknowns all the time. So, it is possible to say that we have some intuition about whether this probability is very high or very low, in general. If we believed that more people were socially conscious like Sam Obisanya ("Do the Right-est Thing"), then maybe we'd weigh more in the direction that humanity will avoid our more destructive urges. If we're of a more cynical bent, believing that we all have a horrible little Rupert in our soul, the probability might reflect that we're all going to die.

The extinction point is technically unnecessary. If the human species is very likely to go extinct before reaching this advanced technological stage, then it is inherently impossible that they would "run a significant number of simulations of their evolutionary history." Extinct societies run very few simulations, so you could account for the "extinction" scenario as part of the probability of creating simulations.

That is the point of the second question above. What happens in a society that does reach this technological point? How interested would such a species be in running simulations of this kind? This is just as important as the brute (but as yet unknown) fact of whether a human species would reach the technological ability to do so. We might think, after all, that a species with such advanced technology would have little interest in running historical simulations and using that processing power to create massive numbers of fully-fledged simulations of individuals throughout their histories. Bostrom quantifies this as the probability that an advanced civilization will want to run ancestor simulations.

Again, it's important to point out that this number too has to be estimated by intuition, because there's no way to observe it. We've never witnessed an actual society at this technological stage and have no empirical idea of what might motivate them. We are guided only by intuitions, based on the degree to which our current human society engages with far less sophisticated simulations. Consider the amount of time and energy fans spend on soccer games or fictional television series—or a fictional television series about soccer.

This reliance on intuition isn't some sleight-of-hand on Bostrom's part. It's his key point. We have intuitions on the probabilities of those two things. If the probability that a species will ever make simulations is zero (either because they can't or don't want to), then the answer to whether we live in a simulation is trivially easy: We don't, because no such simulations will ever exist. However, if we don't set these two probabilities at (or near) zero, then we have to consider the possibility that complex simulations will exist. And if they exist, we have to consider the possibility that we could exist within one. Something that Coach Beard, at least, is completely comfortable with, even without looking at the math behind Bostrom's argument—although for all we know, math books are among the many titles on Beard's never-ending reading list.

Bostrom's Simulation Equation (Without the Math)

With these two probabilities in consideration, Bostrom dives into the math.[2]

Consider the total of all people, or at least pre-simulation people. The total number of all people would be the simulated people plus non-simulated people. The non-simulated people are all of those humans who actually lived through human history prior to the point the species reached a status where they began to be able to create simulations. To find the percentage of all people who are simulated people, you'd divide the number of simulated people by the number of all people.

If the number of simulated people is close to zero, then the probability that you yourself are a simulation will be close to zero. In other words, this mathematically demonstrates the intuition from earlier: If no one ever creates a simulation (or doesn't create many of them), then it's very unlikely that you are a simulation.

Some people feel like this really resolves Bostrom's trilemma (a dilemma with three outcomes), with no need to look any deeper. Theoretical physicist Marcelo Gleiser, for example, discounts the idea that advanced intelligences would have any interest in running such simulations: "Why would they, exactly?" he asks. "Would they expect to gain some new information about their reality by looking at their evolutionary past?"[3]

But what if assumptions about inability or unwillingness to create a simulation were not small? These societies would have the ability to create a large number of simulated people. And it doesn't take many large-scale simulations of this type for us to get concerned about our status. If in all of the future, only ten motivated people decide to run full-scale simulations of their human ancestors, then there are ten times as many simulated humans as real humans, resulting in a ten-to-one chance that you're a simulation human. And if those simulators are running significantly more simulations, there's even greater likelihood that our world is a simulation ... and so are all the people within it.

Including Beard and his drinking companions.

Just to be clear, this line of reasoning doesn't mean that we (or Gleiser or anyone other than Coach Beard) have to believe we're living in a simulation. It means that we have to believe either one (or more) of the following:

1. It is very unlikely that humans will ever reach the point where they have the technology to simulate worlds of simulated people.

2. It is very unlikely that advanced societies would choose to run simulated worlds of simulated people.
3. It is very likely that we are simulated people living in a simulated world.

It may be that someone holds belief 1 and just doesn't believe in people with this advanced technology level. (But, as Ted would say, it's more important that they believe in themselves.) So, it is certainly possible that you don't adopt point (3) above, but it logically suggests in doing so that it's because you believe either (1) or (2), or both. Gleiser, for example, clearly embraces (2) as a way of refuting (3), which is perfectly consistent with Bostrom's reasoning.

Coach Beard, in strongly embracing (3), seems to make his position loud and clear.

Is Led Tasso Real?

One thing that's noteworthy about Bostrom's argument is that it completely falls apart if you try to argue that we are somehow a particularly *unique* simulation, or even a rare one. It assumes that once a civilization reaches the point where it can create these complex simulations, it will be running a lot of them. If a civilization is disengaged from this wondrous technology and runs just a simulation or two, then the math doesn't compel a person to assume that they're one of those simulated people.

But it's reasonable to assume that if the technology became available, then people would want to run all sorts of weird scenarios. They might want to see what would happen, for example, if you took a Kansas football coach and made him the coach of a British soccer team. How would all the other people in that environment react? Sounds like a pretty cool concept.

In simulated world 1, then maybe Ted Lasso is still coaching football in the United States, still married to his wife, and able to tuck his son in every night. In simulated world 2, we instead have a Ted Lasso who is divorced from his wife, separated from his son, and living in Richmond coaching a soccer team. Both may have the same personality and demeanor, but they exist in different worlds, and different outcomes are unfolding due to those different life paths. Simulated world 2 is the world that fans are watching play out, of course, when watching the television series *Ted Lasso*.

Similarly, there could be another world where Ted Lasso reacted differently to his father's suicide, and instead of becoming an intensely positive person, he assumed particularly dark character traits, becoming a shouting rage monster who rivals the likes of Roy Kent on his worst day. We have seen a glimpse of this dark reflection of Ted Lasso when he briefly assumes the persona of Led Tasso in an effort to encourage his team to unite ("Do the Right-est Thing"). But in a scenario where we have hundreds of thousands of historical world simulations, it may well be there would be some of those worlds where this is the person that Ted Lasso becomes.

The philosopher who is most strongly associated with thinking about these sorts of multiple world scenarios is David Lewis, who used such thinking to develop a curious theory, called modal realism, which focused on how to think about different possible worlds. The book Lewis wrote primarily focusing on these concepts was published in 1986.[4] This is a mere two years after the publication of William Gibson's novel *Neuromancer*, often credited with the creation of the cyberpunk genre. Digital worlds play a significant role in cyberpunk fiction, though Gibson wasn't the first author to toy with this idea.[5] Given that the ideas about virtual worlds were out there, you'd think that Lewis himself would have focused strongly on such worlds, but he was thinking of multiple worlds in a very different sense.

Lewis was thinking about hypothetical worlds, which describe things that don't actually exist. In the actual world, there is no Coach Beard, but there is an actor and writer named Brendan Hunt. Brendan Hunt is an actual person, and that actual person helped create a television series called *Ted Lasso*, which describes a possible world. He plays the role of Coach Beard, one of the possible people who are depicted as residing within that world.

The main thrust of David Lewis's work was to make the argument that these possible worlds, and the possible people within them, should be considered real. They aren't part of this world, which means they aren't this-worldly, or aren't "actual." But that doesn't mean they aren't real in a more fundamental sense.

Specifically, Lewis pointed out that most of what we do in life is think through counterfactual experiences that haven't happened yet (and may well never happen). If those counterfactuals we're thinking about have no claim to "reality," then it places a lot of our regular thinking on a particularly precarious foundation.[6]

So, Lewis argued, the better way to approach this problem is to assume the actual world exists (which would seem obvious to anyone who isn't a professional philosopher), but to also assert the reality of any other possible worlds that may exist as well. If a world is impossible, then fine, we can discount it, but as long as it's possible we have to take those possible worlds seriously as having a real existence.

Again, Lewis wasn't talking explicitly about digital simulated realities, but about hypothetical future extrapolations, counterfactual claims about the past, and similar situations. Determinism aside, people look at their own life, or the world, and think that if only things had gone a little differently, there would have been significantly different outcomes. By definition, other possible worlds have to be possible. A truly impossible world wouldn't fall within the set of all possible worlds.

The worlds discussed thus far all fall within the realm of realities that are possible, whether they feature the actor Jason Sudeikis, a happily-married Ted Lasso, Ted Lasso as an upbeat British soccer coach, or Led Tasso as a bitter soccer coach. According to Lewis, the different people in these realities all really exist. Even Led Tasso.

Tipping Coach Beard's Cap

Paul's question to Beard ponders an existential crisis. "How do you cope knowing the universe is infinite, but your consciousness can end in a second?" Beard's reply ultimately comes to rest on the simulation hypothesis, and the claim that "all we can do is tip our caps to the rascal pulling the strings."

Certainly, the simulation hypothesis can trigger an existential crisis. Some claim, as Gleiser does, "The simulation argument messes with our self-esteem, since it assumes that we have no free will, that we are just deluded puppets thinking we are free to make choices."[7] But there are a lot of philosophical arguments that we don't have free will, and you don't need the simulation hypothesis to ground that claim. There's nothing in the simulation hypothesis that implies our free will is any less real than if we were real people. The level of computational power available in the advanced technology civilization could be enough to generate real agency in the simulated people. We just don't know enough about either free will or our hypothetical advanced technology to definitively rule out free will within a simulation. Despite that, Gleiser and Beard both seem to conclude that in a simulated world, we're having our strings pulled by some unseen force.

But it is worth noting that under the strongest case in favor of the simulation hypothesis, the "rascal pulling the strings" comment doesn't really hold much weight. Yes, if Coach Beard's world were indeed a simulation, then obviously someone had to have created the simulation and be running it. (Someone other than Apple TV+, that is.) But it's one of a vast number of such simulations being run, and there's nothing particularly unique or rare about it. The "rascal" that is in charge of running the simulation is unlikely to be taking note of any particular single simulated person, and the majority of the details within the simulation are likely happening algorithmically, rather than having any strings pulled by the whims of any single godlike rascal.

Even still, the simulation hypothesis does give some possible solace in response to Paul's existential question. Rather than being a bleak prospect, there is hope when we consider the role of a simulated person's consciousness within such a scenario.

If we are simulated beings, then the key feature of this simulation is that it is able to simulate consciousness (and, perhaps, free will). That is to say, it has done so by creating actual simulated beings. Namely, us. We are conscious entities. Nothing about the simulation hypothesis suggests that the consciousness we experience is an illusion. Rather, the society has the computing power to actually create (or replicate) consciousness. We think, therefore we are. Even if we are simulated.

Beyond that, if we are simulated people, then our experience has real meaning.[8] We know this for a couple of reasons, even without having to rely on David Lewis's claim about all possible people being real. Primary among the reasons is simply this: we are ancestor-simulations of a people who made it and survived. The human experience, which we represent, was not a temporary, meaningless flash of intelligence and consciousness on a distant backwater third planet from an insignificant star. The computing power needed to run high numbers of ancestor-simulations suggests that we found a way to fix our most intractable problems. We clearly found a way to dodge extinction. We found a way to harness the immense power of the cosmos to fuel our technology, which almost certainly means we have transcended the limitations of a single planet.

And those vastly-evolved people of the future find value in our experiences. Whatever the motivation for the simulations—entertainment, historical curiosity, or a better understanding of their own psychology—those advanced civilizations have decided that there is merit in looking to our experiences. We are remembered.

So instead of tipping a hat to the rascal pulling the strings, perhaps it's better to think of it this way: The simulations are those future rascals tipping their hats to us.

Notes

1 Nick Bostrom, "Are You Living in a Computer Simulation?" *Philosophical Quarterly* 53 (2003), 211.

2 Ibid.

3 Marcelo Gleiser, "Why We Are Not in a Video Game – And Why It Matters," *NPR, Cosmos & Culture*, March 9, 2017, at https://www.npr.org/sections/13.7/2017/03/09/519376356/why-reality-is-not-a-video-game-and-why-it-matters.

4 David Lewis, *On the Plurality of Worlds* (Malden, MA: Blackwell Publishing, 1986).

5 Andrew Liptak, "How Science Fiction Writers Predicted Virtual Reality," *VentureBeat*, July 3, 2015, at https://venturebeat.com/2016/07/03/how-science-fiction-writers-predicted-virtual-reality/.

6 David Lewis, *Counterfactuals* (Malden, MA: Blackwell Publishing, 1973).

7 Marcelo Gleiser, "Why We Are Not in a Video Game."

8 Sam would explicitly choose a meaningful simulated experience over the alternative. When Richmond is on the verge of winning the Premier League, he quips, "If this is the Matrix, don't unplug me" ("Mom City").

15

Kansas City Candide Meets Compassionate Camus

Kimberly Blessing

Ted Lasso is an unwavering optimist. He's a good man who has been thrown into an impossible situation. He has little knowledge of football (soccer) or of the UK's passion for the sport. "Heck, you could fill two internets with what I don't know about football." Worse, Ted Lasso has no idea he is being manipulated by Rebecca Welton, the owner of his new club, AFC Richmond. His players ridicule him, referring to him as "Ronald Fucking McDonald." Richmond fans refer to him as a ... man who likes to be alone with his thoughts. In the media, he is mocked and chastised. He also misses his wife and son, who live in the States. Despite this, Ted maintains an upbeat attitude. "I do love a locker room. Smells like potential" ("Pilot").

The show was a welcome salve, coming as it did during the Covid-19 outbreak. Audiences devoured this feel-good comedy as eagerly as Rebecca devoured Ted's homemade biscuits. But *Ted Lasso* is no fairy tale. It depicts failed marriages and broken hearts, a teen whose father committed suicide, an aging soccer star coming to terms with the end of his career, a scorned woman continuously mocked by a cruel ex-husband, a homesick Nigerian player reminding us of the evils of imperialism, a star athlete who can't win his abusive father's love and approval, an insecure and power-tripping assistant coach, and a team that doesn't win. Still, the show retains its infectious joy and comedy, and Lasso his sunny disposition. "Oh, boy. I tell you, man. I feel like we fell out of a lucky tree, hit every branch on the way down, ended up in a pool full of cash and Sour Patch Kids" ("Two Aces").

Ted's radical optimism is not unique. It resembles the naive optimism satirized by Voltaire in his masterpiece *Candide*. Like Voltaire's protagonist Candide, Lasso and his players eventually see that

Ted Lasso and Philosophy: No Question Is Into Touch, First Edition.
Edited by Marybeth Baggett and David Baggett.
© 2024 John Wiley & Sons, Inc. Published 2024 by John Wiley & Sons, Inc.

optimism has its limits. For an alternative, we'll turn to Albert Camus's pandemic must-read, *The Plague*. While he shares a love of football, Camus does not endorse Lasso's belief in hope. Instead, Camus places his faith in the power of collective human decency, a move right out of Coach Lasso's playbook.

Rom-Communism[1]

Ted describes himself as a believer: "I believe in belief" ("The Hope That Kills You"). Even the crooked sign "BELIEVE" that he hangs over his office door champions that spirit. "Gentlemen, I am, by nature, a believer. Ghosts, spirit guides, aliens. Still, I can't actually tell you what lives beyond our physical world and what doesn't" ("Two Aces").

Lasso refers to his upbeat worldview as "rom-communism," which is all about "believing that everything's gonna work out in the end" ("Rainbow"). But just as Voltaire's main character Candide eventually realizes the cock-eyed optimism advocated by Professor Pangloss is untenable, so too for rom-communism. For Ted comes to realize that he is "not in Kansas anymore" ("Pilot").

By Season 2, there are cracks in Ted's cheerful veneer, with his sunny disposition masking psychological issues and pain. Ted suffers from debilitating anxiety that likely stems from his father's suicide when Ted was a teenager. Ted's anxiety is hinted at late in Season 1 when he suffers a panic attack after receiving divorce papers from his wife ("Make Rebecca Great Again"). By the following season, however, Ted's anxiety disorder is on full display. Following a crucial match, he is curled up in a ball in team psychologist Dr. Sharon's office, asking for help. In Season 3, he tells a room full of reporters: "Regarding my panic attacks, I've had more psychotic episodes than *Twin Peaks*" ("Smells Like Mean Spirit"). This anxiety indicates that Ted does not truly believe "everything's gonna work out in the end." As it turns out, life is *not* an infinite series of happy endings, lucky branches, Sour Patch Kids, and pools of cash.

Candide

Candide, originally titled *Optimism*, challenges Ted's rom-communism.[2] Voltaire, the penname for François-Marie Arouet (1694–1778), was one of the most influential writers of the

18th century. Written in only three days in 1759, *Candide* is one of the most frequently taught works of French literature and, by some metrics, one of the top 100 most influential books of all time.

Voltaire wrote *Candide* against the backdrop of a debate about philosophical optimism. To be clear, philosophical optimism is not what we usually we mean by the term "optimism" these days. Philosophical optimism does not refer to a psychological feeling or disposition—a "glass half full" attitude or belief that future conditions will work out for the best. Instead, it refers to a metaphysical doctrine concerning the nature of reality. Optimists of this era believed God created reality to be perfect, or the best it could be, the term deriving from the Latin *optimum*, which means "best."[3]

Voltaire was initially drawn to optimism, but the devastating earthquake of Lisbon (November 1, 1755) led him to change his mind. As a result, he conjured up the character Pangloss ("all tongue"), a professor of "metaphsyico-theologico-cosmolonigology." Pangloss, the ultimate optimist, "demonstrated beautifully that there is no effect without a cause" and that this is the "best of all possible worlds."[4]

Principle of Sufficient Reason

In Voltaire's work, Pangloss represents—in satirical form—the position of German philosopher Gottfried Leibniz (1646–1716).[5] In *Théodiceé* (1710), Leibniz reasons that God could have created only the best of all possible universes and one that would be good for humans to inhabit. "Leibniz could not have been wrong, and moreover the pre-established harmony is the most beautiful thing in the world."[6]

If God could have created a better world but chose not to, he would not be the all-good or all-powerful being that classical theists (those who believe in God) believe him to be. In explaining this, Leibniz coins the *Principle of Sufficient Reason*, which states that God had a sufficient reason for everything in this imperfect world that he chose to create. Leibniz believes humans, due to our limited understanding, cannot appreciate how the evils encountered in everyday life contribute to the best of universes and universal harmony.

Greater Goods Theodicy

Many people were drawn to optimism at Voltaire's time because it answered a deep philosophical question raised by the Problem of Evil. If God is all-powerful, all-knowing, and all-good, then why is there so much evil in the world? Philosophical optimism provides a way out: God created everything for the best, using personal misfortune to bring about the greater good. It's similar to the Dutch football saying that Rebecca introduces to Ted, "Every disadvantage has an advantage." To which Ted responds, "Ooh, I like that" ("The Hope That Kills You").

Leibniz believed that evil, pain, and suffering were inevitable. But they exist only to bring about a greater good, hence the Greater Goods Theodicy. A *theodicy* is an account of God's reasons for permitting evil. That evil may exist to bring about a greater good is "kind of like back in the '80s when 'bad' meant 'good'" ("Tan Lines").[7]

Candide (think Buddy in the movie *Elf*) adheres to his professor's teaching, despite his trials and tribulations. When he discovers Pangloss has contracted syphilis, he asks if the Devil is to blame. Pangloss responds, "If [in America] Columbus had not caught ... this disease that poisons the genital organs, and that often even makes people sterile," then we would not have chocolate.[8]

Again and again, Voltaire's searing satire underscores the absurdity of the optimist's logic. "That's how things have to be ... the misfortunes of individuals go to make up the welfare of the whole, in such a way that the more personal misfortunes there are, the more everything is for the best."[9]

Problems with Panglossian Optimism

According to Voltaire, no serious person—or perhaps only a philosopher—could believe this imperfect world is the best it can possibly be. Panglossian optimism flies in the face of the vast and diverse torment and evil that Candide witnesses firsthand. Voltaire thinks that optimism denies the human reality that experience has taught: a world filled with unredeemable pain, injustice, and cruelty.

As his faith in Pangloss begins to wane, Candide asks Martin, the pessimist, "Do you believe that men have always massacred each other as they do today? That they have always been liars, cheats, and robbers, unreliable, ungrateful, weak, fickle, lazy, envious, greedy, drunken, avaricious, ambitious, violent, debased, fanatical, hypocritical, stupid, and with nothing good to say to each other?"[10]

Voltaire believes that philosophical optimism equals fatalism. "There is no effect without a cause, everything is linked together by necessary connection, and arranged for the best. It was inevitable that I would be driven away from Miss Cunegonde's [Candide's lover] side, that I should have to run the gauntlet, and it is necessary that I beg for food until I can earn my own keep. All this could not be otherwise."[11] If the world is already the best it can possibly be, we lose our ability to change it for the better, leaving God to remedy injustice and ensure that, in Ted's words, "It's all gonna work out in the end."

Moreover, if there were a "sufficient reason" for evil and suffering, there would be no incentive to improve the lot of those who suffer evil and injustice. "It can be demonstrated, Pangloss would say, that things could not be other than they are; for everything has been made to serve a purpose and so nothing is susceptible to improvement."[12] We see a similar kind of fatalism in Ted's coaching philosophy. "[I]t will all work out. Now, it may not work out how you think it will or how you hope it does, but believe me, it will all work out. Exactly as it's supposed to. Our job is to have zero expectations and just let go" ("Rainbow").

Candide eventually rejects Panglossian optimism after witnessing the evil of slavery. "Oh Pangloss! You never imagined such an abomination could exist.... [I]n the end I have no choice but to give up your optimism. [This] madness that leads one to maintain that all is well when one's own life is dreadful."[13] At the end of the novel, Pangloss inexplicably maintains his view "although he doesn't believe it for a moment." And the entire group accepts the pastoral lifestyle, eating "roasted pine nuts and pistachios."[14]

Voltaire wants secular humanism to replace rationalist metaphysics and the theology of his day. So, for Voltaire, our love and devotion should move from God to humanity. Candide, who no longer believes in optimism, is redeemed, not by God, but by work, hence Candide's famous last line: "That's well said ... but we must work our land."[15]

Because there is so much wrong with our world, we must put aside our philosophizing and work to improve things. Voltaire advocates *meliorism*—the belief that things can be made better—instead of philosophical optimism, the belief that everything is already as good as it could be.[16]

Can Don't

As things fall apart in Season 2, we see that Lasso's can-do optimism can take him and his team only so far. Roy and Keeley's sweet relationship starts to fall apart. Coach Beard's self-loathing and self-destructive tendencies are on display. Nate becomes a bully after feeling abandoned and betrayed by his mentor. And the supremely likable Dani Rojas kills the team mascot Earl the Greyhound, shifting the worldview from "*fútbol* is life" to the darker view "*fútbol* is death." Dani's "yips" cannot be cured by the goldfish philosophy that worked so well with Sam. So, AFC Richmond must turn away from their coach's belief in belief and seek assistance from Dr. Sharon Fieldstone.

Ted's biscuit offensive will not win over the no-nonsense therapist. He finds it difficult to let down his guard of persistent positivity when he finally agrees to go to therapy. Ted flees the office during his first session because he fears facing the truth. Dr. Fieldstone warns him, "The truth will set you free, but first it will piss you off" ("Headspace").[17]

When he is triggered by witnessing an argument between Jamie Tartt and his abusive father, Ted doesn't invoke the goldfish or try to smooth things over. Instead, he calls Dr. Fieldstone in tears, confessing to her that his father took his life when Ted was 16. He can no longer hide behind his cheerful facade. Rom-communism is no match for the real world. Ted is now ready to face the truth, no matter how much it may tick him off.

Fans of *Ted Lasso* found escape from the cruel reality of Covid and a polarizing political landscape. This fictional universe, where kindness was king, was a welcome respite. Reality sets in, however, and Ted's escapist optimism is ultimately unsustainable and ineffective in addressing the real problems Richmond players and coaches face. This theme continues to play out in Season 3. In the end, "Belief can't score goals, Coach" ("Hope That Kills You"). Still, we need not despair.

The Plague

While many were watching *Ted Lasso* during the pandemic, others were reading Albert Camus's novel about a fictional pandemic in the North African city of Oran. Albert Camus (1913–1960) is often associated with the 20th-century intellectual movement known as existentialism, though Camus himself rejected this label. Camus's 1947 novel *The Plague (La Peste)* reveals a tempered optimism that sets him apart from his pessimistic peers, such as Jean-Paul Sartre.[18]

Dr. Rieux,[19] like Coach Lasso, is a good man thrust into an impossible situation: a medical doctor trying to save lives amid a plague. Camus's novel is an allegory for Nazism that was sweeping Europe. The rodents that bring the disease to Oran are referred to as "*pestes brunes*" ("brown rats"). This is the French term for the brown-uniformed Nazi soldiers—the same soldiers who referred to Jews as rats or pests. While corpses begin to pile up in the streets, Dr. Rieux remains steadfast in his commitment to "endless defeat," struggling with all his "strength against death," refusing to raise his "eyes to heaven and to God's silence."[20] A situation that Camus would call Absurd.

The "elusive feeling of absurdity" arises due to the fundamental rub between the human need and desire for meaning in life and a silent universe. As intelligent beings, we want a "sufficient reason" or explanation for everything that happens, including evil and human suffering. But a godless universe provides no answers.

Sisyphus, whose fate is to roll a rock endlessly up the hill only to have it come back down, best exemplifies absurdism. Camus considers Sisyphus to be absurdly heroic. He admires Sisyphus because he is aware of his plight. Nonetheless, Sisyphus chooses to continue his futile task of rolling rocks, refusing to hope for a better future. The fact that Sisyphus accepts his absurd situation with eyes wide open is why, in Camus's words, we must "imagine Sisyphus happy."

Affirmative Atheism

Rieux, too, accepts the absurdity of his situation and refuses to hope for something better. In dialogue with a Jesuit priest Father Paneloux, Rieux respectfully rejects Paneloux's Christian or faith-based approach that justifies evil. He cannot, like Paneloux, love "what he does not understand." Instead, Rieux has a "different notion of love: and to the day I die, I shall refuse to love this creation in which children are tortured."[21] Rieux echoes Voltaire's belief that placing one's faith in God discourages us from attempting to improve the world. If he had faith in an all-powerful God, "He [Rieux] would stop healing people and leave it up to Him."[22]

Camus, like Voltaire, places his faith in humanity, believing that "people are more often good than bad."[23] With eyes wide open, Dr. Rieux accepts that "the plague bacillus never dies or vanishes entirely." In a world where evil and human suffering are ever present, Camus writes his last line. The day will come when, "for the instruction or misfortune of mankind, the plague will rouse its rats and send them to die in some well-contented city."[24]

Camus does not believe that ours is the best of possible worlds. There is no God who lovingly created this world with us in mind. There is no greater good. No universal harmony. No justification for evil and human suffering. So we are all faced with a choice. "[T]here are pestilences and there are victims—and as far as possible one must refuse to be on the side of pestilence."[25] As Ted says, "Every choice is a chance" ("Inverting the Pyramid of Success").

Doing the right thing or being a good person does not require heroism or sainthood. Instead, Rieux says, "What interests me is to be a man."[26] For Camus, belief in human decency and goodness is the only antidote to despair. "It may seem a ridiculous idea, but the only way to fight the plague is with decency."[27]

Hope Is Suicidal

Dr. Rieux is no rom-communist. Because life is absurd, he harbors no hope that "it's all gonna work out in the end." Instead, Rieux believes "it's the hope that kills you," a point of view Coach Lasso rejects. "So I've been hearing this phrase y'all got over here that I ain't too crazy about. 'It's the hope that kills you.' I think it's the lack of hope that comes and gets you. See, I believe in hope. I believe in belief" ("The Hope That Kills You").

In contrast to Lasso, Camus believes that hope—"an idiotic faith in the future"—is a form of philosophical suicide. Suicide in any form is an act of escapism. And religious believers who hope for life after death deny our mortality. For Camus, refusing to take the world as it is amounts to nihilism.[28] Absurd heroes embrace their mortality. Even though life could end at any moment, they choose to live and, while alive, "refuse to be on the side of pestilence."[29]

A Strange Hope

Camus refuses to give in to hope. He also refuses to give in to despair and the subsequent quietism reflected in the works of his gloomy existentialist colleagues. Rieux acutely attends to human suffering and commits to being a fully engaged human being. A kindred spirit with Ted in this respect, Rieux maintains his faith in humanity and chooses to believe that "there is more in men to admire than to despise."[30]

Camus's "étrange espoir" ("strange hope") redirects naive optimism's focus on future goods toward present possibilities. Rieux is motivated by this strange hope and struggles to continue the futile task of saving lives. Camus's affirmative atheism is a type of humanism that confirms our solidarity with our fellow humans.[31] We are together in our suffering but also in finding relief from that suffering. For Rieux, joining the health teams "was the only thing to be done and not doing it would have been incredible at the time."[32] Camus, like Voltaire, calls on us to be more engaged human beings. We need to stop talking and do the work. It's what eventually propels the Greyhounds to victory. "I'm telling you, man, if y'all play hard, play smart, play together and just, you know... Just do what y'all do, and we'll go out with the peace of mind knowing we did our best. Right? That we tried. Yeah?" ("So Long, Farewell")

One Is the Loneliest Number

Camus's humanism echoes *Ted Lasso*'s heartwarming sentiment: the goodness of people comes to the surface when we join together as a team. "Doing whatever you have to so everyone in your life can move forward with theirs" ("Tan Lines"). Citizens of Oran can resist the plague by banding together and joining sanitation squads to help prevent suffering and loss of life.[33] We, too, can resist being on the side of pestilence by working together to relieve people's burdens and ease their suffering.

If we try to go it alone, we suffer. For Ted, the only thing worse than being sad "is being alone and being sad" ("The Hope That Kills You"). Camus eloquently describes the feelings of exile and extreme loneliness once the plague takes hold. His words resonated deeply during our own pandemic and quarantine. "Hence each one of us had to accept living from day to day, alone in the sight of heaven. This general abandonment, which might in the long run form character, began however by making life futile." A few weeks before their pandemic, Oranians were not alone and "the other person who lived with them stood at the front of their universe. From this moment, however, they seemed to have been handed over to the whims of the heavens, which is to say that they hoped and suffered without reason." In these "extremes of loneliness" one cannot "hope for help from his neighbor," which leaves everyone "alone with his anxieties."[34]

Belief in the Collective

We see Ted deteriorate when he is left alone with his anxieties. Even Ted's therapist is cured of her own demons after bonding with Ted. Similarly, Keeley reaches out to the brunette Oscar-the-Grouch Roy.

Roy himself develops a deep connection with his niece. Season 3 sees grumpy Roy develop a heat-warming bromance with egotistical Jamie. In the Christmas special, Rebecca, who knows the loneliness of divorce and separation, rescues Ted and takes him on a gift-giving pilgrimage through the town. The series culminates in seeing the team, including the estranged yet redeemed Nate, join together to secure a second-place victory for AFC Richmond. Again and again, characters are saved by their "teammates."

Coach Lasso understands the importance of teamwork. Ted benched Jamie for failing to pass the ball to his teammate. Ted reminded his talented young player that soccer is, at its core, a team sport. "I think that you might be so sure that you're one in a million that sometimes you forget that out there, you're just one of eleven. And if you just figure out some way to turn that *me* into *us*, whew … sky's the limit for you" ("Biscuits"). In Season 3, when they bring in the superstar, ball-hogging Zava to secure a winning season, it doesn't work. The Greyhounds work best when they work like a team, as when they join together to save Sam's vandalized restaurant.

Lasso, like Camus, believes in the power of the collective over the individual. "What about you, Nate? You believe these guys can win?" Nate responds, "I believe this team can do anything" ("Make Rebecca Great Again"). We might read into this that Ted believes in miracles. Maybe not. Maybe he simply believes in our collective humanity. It's a winning strategy for life.

No "I" In Team

The perpetually askew BELIEVE sign above Coach Lasso's office door doesn't necessarily advise us to adopt a particular outlook on the world—optimistic or pessimistic. For a predetermined worldview or attitude can mask reality in ways that are detrimental and ultimately untenable, as we have seen with Ted's naively optimistic rom-communism.

Belief doesn't have to be about assenting to a particular state of affairs: victory over defeat, love over loss, parental approval over rejection, youth over old age, success over failure. Instead, we can believe in people's goodness and abide by a "strange hope" that most people will choose decency. Having faith that they will not look past the pain and suffering of others and will work together as a team to improve the world. Lasso, like Camus and Voltaire, has faith in humanity. Ted tells Nate, "Sorry, I have a real tricky time hearing folks that don't believe in themselves." He says the same thing when he explains why he loves coaching. "For me, success is not about the wins and losses. It's about helping these young fellas be the best versions of themselves on and off the field. And it ain't always easy, Trent, but neither is growing up without someone believing in you" ("Trent Crimm: The Independent"). Ted returns to this idea in Season 3. "To believe in yourself. To believe in one another. Man, that's … that's fundamental to being alive" ("Signs").

For Camus, decency, compassion, solidarity, and brotherhood alleviate the agony of loneliness and the unavoidable evil and suffering in the world. But we must pay attention to human suffering. These same humanist themes and values, hallmarks of Voltaire's Enlightenment, resonate with the kindness, empathy, teamwork, brotherhood (and sisterhood) exemplified in *Ted Lasso*. Actress Hannah Waddingham (Rebecca Walton) describes the show as "a hug to humanity." "I think it's what everybody needed at the time. They needed a hug and a reminder to be kind to each other. A reminder to include each other. A reminder to check in with each other, even if you think someone's got their stuff together, they haven't."[35]

AFC Richmond will not win, the world will not improve, and people will not stop dying from the plague simply by believing that "it's all gonna work out in the end." Belief is not enough. Instead, we must band together and do the work. One biscuit at a time.

Notes

1   This is short for "romantic comedy-ism."
2   Voltaire, *Candide and Related Texts*, trans. David Wootton (Indianapolis: Hackett, 2000).
3   The first recorded use of the French *optimisme* is 1737. "The publication of *Candide* was followed promptly by the invention of the word *pessimisme* (1759)." Wootton, 1n1.
4   Wootton, 2.
5   *Candide* is a satirical and fictional work, and scholars debate the extent to which Voltaire accurately represents Leibniz's points of view.
6   Wootton, 75.
7   Ted offers this quip in a different context from what I am suggesting here.
8   Wootton, 9.
9   Ibid., 10.
10   Ibid., 49.

11 Ibid., 7.

12 Ibid., 2.

13 Ibid., 43.

14 Ibid., 79.

15 Ibid.

16 Ibid., xv.

17 Dr. Fieldstone is borrowing this line from a book title, written by feminist Gloria Steinem.

18 Albert Camus, *The Plague*, trans. Robin Buss (London: Penguin Classics, 2013).

19 To pronounce his name "Rieux," say "ree – yuh."

20 Ibid., 98.

21 Ibid., 169.

22 Ibid., 97.

23 Ibid., 101.

24 Ibid., 237–8

25 Ibid., 195.

26 Ibid., 197.

27 Ibid., 125.

28 In his *Notebooks*, Camus writes: "We must pay and dirty ourselves with the meanness of human suffering. The dirty, repulsive, and slimy universe of pain." Albert Camus, *Notebooks 1935–1942*, trans. Philip Thody (New York: Knopf, 1963).

29 Camus (2013), 195.

30 Ibid., 237.

31 Claudia Bloeser and Titus Stahl, "Hope," *The Stanford Encyclopedia of Philosophy* (Summer 2022 Edition), Edward N. Zalta (ed.), forthcoming URL = https://plato.stanford.edu/archives/sum2022/entries/hope/.

32 Camus (2013), 101.

33 Ibid, 102.

34 Ibid., 59.

35 Norah O'Donnell, "The Gospel According to Ted Lasso: Behind the Scenes of the Uplifting Show that Changed Hollywood," *60 Minutes* (March 13, 2022).

16
Ted's Chestertonian Optimism

Austin M. Freeman

In his 1912 novel *Manalive*, G. K. Chesterton says of his protagonist Innocent Smith, "This man's spiritual power has been precisely this, that he has distinguished between custom and creed. He has broken the conventions, but he has kept the commandments."[1] There is no denying that Ted Lasso breaks the conventions of the soccer establishment, and his merry iconoclasm reshapes those around him into recovering the *true* nature of sport, teamwork, and friendship.

Indeed, it is precisely in Ted's breaking the conventions that the true "commandments" are made manifest. Ted models the ancient literary type of the holy fool: a figure seemingly naive and incompetent, but whose deep insight into the reality of the human condition pierces the veil of the false and results in emotional healing and wholeness. No contemporary thinker has deployed the holy fool archetype more effectively than G. K. Chesterton (1874–1936), and in the same humorous and delightful tone as *Ted Lasso*. But Chesterton is more than a humorist. He uses his holy fools to lay out perhaps the most preeminent case for philosophical optimism in the last several centuries.

Inverting the Pyramid

The holy fool archetype has a long history, cropping up most prominently in Dostoevsky's *The Idiot* (1869) and Miguel Cervantes' *Don Quixote* (1605). In both novels, the protagonist's seemingly foolish idealism has discerned something about the world that the ostensibly more clear-headed secondary characters haven't.

Ted Lasso and Philosophy: No Question Is Into Touch, First Edition.
Edited by Marybeth Baggett and David Baggett.
© 2024 John Wiley & Sons, Inc. Published 2024 by John Wiley & Sons, Inc.

Chesterton, a British journalist and well-known public figure of his day, made another such contribution to the holy fool tradition in *Manalive*.[2] In brief, the plot concerns the residents of a boarding house in contemporary London and the disturbances in their lives caused by the arrival of one aptly-named Innocent Smith.

Smith brings the otherwise solitary residents together in a *joie de vivre* never before experienced, so that it comes as a crushing blow when the police arrive and accuse Smith of all sorts of heinous crimes: burglary, spousal desertion, polygamy, and attempted murder. As it turns out, Smith is innocent of all of these crimes, for increasingly fantastical reasons. But his perspective on the world changes the lives of those around him for the better. Clearly, the holy fool is not *merely* a literary stereotype or social role. These figures offer insight into the nature of reality and act as fixed points through which the world comes to be reinterpreted. Their strange views are, by dint of their formal position within the narrative, also metaphysical valuations endorsed by the author.

This is true of Ted as well. Take his seemingly mind-boggling decision to bench Jamie Tartt, the team's top scorer. What is immediately dismissed as foolishness actually manifests as wisdom, giving the other players the confidence needed to work together as a team. Or take any number of Ted's folksy comments, such as his paradoxical statement to a reporter: "Well, Sarah, I believe you can outscore your opponent and still lose. Just like you can score less than them and win. But last week we definitely won, which is pretty darn fun" ("Two Aces"). What seems at first blush to be nonsense is in fact a comment about the true nature of winning and losing, and a reevaluation of what truly matters in the game.

Insofar as he upsets our perspective on sport, Ted also reorients our view of the real as a whole. He encapsulates a philosophical optimism that delights in life. We find a fuller articulation of such a philosophy in Chesterton's many writings.[3]

Interestingly, Chesterton first introduces Smith in the context of both sport and (English) football. The lodgers are standing in the garden on a windy day when a hat comes blowing over the garden wall. One of the lodgers stoops to retrieve the hat when in a flash Smith has "bounded the wall once like a football, swept down the garden like a slide, and shot up the tree like a rocket."[4] He bellows to leave the hat alone. "Unsportsmanlike! … Give it fair play, give it fair play! … sport of kings … chase their crowns."[5] Smith wants the challenge of catching the hat himself.

But this passage does more than introduce Smith's personality. It also illustrates how Chesterton embodies philosophy in literature. Several years before the story of Innocent Smith, Chesterton had published an essay titled "On Running After One's Hat." In it, he states:

> [T]here is a current impression that it is unpleasant to have to run after one's hat. Why should it be unpleasant to the well-ordered and pious mind? Not merely because it is running, and running exhausts one. The same people run much faster in games and sports. The same people run much more eagerly after an uninteresting little leather ball than they will after a nice silk hat. There is an idea that it is humiliating to run after one's hat; and when people say it is humiliating they mean that it is comic. It certainly is comic; but man is a very comic creature, and most of the things he does are comic—eating, for instance. And the most comic things of all are exactly the things that are most worth doing—such as making love. A man running after a hat is not half so ridiculous as a man running after a wife.[6]

Smith, the holy fool, in fact sees the world more reasonably, and turns comically running after his hat into a delight, much like Ted relishes taking laps on the riding mower.

Chesterton describes Smith as "a kind of fanatic of the joy of life," taking his play very seriously. Here too Chesterton brings his philosophy into his fiction, distinguishing between naive optimism and a considered delight in simple life as such. "Though not an optimist in the absurd sense of maintaining that life is all beer and skittles, [Smith] did really seem to maintain that beer and skittles are the most serious part of it. 'What is more immortal,' he would cry, 'than love and war? Type of all desire and joy—beer. Type of all battle and conquest—skittles.'"[7]

Ted is a fan of the same sort of traditional pub activities, such as ale and darts, under Mae's kindly patronage. Not to mention soccer itself. And Smith draws the same reactions as Ted—annoyance and cursing, but also admiration and allegiance.[8] He possesses what Chesterton elsewhere calls a "mystical minimum of gratitude" for life and existence as such. He revolts against pessimism because he has an existential impulse that *Being itself* is good, even extraordinary.[9]

Chesterton's Relentless Delight

As holy fool, Smith illustrates Chesterton's optimism as founded in this delight in Being itself, as Chesterton would put it. This is one of his most consistent themes, manifest in his literary analyses of Robert Browning and Charles Dickens, and also in his biography of Thomas

Aquinas (1225–1274).[10] It is the basis of the optimism that recurs throughout his work, and this optimism always makes a few characteristic moves.

Chesterton begins with the observation that the traditional definitions of optimism and pessimism cannot be taken at face value. Nobody actually believes that everything is good or bad. This is pure common sense. Not even Roy Kent hates everything. Chesterton quips that he came to the conclusion that "the optimist thought everything good except the pessimist, and that the pessimist thought everything bad, except himself." In characteristic style, this aphorism hides substantial depth. A naive optimist alleges that all things are good, yet condemns a denial of that statement, and so falls into self-contradiction. A naive pessimist condemns the world in which she finds herself, yet neglects to include herself in this judgment, setting her own position up as correct, as good, and thus in some sense free from the distortion that veils the rest of reality.[11] Ted falls victim to neither of these traps. He offers condemnations of evil, such as when he defends Rebecca from Rupert. He also refuses to become jaded by his own divorce or his tragic past with his father.

Chesterton's second move expands this critique of naive optimism and offers instead an optimism founded in the nature of reality—in the metaphysics of evil, in fact. Chesterton is fervently against what he calls vulgar optimism, "an attempt to whitewash evil" and obscure its harm.[12] "It is the optimism which denies that burning hurts a martyr."[13] Instead, he insists that if there is no such thing as real evil, then there is also no distinct good, and nothing in which we can take joy over and against the rest of bland existence.

If tea is as good as Kansas City barbecue, then barbecue is as horrible as that dreadful garbage water. "Against such an aching vacuum of joyless approval there is only one antidote—a sudden and pugnacious belief in positive evil."[14] Ted's own approach to the world is likewise highlighted and rationalized by other characters' encounters with evil. Think here of Jamie's transition from narcissistic gloryhound to team-oriented Greyhound, a transformation at least partially based in his evaluative comparison between his father figure Ted and his real father.

Against naive optimism and as a response to the presence of evil, Chesterton makes his third move and sets forth "the real and profound philosophical optimism of the universe." It's based on his Christian insistence that human life is not the way it was originally meant to be, that evil is *real* but not *ultimate*.[15] An honest pessimism is in fact the basis for real optimism, which must consist in a mixture of joy and sorrow in a reflection of real life, and a faith in the infinite depth and value of the human soul.[16]

This weird paradox, of simultaneous happiness and unhappiness, works an unexpected wonder.[17] Humility, the realization that things can be dark, highlights the sensational presence of goodness. Only a man who considers blindness can begin to marvel again at seeing the sun.[18] Naive optimism attempts to prove that we fit into the world as it is, that things are in fact okay. Chesterton's Christian optimism denies this—we *do not* fit into this fallen world.[19] We were made for a better one. And furthermore, the existence of any world at all is a contingent fact, not a necessity, and thus an extravagant gift. "One optimism says that this is the best of all possible worlds. The other says that it is certainly not the best of all possible worlds, but it is the best of all possible things that a world should be possible."[20]

Chesterton calls this form a higher optimism, and marks in it not merely an admiration for the universe, but an intense love and loyalty toward it.[21] This is his final move. We cannot stand in evaluation of the world as if we are evaluating a new apartment—or a soccer club. We already belong to it, have already fought and suffered for it.[22] In other words, the real optimist's delight in being is not a matter of mere approval but of patriotism. "The world is not a lodging-house at Brighton ... it is the fortress of our family, with the flag flying on the turret, and the more miserable it is the less we should leave it."[23] Much like the diehard fans of AFC Richmond on the verge of relegation, the world is our team, come what may. Greyhound 'till I die.

Optimism and pessimism, in the naive sense, are irrelevant. "The point is not that this world is too sad to love or too glad not to love; the point is that when you do love a thing, its gladness is a reason for loving it, and its sadness a reason for loving it more."[24] Pessimists are not the true counter-culturalists, because pessimism appeals to the weaker impulses and to despair. "The person who is really in revolt is the optimist, who generally lives and dies in a desperate and suicidal effort to persuade all the other people how good they are."[25]

This is why so many people don't know what to make of Ted. He takes the less common path. The optimist is the real reformer. The one who believes life worth living is the one who will take the trouble to change it.[26] An age of skepticism and cynicism—what Richmond endured under Rupert and Coach George Cartrick—actually undermined significant reform, since nobody believed the team worth improving. As Chesterton remarks, "No man ever did, and no man ever can, create or desire to make a bad thing good or an ugly thing beautiful. There must be some germ of good to be loved, some fragment of beauty to be admired ... things must be loved first and improved afterwards."[27] But why exactly does Ted possess this nigh unflappable belief in the goodness of the world? It seems clear that Ted adopts most of Chesterton's moves but without the crucial theological grounding, making Ted's final existential loyalty unfounded.

Believe in What, Exactly?

In the pilot, Keeley finds Ted alone in the locker room, hanging up his sacrosanct Believe poster. "How lovely," she comments, "though I 'believe' it's crooked." Ted responds with the most explicit formulation of his Chestertonian philosophy yet. "Now here I am thinking it was the room that was all outta whack," he quips. It is the world that has gone crooked, the world that ought to align itself with his optimistic perspective. His role as the holy fool is meant to turn the upside-down world back upright. Ted of course believes that his perspective on life and ethics is correct, and that the perspectives of people like Rupert or Edwin Akufo are wrong.

As such, Ted's philosophical optimism is founded in a form of essentialism, a belief that there is indeed a fact of the matter, a correct perspective about a subject. Certain things have essential properties that must be present in order for them to be what they are. In order for a bed to be a bed, for instance, it must have the capacity to be slept in. If soccer is to be soccer, it must involve goals and not involve hands.

Those sorts of examples are less controversial, but what is the essence of happiness? Of health? Of sport? Of the human person? Ted's judgment that Rupert's view of sport is wrong entails that Rupert is mistaken in his definition. For Ted, sport involves human growth and development through teamwork and competition. But who is to judge whether Ted or Rupert is right? More broadly, who is to judge whether the world is the way it is meant to be? "Meant" by whom?

An Adequate Foundation

Chesterton's optimism finds such a foundation for judgment in Christianity. It strains credulity to be an optimist without God. A universe of progress would be an eternal coincidence more miraculous than any real miracle.[28] More than this, the very idea of progress, of better and worse, relies on some standard or direction. "And there is no such direction, unless it be in quite transcendental things, like the love of God," he asserts.[29] Even our sense of imperfection implies a design of perfection, of what is truly right.[30] Chesterton insists on the existence of abiding objective facts on which to build.[31]

Ted has no such option. In "Two Aces," Ted comments, "Gentlemen, I am, by nature, a believer. Ghosts, spirit guides, aliens. Still, I can't actually tell you what lives beyond our physical world and what doesn't. What I can tell you, is that with the exception of the wit and wisdom of Calvin and Hobbes, not much lasts forever."[32] Ted's predisposition toward belief for its own sake is made explicit a few episodes later. In the finale of Season 1, Ted gives an inspiring speech to the team. Critiquing the British idea that hope is what kills you, Ted responds, "See, I believe in hope. I believe in belief." He offers his own counter-proverb, "Do you believe in miracles?" Then he asks each player to decide for themselves. They all do, of course, and go on to play amazingly well against an overwhelmingly superior team. Such is the nature of the narrative.

But despite his invocation of the miraculous, Ted seems to lack any sort of firm religious belief. His quip in the same episode that "[i]f God wanted games to end in a tie, she wouldn't have invented numbers," might imply a sort of theism, but this is countered by Ted's skepticism in "Goodbye, Earl." When Nathan asks if he can pray, Ted responds, "Yeah, of course. But to which god and in what language, you know?"[33] Beard adds that Nathan might simply cross his fingers and make a wish, and Ted accepts this as a legitimate alternative. It is the belief itself that matters, not its object.

This is of course absurd. Notwithstanding the psychological benefits of genuine religious belief as such, *Ted Lasso* as a whole depicts a universe in which people succeed at what really matters, become fulfilled, and receive a happy ending. Ted affirms this sentiment in his post-game talk after Richmond's disappointing loss to Manchester City in Season 3: "The belief that I matter … regardless of what I do or don't achieve … that we all deserve to be loved, whether we've been hurt or maybe we've hurt somebody else. Or what about the belief of hope? … That things can get better. That I can get better. That we will get better…. To believe in yourself. To believe in one another …. That's fundamental to being alive" ("Signs"). But in the real world, a belief in the Flying Spaghetti Monster, for instance, can secure none of these things.

At best, *Ted Lasso* can offer a lesson in psychological health, but in a world without the guarantee of ultimate safety from tragedy and disaster, such health would not last for long. Why should Ted not be fired due to his performance and the realities of the economics of professional sport? Why should he not be abandoned by his players and the fans? Coach Beard, and eventually Nathan in a much more shocking way, both challenge Ted's dismissal of the demands of the job in favor of mere personal growth.

Optimism can exist only when a good outcome can be seen and accepted as a legitimate possibility—and not an utterly remote one. More than this, it can exist only within a universe we believe to have a good purpose and a happy ending. In a not-so-different sort of world, and for people in circumstances not scripted by television writers, such outcomes become increasingly alien. What basis for philosophical optimism should there be for the preteen girl kidnapped by Boko Haram?

This is not to say that Ted Lasso, any more than Chesterton, operates under a cloud of philosophical naiveté. Ted grapples with divorce and panic attacks over his father's suicide. But he continues in his belief that things will turn out well. He does reap certain benefits from his belief in the psychological and emotional power of his own optimism, regardless of its truth or falsity. But as human beings, we have long accepted that it is better to live in sorrow and truth than in happiness and delusion. In order for Ted's optimistic philosophy to be good, it must be true. Ted Lasso does seem to believe that its philosophy is true, but it cannot justify such optimism, only intuit it.

Notes

1   G. K. Chesterton, *Manalive* (New York: John Lande, 1912), 301.

2   Robert Wild, in his book *The Tumbler of God* (Tacoma, WA: Angelico, 2013), argues that Chesterton himself was a holy fool, a mystic gifted by God with preternatural insight. Such a claim is beyond the scope of this chapter.

3   Can we speak of Chesterton as a philosopher? Hugh Kenner was perhaps the first to study Chesterton as a thinker of real philosophical heft (*Paradox in Chesterton* [London: Sheed & Ward, 1947]). Quentin Lauer argues that Chesterton deserves to be considered a philosopher because he spoke about fundamental principles in light of current issues (Quentin Lauer, *G. K. Chesterton: Philosopher without Portfolio* [New York: Fordham University Press, 1991], 7–8). Wild affirms this as well.

4   Chesterton, *Manalive*, 20.

5   Ibid., 17–18.

6   G. K. Chesterton, *All Things Considered* (New York: John Lane, 1913), 33–34.

7   Chesterton, *Manalive*, 226.

8   Ibid., 231–232.

9   G. K. Chesterton, *The Autobiography of G. K. Chesterton* (San Francisco: Ignatius, 2006), 98. Cf. also *The Common Man* (London: Sheed & Ward, 1950), 241. We find Ted embodying his own philosophy in literature quite frequently. His gift to Roy of *A Wrinkle in Time* is the way Roy finally realizes Ted's reasons for not intervening in the team's bullying of Nathan.

10   G. K. Chesterton, *St. Thomas Aquinas* (New York: Image/Doubleday, 1956), 88–89.

11   G. K. Chesterton, *Orthodoxy* (New York: John Lane, 1909), 119–120.

12   G. K. Chesterton, *Charles Dickens* (London: Wordsworth Editions, 2007 [1906]), 142.

13   G. K. Chesterton, "Charles Dickens" (London: Hodder and Stoughton, 1903), 8.

14   Chesterton, *Charles Dickens*, 143.

15   Chesterton, "Dickens," 9.

16   Chesterton, "Dickens," 6; *Charles Dickens*, 9.

17   Chesterton, *Charles Dickens*, 26.

18   G. K. Chesterton, *Heretics* (New York: John Lane, 1909), 164.

19   Chesterton, *Orthodoxy* (New York: John Lane, 1909), 146. Cf. also *The Catholic Church and Conversion* (New York: Macmillan, 1926), 105.

20   G. K. Chesterton, *G. F. Watts* (London: Duckworth & Co., 1904), 146.

21   Chesterton, *Charles Dickens*, 22.

22   Chesterton, *Orthodoxy*, 129.

23   Chesterton, *Orthodoxy*, 121.

24   Chesterton, *Charles Dickens*, 5.

25   G. K. Chesterton, *The Defendant*, 3rd ed. (London: J.M. Dent, 1907), 4.

26   Chesterton, *Charles Dickens*, 5.

27   Chesterton, *Defendant*, xii.

28   Chesterton, *What I Saw in America* (New York: Dodd, Mead, & Co., 1923), 236–237.

29   G. K. Chesterton, *Fancies versus Fads* (New York: Dodd, Mead, & Co., 1923), 192–193.

30   G. K. Chesterton, *Robert Browning* (New York: Macmillan, 1904), 179.

31   Cf. Chesterton's remarks on truth (and soccer) in G. K. Chesterton, *The Uses of Diversity* (New York: Dodd, Mead, & Co., 1921), 119–120.

32   Here we find another amusing consonance. Chesterton writes, "I believe in the supernatural as a matter of intellect and reason, not as a matter of personal experience. I do not see ghosts; I only see their inherent probability" (*Tremendous Trifles* [New York: Dodd, Mead, & Co., 1909], 25). When asked if he believes in ghosts, Ted replies, "I do. But more importantly, I think they need to believe in themselves."

33   Ted's visionary experience of a (female) god in "Sunflowers" may or may not change the situation for him.

Part V

SMELLS LIKE POTENTIAL

17

What To Do with Tough Cookies

David Baggett and Marybeth Baggett

When we first meet Trent Crimm, he's among a throng of journalists champing at the bit to expose the inexperienced and unprepared new coach of AFC Richmond. With fashionable glasses and an impressive head of hair, Trent distinguishes himself with his memorable catchphrase: "Trent Crimm, *The Independent*." From that first press conference on, Trent emerges as the hardest hitting reporter of them all.

"I just want to make sure I have this right," Trent begins. "You're an American who's never set foot in England, whose athletic success has only come at the amateur level—a second-tier one at that—and is now being charged with the leadership of a Premier League football club, despite clearly possessing very little knowledge of the game." Trent wants to know if this is just an enormous joke. By asking the question, Trent captures the incredulity felt in the packed press room and in the Crown & Anchor. "Thank you, Trent!" cries Baz, Richmond fan. "I love journalists," adds Jeremy. On another occasion, Baz and Jeremy warn their friend Paul not to humanize Ted.

The scene that follows exaggerates the worst impulses of journalism as the reporters inundate Ted with questions trying to trip him up. It's "gotcha journalism" playing in real time, and it echoes the press's mistreatment of Rebecca and others. Trent is no tabloid muckraker, but this opening scene suggests there are incentives in journalism that if taken to their logical conclusion desensitize journalists to the humanity of their subjects and inflict deleterious effects on themselves. In the third season Trent admits that his hit piece against a

Ted Lasso and Philosophy: No Question Is Into Touch, First Edition.
Edited by Marybeth Baggett and David Baggett.
© 2024 John Wiley & Sons, Inc. Published 2024 by John Wiley & Sons, Inc.

young Roy Kent was an effort to be edgy and make a name for himself, when all he was really doing was looking for the worst in people. It is Ted's authenticity and transparency that soften Trent's attitude, reduce his cynicism, and eventually contribute to his desire to get a better sense of what he was meant to do.

A Salty Bunch

Rebecca finally puts a stop to the press conference debacle, saying Ted "must forgive my fellow countrymen. Somewhere over the last few years we seem to have abandoned all sense of manners and hospitality. My, my, aren't you a salty bunch?" ("Pilot"). Given Rebecca's history with the tabloids, viewers would assume she is taking Ted's side. "He gets the bimbos, she gets the bozos." That's how the tabloid on Rebecca's desk in the pilot episode sensationalizes the details of her painful divorce.

Presumably, attendees at the press conference are legitimate sports journalists, not muckraking tabloid writers aiming at sensationalist headlines. But that dividing line may be thinner than imagined. In case you've missed the repeated reminders, Trent is from *The Independent*. This is the more reputable paper owned by the same company that also owns *The Sun*, a publication rife with scandalous captions and misleading innuendo. A subtle hint that when news becomes a commodity to sell, the lines between journalism and rumor sheets easily grow fuzzy. Good and bad journalism may be more a continuum than rigid dichotomy. Indeed, readers often find both in the same pages.

Across the pond, late 19th-century American journalists coined the term "yellow journalism" to castigate these questionable practices deployed primarily for profits' sake. The rivalry between William Randolph Hearst, publisher of the *New York Journal*, and Joseph Pulitzer, publisher of the *New York World*, normalized the practice. As each publisher sought to increase their market share, big personalities, shameless self-promotion, and dubious webs of lore and spin became increasingly commonplace. Sensationalist and salacious scoops, stories aimed at inflaming passions, and pandering to the hoi polloi were the rage.

While it's tempting to think the battle over the soul of journalism is behind us, it isn't. *Ted Lasso* is a gentle and humorous reminder that just as principled journalism is a noble endeavor, dubious journalism is alive and well.

Trent Crimm, *The Independent*

Trent's character arc provides a case in point. He's an excellent reporter who loves to write and is darn good at it. He asks incisive questions, has a nose for a story, and brings the heat. But he can also be harsh, as in the first press conference. He is often cynical and can be preoccupied with wandering around and looking for dirt, like a Roomba.

If Roy Kent's right, Trent is a colossal prick and always has been. But perhaps Roy shouldn't be taken too seriously. There's often healthy tension between reporters and the subjects of their investigation, and Roy's an equal opportunity critic. Trent seems more good than bad, even if he has some things to learn.

All in all, Trent seems to be a stand-up guy and a genuinely good reporter. We catch a glimpse of this in "Do the Right-est Thing." After Sam takes his courageous stand against a corporate sponsor, Trent asks if that protest might have contributed to the loss. Sam makes it clear that the issue at stake is much larger than a game, and Trent's follow-up underscores the import of Sam's words. He asks a penetrating point-blank question about corruption in the Nigerian government, a significant and newsworthy story. A free press is vital to a healthy society, and reporters must be able and willing to ask tough questions to get to the bottom of things. This is true in England as well as America, notwithstanding different burdens of proof in libel cases.

Trent doesn't start out as a fan of Ted, but the day they spend together begins to change that. Rebecca had arranged the interview in an effort to embarrass Ted. She knew from first-hand experience what it's like to be the target of intrusive, abusive tabloid journalism that relishes the prospect of exploiting vulnerability and exacerbating personal pain to make money. Where Ted was concerned, she wanted the press to be as prickly as the cactus Keeley gives her. Though she knew Trent was no sensationalist, she was still sure that his hard-hitting style would expose Ted as an amateur. But things didn't play out as she hoped.

From the start of their day together, Ted's transparency and charm disarms Trent. Ted doesn't try to hide that his unassuming kit man is the one who came up with the decoy play they were practicing. He twice makes it clear that winning games isn't his highest goal. Ted's authenticity and concern for community becomes all the clearer as the day wears on, taking Roy's abuse without defensiveness and letting Roy be the star of the show at the school they visited. Ted puts on no airs, allows himself to be vulnerable, and shows people respect. Time and again Ted gives people the opportunity to be their best self, and at the end of the day he tells Trent how much he enjoyed their time together. "You mean that, don't you?" Trent asks, almost surprised that Ted's warmth is real.

Ted did all of this in front of a journalist, for whom cynicism is almost an occupational hazard. Ted knew full well that Trent could have painted him as a bumbling idiot and naive simpleton, a depiction that would have pandered to the prevailing view of the public. It was possible that Trent could have indulged his penchant for cynical skepticism in the face of Ted's countercultural authenticity and transparency. But he didn't, and the profile he wrote instead was eminently positive and rigorously fair. He still thought Ted was being irresponsible and would fail, but he wasn't hoping for it. And that's the difference between a bona fide journalist and a crank or rabid partisan.[1]

Cover-Up Revealed

In a fascinating turn of events, Nate betrays Ted's trust, telling Trent that the real reason Ted left the Tottenham game early was because of a panic attack. Trent then decides to publish the story on the basis of this anonymous source ("Midnight Train to Royston").[2] In journalism keeping sources anonymous is a time-honored tradition, with very few legitimate exceptions. Contrary to this practice, Trent makes a fateful choice to the chagrin of many journalists who are also fans of the show.[3] Out of respect for Ted, he tells him Nate was his source.[4] Whether Trent should have done this is likely the biggest question of journalistic ethics that leaps to mind from the show.

For many viewers, there's no conversation to be had. Journalists do not reveal their sources, ever. It treads the verge of an inviolable axiom. If you fall in that camp, we hope you'll indulge us a bit as we press the question. We think looking closer opens up an array of bigger issues. The case that Trent was wrong to do what he did might go like this. His decision to reveal his source, contrary to Nate's wish to remain anonymous, was an egregious violation of journalistic ethics. The widely accepted code of journalistic behavior dictates that he had a responsibility not to do that. Journalistic integrity should prevent journalists from outing their anonymous sources whenever they might want to.

The rationale for the underlying moral principle here might concern bad potential consequences—like the undermining of the journalistic profession if anonymous sources don't feel protected. Or considerations that point to the inherent rightness of honoring such sources' wish for anonymity. Whatever the rationale, protecting sources is deadly serious business, sometimes literally. Many journalists have paid high personal prices out of principle to protect their sources.

Of course Trent's choice works well for dramatic purposes, but the ethical question remains. We can certainly understand his desire to share the information, and viewers are undoubtedly glad to see Ted find out the truth. Still, the question is whether Trent was wrong to share it. A few potential answers here might be that Trent was obligated not to share it, rendering it wrong to do so. Or much less plausibly, he was obligated to share it, in which case he was right to share it. Or he was merely permitted to share it, in which case he wasn't wrong (but not obligated) to share it. By way of replying to those who insist he was wrong to share it, we'd like to discuss a few considerations that might complicate the answer and, more importantly, uncover some more fundamental ethical issues.

One reason someone might adduce for Trent's wrongdoing is that he's violating a general principle that holds in nearly all circumstances. "Relationships with sources are sacred," as Nicole Gallucci says.[5] It's a violation of a moral principle; it isn't a legitimate exception. But one might wonder, what *is* the operative principle? This is a problem that arises in Kantian ethics, which says we should act only on those principles that can be consistently applied to everyone in similar circumstances. So we shouldn't, for example, lie because doing so is based on a maxim that can't be universalized.

But doesn't it matter why one's lying? If it's for mere personal comfort, that can't be applied universally, true enough. But what if it's to save an innocent life? Or prevent terrible harm? Or salvage dignity? Aren't there exceptions in such cases? Why can't those moral principles be universalized? One problem is that there isn't just one possible underlying principle corresponding to each action. There are many such principles, some of which can be consistently universalized, some of which cannot.

Trent's underlying rationale, so he says, is respect for Ted—a vague explanation that we could fill with all manner of details. But arguably that's not enough to justify revealing his source. It's broad enough to allow for far too many exceptions. Might Trent have had in mind other reasons to tell him? Perhaps he recognized that there was something corrupt about Nate's disclosure. What was Nate's motivation or end game? Was it simply to undermine Ted's reputation? Or get his job? We don't really know, but it's reasonable to conclude that Trent could have found Nate's traitorous behavior beyond the pale. We might emotionally concur, but still, it's hard to justify Trent's subsequent action on this basis.

The protection of sources as a journalistic principle might be similar to rules as rule utilitarians conceive them. Rule utilitarians think our moral duties come from doing what produces the best overall consequences. Some rules of thumb, on their analysis, if generally followed, will produce the best overall results, even though following such rules may not produce the best consequences in some cases. Still, we should continue following the rule knowing that, by doing so, we'll produce the best overall results. So even if Trent's revealing his source in this case produces better results than not revealing his source, this analysis would still counsel that he shouldn't.

Thus far the considerations seem to weigh more heavily in favor of the view that Trent should not have divulged his source, but consider one further factor. Trent was willing to pay the price of informing Ted. He volunteered the information of his disclosure to his bosses, knowing there could be repercussions, and indeed there were. He lost his job. Disanalogies aside, this almost brings to mind the civil disobedience of Thoreau, Gandhi, or Martin Luther King, Jr.: violating a rule with a willingness to pay the resulting price. Whatever Trent's reasons for telling Ted (and we're left guessing what the full set of reasons were), he felt strongly enough about it to take the fall and pay a steep price.[6]

Might this consideration be enough to suggest that he wasn't wrong after all? He undoubtedly violated a code of professional ethics, but it's not altogether clear how sacrosanct the principle is. Perhaps it's more like a pragmatic rule of thumb. And he did so knowing he would tell his employer and might have to pay a price. He certainly doesn't appear to have been under any obligation to tell Ted, but might his choice to do so have been morally permissible? If so, he wasn't wrong, after all. But we're not advocating this analysis. We find it to be an intriguing possibility, but we don't quite buy it.

Looking for Something Deeper

Relying on an anonymous source is usually a journalist's last resort. Because the journalist (and the publication) is in essence vouching for the source's credibility, without any outside accountability to back it up, the stakes of the story itself are raised.[7] Whether Trent was right or wrong to reveal his source is an interesting question, partly because wrestling with it forces us to consider bigger ethical questions.

A quick way to broach such questions is by asking why Trent wrote the article in the first place. Was it really news?[8] He was surely within his legal rights to write it, perhaps even his ethical rights, but still, why write it? Surely a journalist has an obligation to avoid doing reasonably foreseen harm. And how was this piece not going to harm Ted or the dynamic between Richmond coaches?

Of course a journalist can't be expected to predict the future, and isn't responsible for any and every result that ensues. But in this case, wasn't a certain amount of real harm almost inevitable? And what was the public good of doing so? Trent's strongest temptations to tell Ted of the source are also solid reasons not to use an anonymous source in the first place and perhaps not even to write the piece itself. Is Ted not entitled to a measure of privacy in this matter? Is an article like this the best way to broach delicate matters of mental health in the public square?[9] A concern like this seems to weigh on Ted's mind, as he notes in the press conference. Perhaps most importantly, is such a piece culpably sensationalist?

But let's suppose that Trent, despite all that, felt a professional obligation to write the article. Richmond was his beat. He had become privy to interesting and important information about a public figure. Perhaps he thought the public had a right to know this information, and that Ted had misled people with his food poisoning excuse. The title of Trent's piece after all is "Richmond Coach Cover-Up Revealed" ("Inverting the Pyramid of Success"). So Trent may have felt a duty to write it, despite personal misgivings he might have felt. And in truth, if so, there may have been something laudable about his following through, writing an article he felt he should, despite his fondness for Ted. It's interesting to note that Ted doesn't hold it against him, saying Trent's a good guy just doing his gig.

When Trent loses his job, he doesn't seem to mind. In fact, he says he's looking for deeper, more meaningful work. Perhaps this is a clue to Trent's trajectory. He began as a rather incredulous, cynical, hardened reporter. Better than a sensationalist muckraker to be sure, but still rather suspicious of anyone who seemed too kind or genuine. He ends Season 2 willing to lose his job by divulging his source to Ted, who has perhaps helped Trent see there's a better way to live.

This isn't a point about all journalists, of course, nor is it meant to glorify revealing anonymous sources. But perhaps in Trent's case, doing journalism, at least the way he'd been doing it, put him on a path he didn't like. Admittedly this is conjecture, but it's in the spirit of the show that maybe he wasn't altogether happy with the person he was becoming. Perhaps Ted helped him envision a better Trent, who can use his considerable gifts for ends better than sharing scoops that tread the verge of gotcha journalism. His encounter with Ted encourages him, like Roy, to embrace his own burden of leadership and envision a better way forward.

Trent seems to be taking this momentous occasion to consider what the point of journalism really is. Not sensational scoops or fame-garnering profiles, but achieving a real public good—promoting "a healthy civic space,"[10] which can be perfectly consistent with turning a profit. Perhaps the whole experience with Ted has helped Trent re-evaluate his priorities and values. Maybe he was under a professional obligation to write that article, and perhaps he was constrained by journalistic codes not to tell Ted his source.

But getting to know Ted has changed Trent. This tough cookie has indeed been dipped in milk, one enjoyable chat at a time. It was easy at first to hold Ted at arm's length, judging him and looking down on him, the way Roy thought punditry encouraged. Ted's no longer the mere subject of an article or exposé. He's a real person, and a good one at that. He's become humanized in Trent's eyes, and in the process Trent may be on his way to becoming more human himself.

In Season 3, Trent seems to do just that. He spends the year with the team, to see where Ted's trajectory would take it. He had wanted to focus on something good and laudable, not just find the worst in people. And the book he writes focuses on the Greyhounds' magical season, with all its ups and downs. Initially calling it *The Lasso Way*, Trent reconsiders. Ted's suggestion is better, as he tells Trent, "It's not about me. It never was" ("So Long, Farewell"). *The Richmond Way*, the title Trent lands on, is altogether more fitting. Neither soccer coaches nor journalists should primarily aim at making a name for themselves. Nor should any of us.[11]

Notes

1   As freelance journalist Brandon Ambrosino reminds us, plenty of ethical journalists come across as somewhat mean, and other unethical journalists may appear friendly to or supportive of their subjects. Unlike the show's audience, Trent has a limited amount of time with Ted, and so has to make his writing decisions based only on that.

2   See Matt Carlson, *On the Condition of Anonymity* (Urbana, IL: University of Illinois Press, 2011) for a fuller discussion of the promise and peril of using anonymous sources. Of note in this case is that anonymity thwarts accountability for a source's motives, bias, and framing, which is antithetical to the show's insistence on the importance of being accountable

for one's actions. In some situations, anonymity is necessary for protecting a source and getting a story on record. It's difficult to see how those strictures are satisfied here.

3 Nicole Gallucci, "Trent Crimm of 'Ted Lasso' Did a Major Journalism Don't," *Mashable*, October 5, 2021, https://mashable.com/article/trent-crimm-bad-journalism-ted-lasso.

4 The copy says "sources" (plural). But the headline and Crimm himself imply Nate is the single source. An important question is whether a good reporter should take the word of a single source and write a whole article before reaching out to other sources. We'll set that issue aside for now.

5 Gallucci.

6 We don't mean to suggest that a journalist's willingness to pay the personal price of revealing a source settles the matter. We're assuming enough other conditions are in place—reasonable assurance the source won't be harmed, enough justifications for departing from the normative practice of protecting anonymity, and the like. Whether in Trent's case all the individually necessary and jointly sufficient conditions are satisfied to render his choice permissible remains an open question. This is why we're stopping short of endorsing his decision.

7 We don't learn much of anything about Trent's editors or publisher, but they do provide another layer of accountability for him. Journalists must get approval from senior staffers for stories that they run, and potentially defamatory details will necessarily involve the publication's legal team. Ultimately the journalistic ethics of editors and the publication are implicated by the work of individual journalists.

8 An important test case weighing a subject's right to privacy versus the public good of a news story is Hulk Hogan's suit against *Gawker* for release of a scandalous sex tape (settled in 2016). See more here: https://firstamendmentwatch.org/deep-dive/hulk-hogan-v-gawker-invasion-of-privacy-free-speech-in-a-digital-world/.

9 David Archer, "Privacy, the Public Interest, and a Prurient Public," in Matthew Kieran, ed., *Media Ethics* (New York: Routledge, 2014), 98–112. Archer argues that any journalistic breach of a person's privacy must be outweighed by a public good *and* be the only means of fulfilling that good.

10 UNESCO, "World Trends in Freedom of Expression and Media Development," https://www.unesco.org/reports/world-media-trends/2021/en/journalism-public-good, Accessed August 6, 2022.

11 Our thanks to Adam Snavely, Brandon Ambrosino, and Jeremy Neill for their helpful feedback on an early draft of this chapter.

Stoic Bossgirl

Elizabeth Quinn

TED:	You ever been to a therapist, Rebecca?
TEBECCA:	What for? I can diagnose myself in a heartbeat. I thought being invulnerable would protect me, so I pushed people away for years leading me directly to my greatest fear. Being alone. Big whoop.
TED:	Big whoop. Yeah. I don't get it. Why pay someone to do what a friend should do for you for free?
REBECCA:	Exactly. I mean, that's why you have friends, isn't it? I mean, to burden them with your issues and anxieties, right?
TED:	Right, yeah, yeah. Speaking of ... you got anything you wanna get off your chest?
REBECCA:	No. You?
TED:	... No.
REBECCA:	... See, there you have it. ("Lavender")

Ted and Rebecca may be from different sides of the pond, but they both exemplify traits common to Westerners born between 1965 and 1980. Dubbed Generation X (Gen X), this age group is known for their pragmatic, self-reliant, and self-possessed attitude. Gen X is the neglected "middle child" between the more outgoing Boomer and Millennial generations. But despite their independence, Gen Xers know to lean on their friends for help when they need it, even when it makes them uncomfortable.

Gen X sensibilities permeate *Ted Lasso*. Ted attempts to connect with Rebecca even as she resists that intimacy. This typical Gen X relational tension is captured by Ted's insightful comment early on: "She got some fences all right, but you just gotta hop over 'em" ("Biscuits"). Pop culture references also abound, as when Ted refers to H. R. Pufnstuff as a joke specifically for "people born in the early to mid '70s" ("The Signal"). Gen Xers share a lot, including, as we'll see, a philosophy.

Slacker or Stoic?

Gen Xers like Ted and Rebecca are often described as independent, steeped in irony, and equipped with a Do-It-Yourself gene. Thanks to a hands-off childhood where they had to figure things out for themselves, they have been their own boss ever since their latchkey upbringing. They have also been criticized for standing on the sidelines and withdrawing from activism, which earned them a slacker label.

But what if these Gen Xers were just Stoics in training? One of the core tenets of Stoicism is to accept what you can't control and focus on what you can: your own thoughts, actions, and beliefs. Perhaps what people saw as slacking is better understood as practicing Stoicism. Indeed, as Gen X has aged into mid-life leadership roles, Stoicism has become an even more comfortable fit.

Three of the most prominent Stoic philosophers were playwright and political advisor Seneca (4 BC-AD 65), slave turned teacher Epictetus (50–135), and Roman Emperor Marcus Aurelius (121–180). These thinkers offered guidance for a virtuous life of wisdom, justice, courage, and temperance. Their appeal endures because Stoicism is not just theoretical. It's a philosophy of action with practical applications for daily life.

Stoics often get a bad rap for being unemotional, cold, or indifferent to pain, but that's a misperception. Stoics understand that emotions are a natural part of being human. They simply believe that one should master emotions and put reason, clear judgment, and inner calm over destructive passions. Or as Aurelius said, "Today I have got out of all trouble, or rather I have cast out all trouble, for it was not outside, but within and in my opinions."[1] A Stoic would not condone Ted suppressing his painful emotions, which leads to panic attacks, or Rebecca using her heartache as an excuse to hurt other people. Repressed emotions invariably assert themselves.

Stoicism counsels us to accept reality. For Gen X, "Our Magic 8-ball always replied, 'don't count on it'—and so we didn't."[2] Rebecca's sensibilities are flavored by a dash of the British "keep calm and carry on" attitude with a feminist twist. For this reason, of all the characters, she most embodies the Stoic approach. It's only Rebecca's divorce that's interfering with her natural way of doing things, as she tells Higgins: "I lost my way for a minute. But I'm on the road back" ("All Apologies").

So, sit back, grab a biscuit, and let's explore Rebecca's journey from vengeful ex-wife to feminist Stoic. Or as Nora puts it, Boss Ass Bitch.

The Have-It-All Generation

Can Stoicism and feminism co-exist? While many ancients held regressive views on gender roles, some Stoics saw no difference between men and women when it came to virtue and rational thinking. Roman Stoic Gaius Musonius Rufus (A.D. 25–95) stated in his *Discourses 3.1*, "Women have received from the gods the same reasoning power as men—the power which we employ with each other and according to which we consider whether each action is good or bad, and honorable or shameful."[3]

If Ted is right that meeting people's moms is like "reading an instruction manual as to why they're nuts" ("The Signal"), then we could look to the women of the Boomer and Silent Generation for what makes Gen X women tick. Books like *The Feminine Mystique* by activist Betty Friedan (1921–2006) and *The Second Sex* by existentialist philosopher Simone de Beauvoir (1908–1986) gave these women a voice, an identity, and a sense of community that helped ignite the second-wave feminist movement. Friedan identified "the problem that has no name"—the pervasive unhappiness of women given no options other than "happy housewife." De Beauvoir advanced the idea that woman's oppression is caused by her relegation to being man's "Other," a role that Rebecca sadly succumbed to during her marriage after Rupert made her feel "chosen."

In their response to regressive attitudes, Boomer women may have laid too heavy a burden on their daughters, raising them to believe they could have it all. This included pushing their daughters to become independent women who can pay their own way. Boomer women couldn't even have credit cards without their husbands' permission, so it's understandable that they might push a financially independent lifestyle on their daughters.[4] One woman's historical consciousness is another's feminist torch to carry!

Rebecca aka da Boss

Rebecca's emotions control her personal life in Season 1, but at work she is still the Stoic boss, focusing on the task at hand and presenting a controlled, albeit intimidating, demeanor. These natural strengths and business acumen combined with years of watching Rupert allow Rebecca to step into the owner's role with ease. She can justify hiring Ted because, as she tells the reporters at his first press conference, she has seen Richmond play more than anyone. She also knows whom to fire, promote, and re-hire and is smart enough to see Keeley's talents and offer her a job. A savvy pragmatism guides her business decisions, so it's not surprising that her one decision based on emotions—hiring Ted—backfires.

Rebecca's journey back to herself evolves over several episodes but finally culminates in the episode titled "All Apologies." Rupert stops by Rebecca's office to reveal that he and his new wife are having a baby. In shock, Rebecca lashes out, asks if he's a figure out of the Bible, and reminds him that he hadn't wanted children. With his typical cruelty, Rupert says that he just didn't want children with her. She attempts to maintain her Stoic composure but cannot hide her devastation as the tears well up in her eyes.

This was the wake-up call she needed to accept her reality and bring attention back to what she could control in her life. No matter how far her revenge takes her, she realizes she can never sink as low as Rupert, nor does she want to surrender to her ugliest emotions. She immediately goes to Ted and pulls a painfully transparent mea culpa, confessing the truth about why she hired him. After the briefest pause, Ted reciprocates with a measured, gracious response by forgiving Rebecca. Like the Stoic philosophers, he understands that being hurt or offended by someone's actions is a choice within his control. He knows it's not personal and doesn't let it cause him pain. As he says, "Divorce is hard.... It makes folks do crazy things."

Rebecca has every right to be angry and devastated about Rupert's infidelities and his treatment of her. But she cannot change what happened. Hurting Rupert will not take away her pain, as Higgins flat out tells her in "Diamond Dogs" before he finally quits. Aurelius wrote, "If you are pained by any external thing, it is not this thing that disturbs you, but your own judgment about it. And it is in your power to wipe out this judgment now."[5]

Yes, Rupert treated her terribly. But she is hurting herself by seeking revenge and delaying her acceptance. Ted's immediate forgiveness is so shocking to Rebecca that she hugs him. And she continues to make things right by apologizing to and re-hiring Higgins and promoting Nate. Having put emotion in its place and allowed her reason to rule, Rebecca becomes great again!

We get hints of the real Rebecca as far back as the pilot. Thanks to the writers and Hannah Waddingham's performance, we see Rebecca's vulnerability in the way she stares at the painting she and Rupert bought, and her reaction to Ted asking how she's handling the divorce. These moments reveal that she is not really a villain, just a deeply wounded woman trying to deal with her pain and letting destructive emotions control her. She begins to let her guard down with both Ted and Keeley in "For the Children." Gaining her Stoic equilibrium is a step-by-step process. It doesn't come easily or naturally, but takes time and effort, perhaps prodigious effort.

The entire "Make Rebecca Great Again" episode is an object lesson in Stoicism: "Never value anything as profitable that compels you to break your promise, to lose your self-respect, to hate any man, ... to act the hypocrite."[6] After Rebecca reconnects with and apologizes to her best friend, Sassy, she starts to embrace her true self again. She also sleeps with a hot waiter, sings "Let It Go" at karaoke, and demonstrates genuine care for Ted during his panic attack. Why? Because, as Sassy tells Keeley at their dinner, she hasn't seen the real Rebecca yet. "The real Rebecca is silly. Strong yeah, but not cold."

Girlboss Mentor

When she's not plotting to destroy AFC Richmond, Rebecca rocks at being a boss. Leaning into that Stoic and generational trait of self-reliance serves her well in business, and she continues to grow as a mentor to her employees. But even though Rebecca, as Nate puts it, commands every room she walks into, she still encounters sexism and double standards. "Every time I walk into a meeting with a bunch of football club chairmen, they look at me like a schoolgirl with pigtails" ("Rainbow"). Admittedly she'd look great in pigtails.

Fortunately, she lives by Aurelius's advice: "Begin the morning by saying to yourself, I shall meet with the busybody, the ungrateful, arrogant, deceitful, envious, unsocial. All these things happen to them by reason of their ignorance of what is good and evil."[7] Before she goes into a meeting, she finds a room, stands on her tiptoes, and makes herself as big as possible to feel her own power. As she demonstrates her technique to Nate and Keeley, she embodies her animal of choice, a fierce lion, "Lions are powerful and majestic and rule the jungle" ("Biscuits").

In Season 2, Rebecca continues mentoring Keeley as well as her Gen Z goddaughter, Nora. To help repair their relationship, Rebecca brings Nora to work with her. To Rebecca's surprise, Nora has always wanted to see what it's like to run a football club ever since Rebecca started doing it. It's a nice callback to Ted's commentary on Rebecca's photo shoot for *The Football Financial Quarterly*: "Being a role model's a huge deal. Don't you realize that there's probably a little girl out there somewhere rocking a tiny eggplant-colored power suit, and she's just dreaming about becoming a sports executive someday? She's gonna read this article and she's gonna think, Holy smokes. My dreams are possible" ("All Apologies").

Another key teaching of Aurelius is to prize action over mere talk: "No longer talk at all about the kind of man that a good man ought to be, but be such."[8] Rebecca does just that in her mentorship of Nora. She gives the teen solid tips on leadership: reacting to and anticipating situations, being three to four steps ahead of everyone else. Her advice is tested when Sam backs out of a Dubai Air campaign after discovering its parent company is destroying the environment of his home country of Nigeria ("Do the Right-est Thing"). Rebecca must step in to do damage control, yet she knows it's not her business acumen that will help her. It's whether Richard Cole, the Dubai Airlines CEO and Rupert's friend, will still find her charming. When the CEO tells Rebecca to get rid of Sam, it is Nora who encourages her to "do the right thing even if you lose" and who labels Rebecca a "Boss Ass Bitch." Stoicism strikes again as Rebecca accepts her reality, focuses on what she can control, and does the right-est thing no matter the cost.

Rebecca's mentorship of Keeley is so successful that Keeley gets an opportunity to start her own PR firm. In Season 1, Rebecca's emotions ruled her biggest work decision, but in Season 2 she doesn't let her sadness hold Keeley back. The only advice Rebecca gives her for being a boss is to "hire your best friend," showing her professional and personal growth in one beautiful sentence ("Inverting the Pyramid of Success").

Keeley has gone from being intimidated by Rebecca, to loving and appreciating her, as she tells Rebecca, "You helped this panda become a lion." Keeley tells Nate on their shopping trip in "Midnight Train to Royston" that Rebecca inspired her to want to be a boss. Perhaps Keeley took a cue from Seneca when he said, "Choose as a guide one whom you will admire more when you see him act than when you hear him speak."[9] Stoicism in the workplace is a win-win, but can it help your love life, too?

Being the Boss on Bantr

Rebecca may be Keeley's professional mentor. But Keeley is Rebecca's romantic guru, encouraging her to be open to love again, and reminding her that she is beautiful, amazing, and mad fit. Being newly-single in mid-life means that Rebecca must rely on her friend to help her navigate the contemporary dating landscape. Keeley is fearless in this area and, as a Millennial, thinks everything is about branding—even dating.

Rebecca finds success on Bantr with its focus on words and personality instead of photos. Letting reason drive the attraction helps invoke the mystery that Rebecca wants in romance. Or, as Keeley puts it after Rebecca is smitten by her suitor's Rilke quote, "That's so Bantr, a place where minds come to undress" ("Rainbow"). Taking what she's learned from her marriage, this time around, Rebecca is going to be a boss in her love life, right down to her Bantr handle: Bossgirl. And she is determined to enjoy dating and have some fun in life. Stoics are not immune to emotions, especially joy as highlighted by this Aurelius quote, "Dwell on the beauty of life. Watch the stars, and see yourself running with them."[10]

Watching her ex-husband pursue fatherhood while she's past childbearing age is hard for Rebecca. But if anything can take the sting out of that, it's a relationship with a younger man. That dynamic is not new, but Gen X women like Demi Moore helped make it less taboo. Instead of being alone, as Rupert predicted, she finds herself dating Sam Obisanya, a man over 20 years her junior who loves her for her authentic self and is comfortable with her taking the lead in the relationship. She decides every step, even when to end it—at her father's funeral no less. But that's the thing about death. It forces you to take a hard look at your life.

The Stoics had a lot of thoughts about death, but at the heart of them all is that knowing we'll die eventually should help us live by the tenets of Stoic philosophy. Perhaps that's why Rebecca finally confesses to her mother that she caught her father being unfaithful. Even worse, her father acted like it never even happened. In turn, Rebecca resented him, even while she followed her mother's footsteps by likewise marrying an adulterer. As Rebecca tells her mother, she was terrified to leave Rupert, but she knew it was necessary and, in time, she has found being alone quite wonderful. Rebecca has learned to "be like the promontory against which the waves continually break; but it stands firm and tames the fury of the water around it."[11]

Rebecca has learned a lot by now, but she's been a great teacher, too. Her advice to Ted in "The Hope That Kills You" is that every disadvantage has its advantage. This may be a quote from Dutch football manager Johan Cruyff, but it's straight out of the Aurelius playbook: "For the mind converts and changes every hindrance to its activity into an aid; and so that which is a hindrance is made a furtherance to an aid; and an obstacle on the road helps us along this road."[12] External obstacles may be out of our control, but Rebecca's journey reminds us that how we view them is both fluid and within our control.

Aurelius said, "That which does not make a man worse than he was, also does not make his life worse, nor does it harm him either from without or from within."[13] Or as Friedrich Nietzsche (1844–1900) put it, "That which does not kill us, makes us stronger."[14] We often don't learn this lesson until we reach middle age and have enough experience to realize that whatever pain life throws our way, we will survive it.

Soccer Mom

In the final season, Rebecca's mom thinks a visit to her psychic Tish will give Rebecca the maternal guidance she desperately needs. But it's Rebecca who provides tough but honest mothering to everyone. When Rebecca tears into Roy after he dodges a press conference, she highlights his pattern of walking away from difficult things. At Edwin Akufo's meeting about the super league, Rebecca chides her fellow club owners for their financial greed, which will rob fans of the happiness that football gives them. She scolds them like little boys who refuse to share their toys, reminding them of the responsibilities club owners have to the community. "I would hate for all those little kids and grown-ups out there to ever lose access to that beautiful, passionate part of themselves" ("International Break").

Rebecca also reveals a shred of humanity in Rupert as she recalls how he snuck into Richmond games as a boy when he couldn't afford a ticket. However, she doesn't let him off the hook when she sees him canoodling with his assistant, Ms. Kakes. "Your daughter deserves better," she insists, "and so does Bex" ("Big Week"). The old Rebecca might not have protected her female successor, but now she won't stand by while Rupert destroys another woman's (or child's) life. When Bex and Ms. Kakes visit Rebecca for advice on how to fight Rupert, she is happy to oblige. We know she has fully moved on when she refuses to give the press, or Higgins and Keeley, a comment about Rupert's upcoming divorce. Growth? As Ted would say, "Heck, yeah."

Rebecca fits so naturally into these maternal roles that we hope Tish's prediction is right: she will become a mother. After all, Tish anticipated the green matchbook, the nonsensical "Shite in knining armor," and Rebecca toppling over into the canal. But when Rebecca's doctor confirms she can't have kids, a wonderful night with a divorced Dutch father makes us suspect it's possible yet. Rebecca thinks Tish is a fraud, but it's hard to ignore the deep emotional connection they shared as they ate and sang together and bonded over past heartaches and "gezellig."

For Rebecca's two favorite people, her mothering is kinder and more unconditional. Rebecca cautions Keeley about Jack's love bombing with expensive gifts. "Sometimes, shiny things can tarnish. Just trust yourself. I ignored so many red flags in the past" ("The Strings That Bind Us"). When a private video of Keeley is leaked on the internet, Rebecca can't restructure how society treats women, but she can listen without judgement and offer Keeley reassurance.

And Ted? Rebecca will miss him most of all. Her maternal guidance helped him deal with Michelle's relationship with Dr. Jacob and endure a surprise visit from Mama Lasso. Like any good mother, Rebecca realizes she needs to let Ted go, but she doesn't have to like it. Who could blame her for trying to tempt him with a huge salary and a life in England that includes Henry and Michelle? Even still, she knows it will never be enough money to pay him for what he means to this club, and to her. And so, in the same outfit she wore the first time she met Ted, all Rebecca can do is pull a classic rom-com "leave-cute" at the airport and say a tearful thank you.

The Stoics believed that our common humanity makes us members of the same family. Marcus Aurelius starts his book, *Meditations*, describing what he's learned from the people in his life. He credits his mother for teaching him, among other things, beneficence. Beneficence is also a central theme in *Ted Lasso* and, by the close of Season 3, a quality that Rebecca exudes. In her case, it's Ted she has to thank for its development. Over the three years he's been in Richmond, Ted has created for Rebecca the family she longed for. It took some time, but she has finally discovered her calling, and she is perfectly suited to it.

Now the team matriarch, with the promise of a family of her own, she has greatly expanded the Richmond household, generously offering fans ownership stake in the club. It's a far cry from her revenge fantasies in Season 1. For that, there's good reason to think that just maybe Rebecca really will get it all.

Notes

1 Marcus Aurelius, *Meditations*, trans. George Long (New York: Dover, 1997), 70.
2 Courtney Dabney, "It Took a Global Pandemic, But Generation X Is Finally Getting Love," *PaperCityMag.com*, December 2020, https://www. papercitymag.com/culture/generation-x-earns-respect-conronavirus-pandemic-stay-home/.

3   Massimo Pigliucci, "Musonius Rufus: Roman Stoic, and Avant-Garde Feminist?" *Psyche* https://psyche.co/ideas/musonius-rufus-roman-stoic-and-avant-garde-feminist, Accessed July 20, 2022.

4   We see something of this dynamic in Deborah and Mae sharing a laugh at Rebecca's expense: "I'd just like some peace of mind for my daughter. And all of her generation," Deborah quips. To which Mae responds, "Oh, must be awful for 'em, lying awake at night haunted by how … easy they've had it" ("So Long, Farewell").

5   Aurelius, *Meditations*, 63.

6   Ibid., 16.

7   Ibid., 8.

8   Ibid., 80.

9   Richard Mott Gummere, "On Choosing Our Teachers," https://monadnock.net/seneca/52.html, Accessed July 25, 2022.

10 Available at https://lawhimsy.com/2019/10/29/monday-mantra-249-dwell-on-the-beauty-of-life/.

11 Aurelius, *Meditations*, 27.

12 Ibid., 33.

13 Ibid., 21.

14 Friedrich Nietzsche, *Twilight of the Idols*, 1889 (CreateSpace Independent Publishing Platform, August 16, 2012), 3.

19

Why a Headbutt Might Have Hurt Nate Less

Georgina Mills

Making a pass at Roy Kent's girlfriend seems like a bad idea. Keeley Jones may be kind, cultured, and amazing at her job, but Roy's superpower is anger. And most reasonable people would steer clear of setting him off. Jamie Tartt and Nate Shelley aren't most people. In a moment of vulnerability at the funeral of Rebecca's father, Jamie professes his love for Keeley. Nate goes as far as kissing her while she helps him shop for a new suit, one that's not too loose in the crotch.

Keeley reciprocates neither advance, and soon tells Roy about them. Roy is left figuring out how to respond. Surprisingly, he forgives them both, but his different response to each case highlights something important about the nature of forgiveness. His anger at Jamie, Keeley's former boyfriend, is palpable, and forgiveness seems to result from an internal battle of the will. Nate's offense, on the other hand, gets almost no notice from Roy. The forgiveness Roy extends to him feels more like a dismissal, which confuses Nate. "Don't you at least wanna headbutt me or something?" ("Inverting the Pyramid of Success") What might account for Nate's incredulity, even offense, at Roy's easy forgiveness?

One plausible explanation is that Roy was less annoyed with Nate because he doesn't pose a threat to the relationship. Maybe Roy sees Nate as less desirable than Jamie. This might be a good reason for Nate to be offended, but it is not such a good reason for Nate to be forgiven.

It's a reasonable explanation, but there may be a better answer for why Roy's quick forgiveness damages his relationship with Nate. Maybe it's not because Roy doesn't take Nate seriously as a romantic rival. Instead Roy's quick forgiveness downplays Nate as a *moral*

Ted Lasso and Philosophy: No Question Is Into Touch, First Edition.
Edited by Marybeth Baggett and David Baggett.
© 2024 John Wiley & Sons, Inc. Published 2024 by John Wiley & Sons, Inc.

agent. And while people aren't equal in other respects, they should usually be seen as equals when it comes to this.

Life's Most Complicated Shape

Some philosophers take a dim view of forgiveness because they think it demeans the perpetrator of the original transgression, demanding contrition and a kind of humiliation from them to settle the score.[1] Nate's unearned forgiveness gives us another angle to consider the moral status of forgiveness.

When Roy learns that Jamie confessed his love for Keeley, Roy confronts him. He has every intention of calling him to account and perhaps even inflicting bodily harm. But before Roy can say anything, Jamie comes clean and apologizes profusely. He pulls a *mea culpa*, making no excuses and telling Roy that he respects their relationship. To top it off, he promises never to do anything like that again. Against his better judgment and every violent impulse, Roy accepts this apology. Forgiveness is an important recurring theme in *Ted Lasso*—Ted forgives Nate, Higgins forgives Rebecca, Sam forgives Jamie, and so on. But Roy's forgiveness of Jamie stands out as the funniest and most expletive-filled. He's clearly averse to doing it.

While Roy is bemoaning his forgiveness of Jamie with the Diamond Dogs, Nate confesses that he kissed Keeley on their shopping trip. Also on her lips. Roy barely reacts, in patent contrast with his soul searching over Jamie's infraction. Important to note is that Nate actually does not apologize. Even after Nate says he deserves some retaliation for the offense, Roy declines. Instead Roy reassures Nate that it's all behind them. They're good.

Three features of these encounters stand out: (1) Nate never apologizes to Roy, only confesses. (2) Roy is angry with Jamie, even though he does forgive him. (3) Roy is never angry with Nate. All of these contribute to Nate's problem: that by being "forgiven" so easily, he is arguably dismissed as a moral agent. Like Jamie, he is forgiven for what he did, but unlike Jamie, he did nothing to earn this forgiveness. He made no apology and didn't even attempt to explain himself. The fact that Roy did not become angry with Nate raises the question of whether this response even counts as forgiveness. The failure to acknowledge the wrongness and harm of Nate's actions devalues him by treating him as someone with diminished capacity for making good moral decisions.

Dismissing Nate's transgression so easily suggests Roy sees him as a pitiable figure, desperate enough for attention and affection to mistake kindness for romantic interest. Too desperate to be blameworthy, even though what he did was every bit as bad as what Jamie did, if not worse. When forgiveness is too easily conferred, it signals a lack of faith in the other's status as a moral agent. To be angry with someone is to take them seriously as a member of the moral community, as Peter Strawson and others suggest.[2] Nate deserves Roy's anger because he could and should have acted better. Nate himself seems to recognize that, and Roy's affirmation could have encouraged him in that direction. What Nate did was hurtful and intentional. He neither expressed remorse nor was expected to. For Roy to forgive him anyway was premature and, in a real sense, disrespectful. Roy revealed lack of faith in Nate's moral character, which might have hurt more than a headbutt.

Change Is Scary

These encounters take place at crucial points of character development for all involved. Jamie has gone from an arrogant, antagonistic rising star who couldn't build Jeff Bridges to a team player interested in earning the respect of his colleagues and respecting them in turn. Recall how Jamie in the first season instigated the bullying of Nate, initially resisting Roy's insistence that he put a stop to it.

Roy has also grown in his willingness to communicate and resolve issues amicably instead of with aggression. Were this Season 1, it seems unlikely that Jamie would have made it to the next game without a serious injury. It's even less likely that he would have apologized. But by the end of Season 2 both Jamie and Roy are better able to resolve their issues in healthier ways.

This growth stems, at least in part, from the influence of Ted and his positive, team-focused coaching style. Nate, on the other hand, is coming apart and morally devolving. Early on, Nate is deferential and bullied mercilessly by Colin and Isaac. After his promotion to coach, he still kowtows to his superiors, but frequently belittles perceived underlings and subordinates. In the process Nate gradually becomes what he had resented. Having been mistreated, he now mistreats. In the words of the team, he's both a prick and a wounded butterfly, which doesn't excuse his bad behavior, even if it helps explain it.

The cruelty he's capable of doling out is disturbingly casual. He is now becoming the tormentor of less exceptional players such as

Colin—but not in the Dr. Sharon sort of way. This increasing pattern goes unnoticed except by Coach Beard, who calls him on his rude, personal, and weird misconduct. Duly reprimanded, Nate asks if Beard told Ted (Beard had not), admits his wrongdoing, and then apologizes to Colin at practice.

The scene is extremely hopeful, making us think that perhaps Nate is on a better trajectory. Being held responsible for his actions seems to help him along, to own responsibility, and to make amends, contributing to the overall morale of the team. It even elicits from Colin a gracious and forgiving response.

But the transformation doesn't last. Nate soon reverts to becoming the consummate bully. This time more privately, targeting Will, the new kit man who is as powerless and vulnerable as Nate had once been. Nate neither empathizes with Will nor protects him. Rather than remembering what it was like to be in that precarious position, Nate exploits it and seamlessly assumes the role of the dehumanizing perpetrator, revealing a serious moral deficiency and intractable mean streak.

Not coincidentally, something in Nate is desperate to get credit for his coaching achievements, perhaps to compensate for lack of affirmation from his dad. As Fred Rogers was fond of repeating, "[T]here isn't anyone you couldn't learn to love once you've heard their story."[3] The father/son dynamics of *Ted Lasso* are ubiquitous, and learning of Nate's family history helps viewers empathize with him and root for his turnaround.

By Season 2, though, Nate's craving for accolades is as rapacious and insatiable as his aversion to criticism, baths, and aging. A single negative tweet among a sea of positives triggers his most hideous and gut-wrenching mistreatment of Will. Preoccupied with garnering attention and credit for his skillful coaching, Nate complains that he *won't* get credit for a tactic. Then complains that he *will* get the blame, ruining his "wonderkid" reputation in the process. By the time he kisses Keeley, Nate has come to resent not being the boss and being denied the glory and attention he yearns for and feels entitled to.

All Apologies

Roy's forgiveness of Jamie does not strain their relationship. If anything, it grows stronger by their humble and sincere exchange—though there's still the requisite headbutt to come before full reconciliation.

This progression is *transactional* forgiveness, which takes place when the perpetrator of some wrongdoing is forgiven after an apology and/or an appropriate attempt at restitution, acknowledging the magnitude of the initial harm.[4] Jamie fulfills these criteria. In her book *Making Amends*, Linda Radzik argues that forgiveness requires the wrongdoer to work to repair the relationship.[5] By properly apologizing, Jamie has done what was needed to fix the damage.

It's harder to make sense of Roy's felt need to headbutt Jamie before he could embrace him and celebrate their promotion together, but perhaps it, too, is somewhat transactional. Roy needed to pay Jamie back in some way before truly forgiving him. Sometimes there's still a price to be paid despite forgiveness.

Or we could understand the headbutt as an outlet for Roy's anger in order to address the psychological and affective challenge of letting it go.[6] Roy, it seems, has forgiven Jamie psychologically, but still holds on to an emotional burden. Only by headbutting Jamie can Roy relinquish this anger. The incident feels too joyful to be characterized as revenge. At this point Roy doesn't seem to want Jamie to be in pain. Roy only wants to take some action to restore their relationship so they can celebrate together. A headbutt from Roy makes more narrative sense than an earnest heart-to-heart. Everything that needed to be said has been said.

Contrast this with Roy's treatment of Nate, which doesn't resemble transactional forgiveness at all. No apology, no amends. Roy makes it clear that he already knows what happened, rendering Nate's confession almost superfluous. Roy has already moved past it.

Though showing neither remorse nor contrition, Nate would still prefer reluctant forgiveness from Roy only after anger and violent impulses. Nate seems to think he's owed a headbutt, as if the headbutt is a badge of honor or recognition. Nate likely sees this instance as part of a recurring pattern of being or feeling dismissed, exacerbating his growing resentment as Season 2 comes to a close.

Can You Make Me Famous?

Nate seems surprised, almost insulted that he was let off the hook so easily. He even tries to highlight that what he did was worse than what Jamie did: "I kissed her, I kissed your girlfriend. All Jamie did was talk to her and you wanted to kill him" ("Inverting the Pyramid of Success").

Kissing Keeley was wrong, regardless of how likely he was to be rebuffed. Being rejected has little to do with the morality of betraying a friend and colleague. Rather than treating it as a serious violation, Roy treats the situation as an embarrassing accident that, like Higgins' chat with Beard about Jane, should never be mentioned again.

Nate's feeling disrespected is plausibly a kind of status insult, much like Ted's knee-jerk snicker when Nate suggested he could be the "big dog" to straighten out Isaac ("Rainbow"). Nate kissing Keeley comes at the moment he feels like a rising star. He has been successful as a coach at Richmond, seen almost as a prodigy. He's out with Keeley to buy a smart suit that symbolizes his status and independence from Ted, who'd bought his first one—not counting his suit as a naked baby. Nate displays a consistent status anxiety, keenly aware of who he can talk down to, and who he must treat respectfully.

Perhaps Nate viewed Keeley as the type of woman who might be interested in him now that he's successful. He increasingly saw himself as an equal to Roy. Previously he felt inferior. While he has always liked Keeley, kissing her signals that he believes himself just as good as Roy or Jamie. For his behavior to be trivialized may suggest to Nate that Roy does not see him that way.

Nate's preoccupation with status and prestige helps explain why this would be a sore spot and why he would be more offended than relieved by Roy's easy forgiveness. Kissing Keeley was a terrible thing for a mate to do, even if she is mad fit. So what is going on here? The dismissal of Nate's actions looks like something more than not taking Nate seriously as a romantic rival or an equal. It seems that Roy doesn't take Nate seriously as a moral agent.

Nate the Great

To take someone seriously as a moral agent is to think they are responsible for their actions. Factors such as age, extreme circumstances, or illnesses might affect one's moral reasoning and diminish responsibility. But short of special circumstances, adults are generally thought to be responsible for their moral behavior and the reasonably foreseen effects of those actions on others.

In the case of Nate, he was aware that kissing Keeley was doing something hurtful to Roy, regardless of how his kiss was received. It was wrong and bad, worthy of one of Henry's classic temper tantrums. According to Strawson, to be angry with someone is to take them seriously as a member of the moral community.[7] Roy does this with Jamie. With Nate, however, Roy never feels anger, only awkwardness and perhaps pity. He does not take Nate seriously as a member of the moral community by being angry at his malicious selfish act.

A headbutt was in order, or at least a signature Roy Kent profanity-laced verbal headbutt. Nate should have had to express some remorse. As a card-carrying Diamond Dog, a colleague of Roy's, and a competent moral agent, Nate should have done better and should have been held accountable. To fail to take him seriously as a moral agent is to judge him incompetent to behave as we might expect from a moral equal. He deserves a headbutt because he deserves to be expected to behave better.

Perhaps Roy still thinks of Nate as the timid, bullied kit man from Season 1 and assumes he got carried away when an attractive woman was kind to him. Or perhaps as someone so desperate for love and recognition that he acted impulsively when he thought he had found it. Whatever the reason, it remains true that Nate kissed Keeley, he shouldn't have, and he knew better. But for some reason, Roy dismissed it out of hand, depriving Nate the recognition that he is not the weak baby Jamie once thought he was.

This pattern of forgiveness continues through season 3, where relationships are resolved and backstories revealed. In some cases, such as for those who trashed Sam's restaurant, forgiveness doesn't require amends. Sam shouldn't fight back, his father tells him, but should rather fight forward. Reopening the restaurant would be the real victory over those who meant him harm.

In cases where forgiveness leads to repairing relationships, forgiveness is not given automatically, but earned. After a frank conversation, Roy forgives Trent Crimm for his edgy takedown of him years earlier. Jamie forgives his father for his own sake, realizing he is no longer beholden to him, and there's a glimmer of hope in their restored relationship once Jamie's father enters rehab. What we learn of Ted's history with Beard extends this theme of forgiveness. In offering Nate a second chance, Beard reveals his past betrayal of Ted, how meaningful it was to receive forgiveness, and how fully that reconciliation has changed his life.

Nate himself provides a paradigmatic example of forgiveness and restoration. He earns back his place on the Richmond sideline through humility, remorse, and honesty. He makes amends with the entire team, starting with covering menial tasks for Will and offering the kit man a sincere apology for having bullied him so mercilessly. Notably, he returns to Richmond as Will's assistant, a mark of how much he has changed. He apologizes to Ted, an apology he insists on voicing despite Ted's protests. He even asks Beard for a headbutt when the coach offers forgiveness and invites him back to the team.

The Hope That Kills You

It's more shown than said that Nate is hurt—by the wonderfully expressive acting of Nick Mohammed.[8] At the start of their conversation, Nate doesn't seem keen for a fight, only to confess. But as soon as his confession is dismissed, he challenges Roy and seems genuinely upset by how easily trivialized his actions were. This fits with the broader pattern of Nate not feeling like he is taken seriously. As a coach, as a man, as a moral agent.

Given Nate's specific sensitivity to how others perceive him, we can see how being subtly dismissed as a moral agent would indeed hurt him. What we can learn from this series of events is that there is harm in minimizing wrongdoing and forgiving too easily. It comes at the expense of the respect for the moral agency of the other party. To not be taken seriously as a moral agent is a hurtful thing indeed. A headbutt might well have hurt Nate less.

Notes

1   Martha Nussbaum, *Anger and Forgiveness: Resentment, Generosity, Justice* (New York: Oxford University Press, 2016).
2   Peter Strawson, "Freedom and Resentment" in *Proceedings of the British Academy, Volume 48: 1962*, edited by Gary Watson (London: Oxford University Press, 1963), 187–211.
3   This quote did not originate with Fred Rogers, even though he popularized it. The original came from Mary Lou Kownacki as explained here: https://quoteinvestigator.com/2022/06/09/heard-story/.
4   Nussbaum, *Anger and Forgiveness*.
5   Linda Radzik, *Making Amends: Atonement in Morality, Law, and Politics* (New York: Oxford University Press, 2008).
6   Amia Srinivasan, "The Aptness of Anger," *Journal of Political Philosophy* 26 (2018), 123–144; Georgina Mills, "Swallowing Traumatic Anger: Family Abuse and the Pressure to Forgive," *Public Philosophy Journal*

2 (2019), n.p. Accessed August 22, 2022, https://pubhub.lib.msu.edu/ read/swallowing-traumatic-anger/section/a4d06ac2-edfd-41ec-b721-c2b327ff4616; Alfred Archer and Georgina Mills, "Anger, Affective Injustice, and Emotion Regulation," *Philosophical Topics* 47 (2019), 75–94.

7 Strawson, "Freedom and Resentment."

8 Mohammed earned well-deserved nominations for an Emmy in both 2021 and 2022 for his brilliant performance as Nathan Shelley.

20

Is Rupert Beyond Redemption?

Marybeth Baggett

Rupert Mannion is charming, handsome, smart, and rich. He's also arrogant, devious, petty, and spiteful. It's a bad combination, and the Greyhounds' former owner consistently leverages his charisma to further his selfish agenda, caring little about the ensuing damage. Indeed, in his interactions with ex-wife Rebecca, damaging cruelty is the point.[1]

Rupert's villainy seems out of place in the feelgood world of *Ted Lasso*. Kind of like little Ronnie Fouch on the playgrounds of Brookridge Elementary School. Mercifully his onscreen appearances are limited. More fundamentally though, Rupert's treachery is essential to the show's plot. Without it, Rebecca would have nothing to avenge and no reason to hire the folksy Coach Lasso as a means of destroying Rupert's beloved soccer team in the most humiliating way possible. And as the show progresses, he becomes pivotal in Nate's character arc.

Beyond tempting Rebecca with revenge fantasies and luring Nate to the dark side, Rupert also provides an important test case for the show's persistent positivity. Ted has an unwavering faith in people and a dogged commitment to improving whatever situations, relationships, and lives he encounters. This hopeful attitude is infectious and surfaces whenever things go off track. Sam's courageous stand against Cerithium Oil, Ted's response to Richmond's relegation, the ceremony to exorcise the training-room ghosts, Dr. Fieldstone's therapeutic practice, even Roy's hunt for a dentist to improve Phoebe's breath. Here and elsewhere, *Ted Lasso* insists that any wrong can be set right. What then do we make of the scoundrel Rupert and the havoc he gleefully wreaks wherever he goes? Is he past the point of grace extended by the show?

Ted Lasso and Philosophy: No Question Is Into Touch, First Edition.
Edited by Marybeth Baggett and David Baggett.
© 2024 John Wiley & Sons, Inc. Published 2024 by John Wiley & Sons, Inc.

Maybe We'll Turn It Around

Not all problems in *Ted Lasso* stem from human wrongdoing. Earl's death may be thought tragic, but Dani did nothing unethical in accidentally causing it. Roy's necessary retirement was simply a matter of age. Hard to accept, but the contingencies of time and the demands of the sport required it. The challenge Rupert poses, however, is of the moral kind. He cheated on Rebecca and persists in his mistreatment of her and others. He continues to cheat on his new wife, Bex. Such egregious harm and injustice requires a moral remedy.

Rupert is not alone in his wrongdoing. Other characters have their moments as well and cause plenty of pain besides. Ted snaps at Nate when the kitman simply shares his thoughts on the upcoming match with Everton. Bernard callously makes fun of Phoebe's bad breath. Keeley uses Roy to provoke Jamie's jealousy. Jamie professes his love to Keeley despite knowing she's involved with Roy. When characters behave in such unacceptable ways, forgiveness is needed.[2]

Ted Lasso is filled with moving scenes of grace given and received. An early memorable instance is what transpires between Ted and Rebecca when she comes clean about her attempts to sabotage him. Few television moments are as beautiful and affecting as this heartfelt interaction. Rebecca vulnerably confesses her duplicity, only for Ted to stamp out the offense with a simple and unconditional "I forgive you" ("All Apologies"). "Divorce is hard…. It makes folks do crazy things." This kindness confuses Rebecca who had braced for resentment and retribution but instead gets compassion and understanding.

Ted's forgiveness doesn't excuse Rebecca's actions. Rather, it puts a distance between what Sassy calls the "real Rebecca" and the unfortunate and damaging choices she's made. In an instant, Ted unburdens her of those offenses and provides a fresh start for the relationship— and for her. This same dynamic plays out between a number of other characters: Nate forgives Ted, Phoebe forgives Bernard, Roy forgives both Keeley and Jamie, and so on. You might even say that kindness is *Ted Lasso*'s mantra, its moment, its mood.

Reverse the Curse

Forgiveness is as wondrous as it is complex.[3] The broad strokes are clear: someone has done someone else wrong, resulting in real harm and injustice that requires correction. Forgiveness attends to those broken places, mysteriously but undeniably repairing the torn moral fabric. Ted's forgiveness stirs something in viewers because we sense that it signals a real change of circumstances—in him, in Rebecca, and in the relationship. But how should we understand the change that forgiveness brings about?

Early accounts like that of Joseph Butler (1692–1752) identify forgiveness as a changed *emotion* toward the wrongdoer, especially with regard to resentment.[4] In forgiving, the wronged party turns away from bitterness and renounces malice. This change of emotion goes further, or at least it should. On the view of contemporary philosopher Eleonore Stump, forgiveness has a positive dimension as well. It not only resists antipathy, it embraces compassion and actively wishes the wrongdoer well.

When Rebecca forgives Higgins for his role in enabling Rupert's infidelity, her heart warms to him. Where once she dubbed him "Shithead," she now greets him as Leslie. That she doesn't take the opportunity to mock his "feminine junior" name shows how much her feelings for him have changed. She stops her barrage of barbed putdowns. Admittedly, viewers almost regret this change of heart, given Hannah Waddingham's brilliant deadpan delivery. When Higgins bumbles Rebecca's tabloid scheme, her comeback is as subtle as it is vicious:

HIGGINS: I'm not a spy, Rebecca. I'm just the director of football operations.
REBECCA: And equally proficient at both.

But Rebecca soon redeploys that humor in better, more productive ways, joking and opening up to Higgins on equal terms after they resolve their conflict.

REBECCA: I lost my way for a minute. But I'm on the road back.
HIGGINS: I can tell. You know what, it suits you.
REBECCA: Unlike that beard. Ooh!

Two other competing theories of forgiveness on offer are *treatment accounts* and *performative accounts*. Treatment accounts emphasize the forgiver's *actions* over emotions.[5] One can have vengeful feelings, but refrain from carrying them out. Such accounts hinge on that very distinction and recognize that, no matter how we emotionally feel about another, we can control how we behave toward them. Ted may still be mad at Rebecca for returning Jamie to Man City. But he hands over her daily biscuits anyway, choosing not to act on the anger he most definitely still feels: "I hope they're not as good as they usually are. But dang it, they're the best batch yet. I finally cracked the recipe!" ("Two Aces"). Forgiveness, on this view, is primarily a volitional matter.

Performative accounts further enrich our understanding of forgiveness, shifting the focus from the personal to the social.[6] These, too, are action-centered, but concerned primarily with how forgiveness is *enacted verbally*. When Ted tells Rebecca, "I forgive you," his words carry a kind of force—both expressing a forgiving posture and committing Ted to abide by the promise it entails. The words accomplish a "performative" function.

Although these accounts developed separately and emphasize different elements of forgiveness, they are not at odds. Emotions, will, and words mutually reinforce one another in the most robust cases of forgiveness. Consider Phoebe's forgiveness of Bernard. Her hurt and shame seem eased by her decision to confront him, express her disappointment, and tell him she forgives him. Interestingly enough, Phoebe's forgiveness precedes and even appears to elicit Bernard's sincere apology.

The range of explanations on offer reminds us that forgiveness operates on a sliding scale. Roy's rage-filled expletive in the face of Jamie's apology counts, even though it'll take him time to warm up to Jamie. In its fullest sense, forgiveness involves all the elements mentioned above, but something else too: reconciliation.[7]

The final goal of forgiveness is society set right, a complete Lego set with not even one figure missing from the sidelines. But reality is messy. It is imperfect people who forgive and are forgiven, and a broken world where these faltering steps take place. For that reason, Stump and others think it best to uncouple forgiveness and reconciliation, at least for practical purposes.

Being Accountable Matters

On Stump's account, forgiveness belongs conceptually within a framework of love. Love requires more than forgiveness, but not less. Just as love for others is often thought to be a moral obligation, so too is forgiveness—even for the most egregious of wrongs. As unspeakably difficult and seemingly counterintuitive as this is, how can it be?

Stump bases her analysis on Aquinas's (1225–1274) understanding of love. For Aquinas, love involves two interlocking desires: (1) the desire for another's good, and (2) the desire for union with another. A forgiving spirit stems from both desires. It may seem unfair to shift the demands of forgiveness to the wronged party, though. Why should Rebecca, the one hurt by Rupert, have to forgive him? Isn't he the one who bears the burden? Imposing on her the responsibility to set things right seems to compound the offense, at least on one framing of the situation. But on another, forgiveness is liberating, empowering the one wronged and allowing her to turn the tables on the offender.

Forgiveness unshackles victims from wrongdoers and from the chains of resentment, freeing them to pursue a better path forward regardless of wrongdoers' attitudes. When Jamie chooses to forgive his father, Ted advises, it's a gift he gives to himself. Whether it's Colin's forgiveness of Nate's insults or Sam's forgiveness of Jamie's mistreatment, the offer or stance of forgiveness doesn't depend on the perpetrator's repentance or apology. But refusal to forgive results only in the wronged party's painful relegation to the status of victimhood bound by chronic bitterness and despair. And relegation's never a good thing. Desmond Tutu explains why such a prospect is so irreme-diably bleak: "It is clear that if we look only to retributive justice, then we could just as well close up shop. Forgiveness is not some nebulous thing. It is practical politics. Without forgiveness, there is no future."[8]

By distinguishing between *desire* (for another's good, for union with the other) and *actuality*, Stump balances a realistic yet hopeful response to wrongdoing. It unflinchingly sizes up the situation—the harm done, the moral standing of the offender, the contingencies of time and circumstance—while aspiring to the well-being of all involved. This means that forgiveness can be one-sided even if recon-ciliation cannot.

The Dark Forest

It is lamentable if reconciliation doesn't happen. But even worse is cheap grace that naively resumes fellowship without counting the cost. Rebecca knows from painful experience that overlooking offense only breeds yet more offense. By turning a blind eye to her husband's infidelity, Rebecca's mother implicitly consented to his behavior. At least that was the practical outcome. Refusal to be party to such bad behavior is what lies behind Rebecca's response to Rupert's betrayals.

Chronic wrongdoers who engage in flagrant abuse, like Rupert, hurt both others and themselves. The pain Rupert causes Rebecca is obvious. But he also hurts Bex, his newborn daughter, and Nate by using them as pawns in his schemes against Rebecca. At first, Rupert himself appears unharmed by his choices, even happy with them. But his character is being malformed. His heart hardens and character calcifies with each dehumanizing strike at Rebecca. James Baldwin captures this effect powerfully: "It is a terrible, an inexorable, law that one cannot deny the humanity of another without diminishing one's own: in the face of one's victim, one sees oneself."[9] The further one goes down this road, the harder it will be to distinguish between their choices and character. In Season 3, these cracks in Rupert begin to show until they break wide open in the finale.

Among the challenges to reconciliation that Stump identifies are the impairments to the offender's intellect, will, and habits.[10] Repeated wrongdoing especially can warp a person's perception and experience of right and wrong, making vice seem morally acceptable and even pleasurable. As Ted might explain, it's a little like thinking tea actually tastes good. This process also corrupts one's habits in a mutually reinforcing and downward spiraling cycle. Eventually, the fences blocking reconciliation become so high the injured party can't just "hop over 'em." The worse the deformation of character, the more radical the healing and deliverance process.

Jamie's difficulty on returning to Richmond sheds comical light on this dynamic. He realizes that to be welcomed back fully, he must own up to his mistakes. So he humbly listens to the team's catalog of complaints about his misbehavior: calling Colin a jaundiced worm (in a profile for his hometown paper), hitting on Bumbercatch's mother (in front of his father), cupping a fart and making Richard smell it (it sounds better in French). Though bad on their own, these offenses point to an entrenched pattern not easily rooted out. The team may forgive Jamie, but restoring relationships and moving in a new direction takes time. It also requires better behavior.

This is not to consign Jamie to permanent shame over the past, but rather to give him a chance to show that he has left those disgraceful behaviors behind. Jamie, too, knows that something's required of him. Not the gifts of PlayStations he naively thinks will help, but something even more valuable. It's his decision to show solidarity with Sam and the other Nigerian players in taking on Cerithium Oil that demonstrates a real turnaround. Stepping up like this is a risky move for Jamie. His position in the soccer world is precarious, after burning so many bridges. His gutsy stand shows that Jamie's priorities have indeed shifted and that he's turned over a proverbial new leaf.

Jamie has come a long way, and his transformation suggests that within the world of *Ted Lasso* freedom from corrupt habits is possible.

Even Jamie's dad is in rehab, chastened and finally happy for his son's success. Perhaps there's hope for Rupert yet, especially as he reaps the consequences of the havoc he's sown. But of course there's a big difference between Jamie and Rupert. Jamie eventually recognized his moral malady. He apologized and sought to make amends. Experiencing the negative consequences of his actions opened Jamie's eyes to his plight: "I'm not just a loser, I'm the loser" ("Lavender"). This humorous line underscores the reality of his situation, as Keeley explains to Roy: "He's so lost, Roy. Just like you. But at least he's tryin' to find his way back" ("Lavender"). Grasping the truth forced a choice, and Jamie responded well. We see no such signs in Rupert. He seems practically incapable of acknowledging wrongdoing, let alone taking responsibility for it.

Like a JIF (Or Is It GIF?)

If we're honest, we see a bit of Rupert in Aristotle's description of the bad person. Such a figure has so repeatedly engaged in bad habits and has so corrupted his reason that he can't even distinguish good behavior from bad. Aristotle's bad person is not one who pursues vice for its own sake, à la Milton's Satan. But one whose mental faculty is so damaged that proper moral determinations are out of reach, at least in an extreme case. As Rachel Barney explains it, this corrupted reason "makes moral truths invisible."[11]

Rupert seems to be in this category, or at least treading its verge, his misbehavior escalating episode after episode. He enjoys crashing the charity auction and surprising Rebecca at the pub. He's so dastardly that it's hard to believe he was ever the magnanimous club owner Rebecca describes who gave a raise to someone who had mistreated him as a boy. All these years and choices later, he takes jabs at her appearance, her drinking, and her tenure as club owner, with a twinkle in his eye. By all indications, Rupert believes he's entitled to treat others the way he does. What else would lead him to push his manager down for refusing to channel John Kreese and order West Ham to "take out" Jamie? Even when Rupert gets his comeuppance in the darts game, he won't acknowledge his misstep in underestimating Ted. Instead he comforts himself with his "consolation prize," his beautiful young fiancée.

Rupert not only persists in his bad behavior. He seems to become increasingly desensitized to the harm it's doing to himself and others. He gets his hooks into Richmond through Bex's shares in order to harass and humiliate Rebecca. All of that is bad enough, but it pales in comparison to his purchase of West Ham and nabbing Nate as head coach. If Rupert is not Aristotle's bad person, he's at least well on his way. Taken to its logical conclusion, such a path would make any sort of turnaround for Rupert highly unlikely.

Every Choice Is a Chance

Sassy seems to agree. To her, Rupert is already past the point of no return. She rightly recognizes Rupert's manipulation when he claims that fatherhood has changed him. But she goes further, reveling in what she sees as his impending perdition: "Rupert, I think about your death every single day. Oh, I can't wait. I'm gonna wear red to your funeral. I will be a beacon of joy to the other three people there" ("No Weddings and a Funeral"). Throughout the show, she relishes Rupert's pain. Even when he's at his lowest, she calls him the worst person she knows and joins in the chant as the Richmond fans humiliate him.

Although some may celebrate what Sassy does, she should provide a reminder of C. S. Lewis's warning against wishing for the worst in others. Lewis describes a reader who encounters a story of atrocity in the paper. She then learns that it may not be true. How she responds says more about her than the story's subject:

> Is one's first feeling, "Thank God, even they aren't quite so bad as that," or is it a feeling of disappointment, and even a determination to cling to the first story for the sheer pleasure of thinking your enemies as bad as possible? If it is the second then it is, I am afraid, the first step in a process which, if followed to the end, will make us into devils. You see, one is beginning to wish that black was a little blacker. If we give that wish its head, later on we shall wish to see grey as black, and then to see white itself as black. Finally, we shall insist on seeing everything— God and our friends and ourselves included—as bad, and not be able to stop doing it: we shall be fixed for ever in a universe of pure hatred.[12]

Rebecca's mother takes a rather different tack with Rupert. She tells Rebecca that "the best way to deal with people like that is to make sure they know they can't get to you" ("No Weddings and a Funeral"). She also invites him to a reception back at their house after her husband's funeral. Worse, she poses a false dichotomy between "being loving" and "being right" in explaining to Rebecca why she treats Rupert so well, as though loving another requires sacrifice of the truth of their condition and overlooking the harm done. Ignoring offense may be helpful in preserving one's dignity and bearing up in the face of harm. At its worst, though, it evades the problem rather than facing it squarely. In so doing, it tips the balance to a saccharine sweetness that may invite yet more harm from the wrongdoer. Should Rupert accept Deborah's invitation to community, he will have more opportunity to lash out at Rebecca.

Both Sassy and Deborah miss the mark and contrast with Ted's balanced approach. Ted sees Rupert's character with crystal clarity. Rupert's passive aggressive treatment of Rebecca at the charity gala, with its covert but savage digs, raises Ted's hackles. "If you could've texted Robbie Williams asking him to come tonight," Ted pointedly notes, "you could've probably just as easily asked him not to come" ("For the Children"). Later, he encourages Rebecca, "You may think that you're the only one that can see who he really is, but you're not" ("For the Children"). Rupert is not fooling Ted.

Even still, Ted resists writing him off and instead gives Rupert an opportunity to recognize and turn from his destructive ways. Ted allows Rupert's pride to set himself up for a fall. He fails to be curious and instead is judgmental, underestimating Ted and overestimating his own superiority. And it backfires, spectacularly. This is actually a kind of tough love, even grace, had Rupert availed himself of it. Jamie's response to his own tragic fall suggests as much. Unlike Jamie, though, Rupert becomes further committed to his treachery in response to his self-imposed embarrassment. Importantly, it was Rupert's choice alone, and Ted sacrificed neither the truth nor his integrity in the process.

Rebecca is an interesting case. She is both in need of forgiveness and of forgiving. And we see much growth in her on both scores. A necessary first step is her turn away from revenge, a striking moment that precedes her confession to Ted. In various religious traditions, giving and receiving forgiveness are interconnected. Rebecca's transformation in this scene hints at how they might be linked.

Rebecca has been unable to bring herself to share her wrongdoing with Ted, even though she knows she must. As she's gathering the courage to do so, Rupert barges in with devastating news intended to rub salt in her wound. He and Bex are having a baby. Knowing full well Rebecca's unmet desire for a child, Rupert disingenuously claims it was concern for her that brought him there to tell her in person. More likely he wanted the thrill of getting a rise out of her and seeing her pain.

In that moment, Rebecca seems to realize the path her vengeance has set her on. Rupert, she recognizes, has been on that path for a while and is so far gone that he is willing to bring a child into the dysfunctional situation, only to be a pawn in his egotistical game. That encounter pulls her back and sets her on the right track, even if she still has a long way to go at that point. It's the only way to fix things and involves accepting Ted's forgiveness. As C. S. Lewis explains, "Progress means getting nearer to the place you want to be. And if you have taken a wrong turn, then to go forward does not get you any nearer. If you are on the wrong road, progress means doing an about-turn and walking back to the right road; and in that case the man who turns back soonest is the most progressive man."[13] We never see Rupert heed this correction, but might he yet?

Aristotle's bad person is a limiting case and cautionary tale, but one we should not eagerly apply to every recalcitrant wrongdoer. An unrepentant wrongdoer's repeated choices can probably put him beyond the reach of grace at some point. As the saying goes, we make our choices but in the end our choices make us. Rupert has gone so far down the road of badness that it will be for him to see the need to turn back. But it is his choice to make, at least for now.

Disgraced, deserted, desolate—come the end of Season 3, Rupert, having hit rock bottom, has every incentive to try something different. While his moral destination remains beyond our pay grade, wishing the best for him does not. We may never know what ultimately comes of Rupert Mannion. But what becomes of *us* just might be intimately bound up in what we hope for him.

Notes

1   Anthony Head is perfectly cast in the role of Rupert. Best known as the loveable Rupert Giles on *Buffy the Vampire Slayer*, Head draws on that same likeability in his portrayal of Mannion, but with a duplicitous twist.

2   Paul Hughes notes that some philosophers are skeptical about the morality of forgiveness. Nietzsche sees forgiveness as an element of a larger moral system that he thinks should be rejected altogether. Martha Nussbaum is skeptical, too. The fuller discussion that such views require exceeds the bounds of this chapter. Paul Hughes, "Forgiveness," *Stanford Encyclopedia of Philosophy*, accessed August 3, 2022, https://plato.stanford.edu/entries/forgiveness/.

3   A helpful primer for this topic is the introduction to *Forgiveness and Its Moral Dimensions*, edited by Brandon Warmke, Dana Kay Nelkin, and Michael McKenna (New York: Oxford UP, 2021), 1–28.

4   Butler laid out his views on forgiveness in two sermons: "Upon Resentment" and "Upon Forgiveness of Injuries." These two texts can be found here: http://articles.ochristian.com/preacher566-1.shtml.

5 For two instances of this approach see the work of Frederick DiBlasio (focusing primarily on the wronged party's decision to turn away from revenge) and Michael McCullough (who points to the motivations). Some interpretations of Butler's work place him in this category as well.

6 See Joram Graf Haber, *Forgiveness* (Lanham, MD: Rowman and Littlefield, 1991).

7 Robert C. Roberts, "Forgivingness," *American Philosophical Quarterly* 32 (1995), 299.

8 Qtd. in Simon Wiesenthal, *The Sunflower: On the Possibilities and Limits of Forgiveness*, Revised and Expanded ed. (New York: Schocken, 1997), 268.

9 James Baldwin, "Fifth Avenue, Uptown," *Esquire* (July 1960), available at https://www.esquire.com/news-politics/a3638/fifth-avenue-uptown/.

10 Eleonore Stump, "*The Sunflower*: Guilt, Forgiveness, and Reconciliation," in Warmke, Nelkin, and McKenna, 172–196. Stump uses the challenging case of John Newton to consider the limits of penance and reparations in the removal of guilt.

11 Rachel Barney, "Becoming Bad: Aristotle on Vice and Moral Habituation," *Oxford Studies in Ancient Philosophy* 57 (2019), 273–307.

12 C. S. Lewis, *Mere Christianity* (New York: HarperCollins, 2001), 118.

13 Ibid., 28–29.

Beard's Bookshelf

Marybeth Baggett

Coach Beard goes through books like Rebecca goes through manicurists. He's often found nose-deep in a strategy manual, ferreting out fun football facts like the difference between practice and training, cleats and boots, out of bounds and into touch. The coach really is a sponge, and his literary tastes extend far beyond the pitch—ranging from fungi to forests, politics to culture, memoir to fiction. With all that reading, Beard can move effortlessly from debates about chess to advice for travel to Las Vegas to disputations on the meaning of life. Yeah, he's got a few thoughts.

Beard may be the most prominent bibliophile at Richmond. But the show's frequent literary appearances and references tell us he's not the only one. Ted doles out books to prod his players toward the best versions of themselves. Bantr users quote poetry to connect on a deeper level. The Greyhounds are quite the bookish lot in fact, and their reading choices offer a glimpse behind the show's creative curtain. Metaphorically speaking, books are the invisible red strings that bind together the show's characters and themes.[1] Voracious book-on-tape listeners and treadmill readers alike will find a wealth of wit and wisdom in the pages of *Ted Lasso*.[2]

You Do Not Want to Judge These Books by Their Covers

A Clockwork Orange by Anthony Burgess (Norton, 1962): Violent, darkly comic, dystopian—just another weeknight for Coach Beard. ("Beard After Hours"[3])

Ted Lasso and Philosophy: No Question Is Into Touch, First Edition.
Edited by Marybeth Baggett and David Baggett.
© 2024 John Wiley & Sons, Inc. Published 2024 by John Wiley & Sons, Inc.

About a Boy by Nick Hornby (Riverhead Books, 1998): If Will Freeman can learn to grow up and get over it, anyone can. ("Headspace")

Arco Book of Soccer Techniques and Tactics by Richard Widdows (Arco, 1983): New to coaching in the Premier League? It would be irresponsible not to get this book. ("Two Aces")

The Beast Beyond the Fence by Marcus Rashford with Alex Falase-Koya (Macmillan, 2022): Why bully your classmates when you can solve mysteries together instead? ("We'll Never Have Paris")

The Beautiful and the Damned by F. Scott Fitzgerald (Scribner's, 1922): Better known in Richmond as *The Fit and the Relegated*. ("Trent Crimm: The Independent")

The Beckham Experiment: How the World's Most Famous Athlete Tried to Conquer America by Grant Wahl (Three Rivers Press, 2010): Zava is like Beckham, if every letter were different and there were a few more letters. ("Big Week")

Bird by Bird: Instructions on Writing and Life by Anne Lamott (Pantheon, 1994): Or, in Latin, *Gradarius Firmus Victoria*. ("Biscuits")

Brilliant Orange: The Neurotic Genius of Dutch Football by David Winner (Harry N. Abrams, 2008): It's fast, it's fluid, it's free. It's Total Football. ("We'll Never Have Paris")

Coach Wooden's Pyramid of Success: Building Blocks for a Better Life by John Wooden and Jay Carty (Baker, 2005) If you don't like this self-help book, you don't like ice cream. ("Pilot")

Coaching Soccer For Dummies by the National Alliance For Youth Sports with Greg Bach (Wiley, 2006): Perfect for the American who has never set foot in England, whose athletic success has only come at the amateur level—a second-tier one at that—and is now being charged with the leadership of a Premier League football club, despite clearly possessing very little knowledge of the game. ("Pilot")

The Club: How the English Premier League Became the Wildest, Richest, Most Disruptive Force in Sports by Joshua Robinson and Jonathan Clegg (Mariner, 2019): When billionaires dared to ask, "Why should football not change? Why should it not evolve? Why should profits not grow exponentially?" ("International Break")

The Da Vinci Code by Dan Brown (Doubleday, 2003): Knights Templar, a geezer with a spiked belt around his thigh, short chapters: the best kind of book to read quietly on the couch or in your girlfriend's office. ("Headspace")

The Dharma Bums by Jack Kerouac (Viking, 1958): Follow your bliss, no mushrooms required. ("Pilot")

Ender's Game by Orson Scott Card (Starscape, 1972): Heavy is the jersey that tapes over the Dubai Air logo. ("Trent Crimm: The Independent")

Entangled Life: How Fungi Make Our Worlds, Change Our Minds & Shape Our Futures by Merlin Sheldrake (Random House, 2021): Now for something different, deeper. ("Midnight Train to Royston")

Fever Pitch by Nick Hornby (Riverhead Books, 1998): When art and sport combine, you have quite the metaphor. ("Rainbow")

Fight Club by Chuck Palahniuk (Norton, 2018): What's the first rule of Ted's fight club? No fight club! ("For the Children")

Finding the Mother Tree: Discovering the Wisdom of the Forest by Suzanne Simard (Random House, 2022): Even trees believe in Rom-Communism. ("Midnight Train to Royston")

Football Against the Enemy by Simon Kuper (Orion, 2003): A kit is never just a kit. ("The Signal")

The Fountainhead by Ayn Rand (Bobbs Merrill, 1943): A real curveball. ("Lavender")

Friend of the Devil by James Kirkland (Meathouse, 2019): More mysterious than David Blaine reading a Sue Grafton novel at Area 51. ("The Strings That Bind Us")

The Greatest: The Quest for Sporting Perfection by Matthew Syed (John Murray, 2019): An outstanding example of Coach Wooden fanfic. ("Goodbye Earl")

How to Change Your Mind: What the New Science of Psychedelics Teaches Us About Consciousness, Dying, Addiction, Depression, and Transcendence by Michael Pollan (Penguin, 2019): A good book to have on hand in case of emergencies, like drinking tea from the wrong pot. ("So Long, Farewell")

Inverting The Pyramid: The History of Soccer Tactics by Jonathan Wilson (Bold Type Books, 2013): Among the best of the shape-based books. ("Pilot")

Johnny Tremain by Esther Hoskins Forbes (Houghton Mifflin, 1943): Johnny and Ted had the same upbringing, but different. ("No Weddings and a Funeral")

Kafka on the Shore by Haruki Murakami (Knopf, 2006): More Oedipal overtones than Jamie and his mom. I mean, barely. It's very close. ("La Locker Room Aux Folles")

Leaves of Grass by Walt Whitman (Rome Brothers, 1855): Be curious, not judgmental. ("International Break")

Les Misérables by Victor Hugo (A. Lacroix, Verboeckhoven & Cie., 1862): Beard is a modern-day Jean Valjean. Watch for the spin-off where Beard, now known as Mr. Battenberg, takes over X (formerly known as Twitter) and becomes mayor of London. ("4-5-1")

Middle Passage: From Misery to Meaning in Midlife by James Hollis (Inner City Books, 1993): As the saying goes, *in concussio veritas*. ("Man City")

The Miracle of Castel di Sangro: A Tale of Passion and Folly in the Heart of Italy by Joe McGinniss (Broadway, 2000): Classic story of David versus Goliath, Rocky versus Apollo, Steve Wiebe versus Billy Mitchell, Pearl Jam versus Ticketmaster. ("Smells Like Mean Spirit")

One Flew Over the Cuckoo's Nest by Ken Kesey (Viking, 1962): Is Beard is a natural-born caregiver like Chief or more of a Taber guy? ("All Apologies")

The Prince of Tides by Pat Conroy (Bantam, 1987): The truth will set you free, but first it'll piss you off. ("Lavender")

Quiet Genius: Bob Paisley, British Football's Greatest Manager by Ian Herbert (Bloomsbury, 2019): Coaching can be subtle. It doesn't have to hit you over the head but can slowly grows until you can no longer ignore its presence. ("Trent Crimm: The Independent")

The Richmond Way: The Unbelievable Season of a Premier League Underdog by Trent Crimm (McCarthy Books, 2023): Featuring a very brief foreword by Roy Kent. ("So Long, Farewell")

Sense and Sensibility by Jane Austen (Thomas Egerton, 1811): No need to destroy a priceless artifact to read this story of two sisters looking for love. Most libraries will have a copy. ("The Strings That Bind Us")

Shoeless Joe by W. P. Kinsella (Houghton Mifflin, 1982): Even cornier than Ted's jokes. ("Tan Lines")

The Ultimate Cockney Geezer's Guide to Rhyming Slang by Geoff Tibballs (Ebury Press, 2008): When you need to know the difference between your Big Ben and your Marble Arch. ("Pilot")

The Wonderful Wizard of Oz by L. Frank Baum (George M. Hill Company, 1900): Ted's not in Kansas anymore! ("Pilot")

A Wrinkle in Time by Madeleine L'Engle (Ariel Books, 1962): A lovely novel of a young girl's struggle with the burden of leadership as she journeys through space. Roy's supposed to be the little girl. ("Trent Crimm: The Independent")

Notes

1   From the start, *Ted Lasso* fans have delighted in identifying book refer-
    ences and sleuthing out their meanings and implications. A quick Google
    search will yield many results in this vein. One especially notable endeavor
    is *Coach Beard's Book Club*, a collaborative effort to painstakingly cata-
    logue every book depicted on the show, no matter how incidental, and to
    podcast about each book one by one. *Coach Beard's Book Club* has a
    presence on X (@BeardsBookClub) and can be found on most podcast
    platforms.
2   This list is by no means exhaustive. It attempts to capture the books most
    significant in shaping the spirit of *Ted Lasso* and to whet viewers' appe-
    tites for discovering more along these lines. For an example of the fruitful
    interchange between books and the show, see my blog series on Season 3:
    https://mb-davis.medium.com/whats-beard-reading-smells-like-
    mean-spirit-29205adb5cf6.
3   The episode titles noted in each entry mark the first appearance or refer-
    ence to the book. Several of these titles re-appear in later episodes.

Starting Lineup

Marcus Arvan is Associate Professor of Philosophy at the University of Tampa. He specializes in ethics, social-political philosophy, and metaphysics, and has published two books, *Rightness as Fairness: A Moral and Political Theory* and *Neurofunctional Prudence and Morality: A Philosophical Theory*. Although he agrees with Ted and Immanuel Kant that doing the right thing is never the wrong thing, he also thinks that if mind-independent moral realism is a joke, he loves it—but if not, he can't wait to unpack that with you later.

Michael W. Austin is Foundation Professor of Philosophy at Eastern Kentucky University. He may not have the sort of CV that we all find acceptable, but he assures us he's just what we need. He specializes in ethics, especially as it relates to character and cultivating virtue. He's also a high school soccer coach, and is thinking about growing a mustache so he can be more like Ted. Michael's waiting on that call from A.F.C. Richmond, if they want to give another more experienced American coach a go. Responsibility for any and all adorable but devastating typos in this book falls squarely on his shoulders.

A flâneur by nature, **David Baggett** is Professor of Philosophy and Director of the Center for the Foundations of Ethics at Houston Christian University, and writes for the *Worldview Bulletin*. The only kid in primary school afflicted with sciatica, he had a gelatinous L4 and 5. Though really bad at impressions, he's a master of semantic satiation.

Marybeth Baggett is Professor of English at Houston Christian University. Her latest project is a biography of Alfonso Ribeiro, arguably the greatest physical comedian of the 19th, 20th, and 21st century. When not teaching or writing, she enjoys curling up on the couch under a weighted blanket, watching *You've Got Mail*, and devouring a box of Snookers.

Ted Lasso and Philosophy: No Question Is Into Touch, First Edition.
Edited by Marybeth Baggett and David Baggett.
© 2024 John Wiley & Sons, Inc. Published 2024 by John Wiley & Sons, Inc.

Robert Begley is the Founder of Speaking With Purpose LLC, where he helps entrepreneurs, executives, and thought leaders deliver more memorable messages. His storytelling presentations about heroes and history change people's lives. Robert has written for *The Objective Standard, Reason Papers*, and even published an essay about Ted Lasso for *Objective Standard Institute*. Barbeque sauce!

Lance Belluomini did his graduate studies at the University of California, Berkeley; San Francisco State University; and the University of Nebraska-Lincoln. He's recently published an essay on *Tenet* in *The Palgrave Handbook of Popular Culture as Philosophy*. He's also contributed chapters to the forthcoming Wiley-Blackwell volumes on *Indiana Jones, Mad Max*, and *Star Wars and Philosophy Strikes Back*. Whenever Lance feels stressed over meeting an essay deadline, he embraces the advice Ted gave Keeley, "Now don't you fret, Boba Fett."

Carrie-Ann Biondi holds a PhD in Applied Philosophy and has more than two decades of teaching experience at the college level. She specializes in ancient Greek philosophy, particularly Aristotle's ethical and political works, which inspire her to support students to become the best versions of themselves in and out of the classroom. Carrie-Ann also works as production editor at *Social Philosophy & Policy* and has published popular culture and philosophy pieces on Sherlock Holmes, Steve Jobs, *Harry Potter*, and *Hamilton*. Her favorite novel is *The Fountainhead*, which is a bit of a curveball, but she can explain it.

Kimberly Blessing is Professor of Philosophy at SUNY Buffalo State. Her research interests focus attention on questions and issues related to the meaning of life. Her primary teaching interests include early modern philosophy, philosophy of religion, and existentialism. Living in Buffalo, you gotta be some kind of optimist. But she'd much rather be in Provence, cultivating her garden and eating roasted pine nuts and pistachios. People gave up trying to figure her out years ago.

Joseph Forte, is Assistant Professor of Philosophy at Rivier University in Nashua, New Hampshire, where for years he's been getting shots for his finger allergy. He is the author of the textbook *Moral Issues and Movies: An Introduction to Ethical Theories and Issues Through the Lens of Film* (Kendall Hunt, 2021), which he sells door-to-door in posh English neighborhoods during the holidays with his wife and children while also shopping for dentists. He's an ancient Greek specialist, he edited a forthcoming *Philosophical News* volume on the humanities and democracy, he lives in southern Maine, and was born and raised in the Bronx (NYC), where he recited gangsta rap while doing power poses in front of mirrors.

Austin Freeman teaches theology and apologetics at Houston Christian University, where he serves as department chair in apologetics. Though his PhD in systematic theology focuses on theological paradox, he is mostly known for his pop culture books and essays, especially on the theology of J.R.R. Tolkien. He would love to be English but is far too optimistic to pull it off.

Like Liverpool, **Caleb McGee Husmann** has much to offer. From writing and teaching to the great academic pastime of overthinking, Caleb does it all! Currently he lives in Raleigh, North Carolina where he is an Assistant Professor of Political Science at William Peace University. In addition to his academic writing he has had two novels published under the name C McGee.

Elizabeth Kusko swears like Roy Kent (never in the classroom, of course), cheer-leads for her people like Keeley Jones, and is as clueless about the offsides rule as Ted himself. She's an Associate Professor of Political Science at William Peace University, researches everything from the Narrative Policy Framework to Shirley Jackson, and believes that we're living in a true golden age of television (and is so grateful that she has gotten to write about fantastic shows like *The Expanse* and *Ted Lasso*).

Corey Latta has an MA in Counseling, a PhD in Literature, a full Fellowship of the Ring backpiece tat, and a can-do attitude. He's written on everything from C. S. Lewis to philosophy in *Doctor Strange* to a small quail hunting farm outside of Oxford, Mississippi. You could fill two internets with what he doesn't know about soccer, but he knows a good TV show when he sees it. He's the author of *C. S. Lewis and the Art of Writing* and *When the Eternal Can Be Met*, and with his action figure-y arms, he's confident he could beat Michelle Obama in arm wrestling.

R. Keith Loftin is a close personal friend of a soccer coach, Mike Austin, who's more like Rupert Mannion than Ted Lasso. Keith is a Professor of Philosophy and Director of the Politics, Philosophy, Economics program at Dallas Baptist University. At fifteen he was an understudy for Anita in his all-boy-high-school's performance of *West Side Story*.

Georgina Mills is an alleged philosopher and nap enthusiast working at Tilburg University in the Netherlands. She mostly works on personality, emotion, philosophy of science, and philosophy of medicine, but she has also written philosophical pieces about Britney Spears, women in punk, and friendship. Like Ted she knows nothing about soccer. However, having recently married a Partick Thistle fan, she continues to know nothing about soccer.

Elizabeth Quinn holds an MFA in Writing and Producing for TV from Loyola Marymount University where she is currently an adjunct screenwriting professor. Her original scripts have been finalists in the PAGE International Screenwriting Awards, Nantucket Film Festival, and Cinequest Film Festival. She is currently in post-production on *Going Reno*, a fictional audio drama series set during the booming Nevada divorce industry in 1932, which she wrote and co-produced. When she's not writing, teaching, or producing, she performs improv comedy in Los Angeles where you can give her the suggestion of "ally" any time. She tries to be a lion at work, and a goldfish everywhere else. It's challenging at times, but it's better than being a panda.

Elizabeth Schiltz is the Purna, Rao, Raju Professor of Philosophy at the College of Wooster in Wooster, Ohio, where she teaches and writes about ancient and world philosophy. It's a job that requires a lot of practice (yes, practice!), but she will know it has all been worth it if and when someone—at least once!—says that she, like Dr. Sharon Fieldstone, has served a "heaping spoonful of truth soup."

Sean Strehlow is the assistant professor of sport management at Messiah University. Sean is a teacher at heart and is passionate about the intersection of faith and learning. His scholarship is concerned with the moral and faith development of college athletes, coaches, and athletic directors. On a personal note, Sean is cute as a button and can rhyme his ass off. It's no wonder people want to destroy him.

Andy Wible is a full-time instructor of philosophy at Muskegon Community College. He teaches and writes on business ethics, biomedical ethics, and LGBTQ+ Studies. As an aging professor, he notices his students are more woke than he is even when they're sleeping in class. An immediate goal is to travel and be more culturally aware, because you gotta get it in there to score three points. His ultimate goal is to go out like Willie Nelson—on a high!

Willie Young is professor of religion and philosophy at Endicott College in Beverly, Massachusetts. When not coaching or thinking about youth soccer, his primary research interests are interreligious friendship, listening, and eternity, which he has been studying for what feels like forever. He has previously written on Philosophy and *South Park*, baseball, and *The Shawshank Redemption*. He runs in his spare time, and when he does he tries to get his knees up to his nipples (which gets easier as he gets older).

Andrew Zimmerman Jones, a science and math communicator and educator, is the former About.com Physics Guide and co-author of *String Theory For Dummies*. He's also written on philosophy across many possible worlds, including *The Big Bang Theory*, *Veronica Mars*, and *The Avengers*. He currently works for the Indiana Department of Education, where he is seen as a strong and capable man, notwithstanding his psychotic eyebrows.

Index

References to Notes will contain the letter 'n' following the Note number,
Characters in *Ted Lasso* are filed under 'characters in *Ted Lasso*' sorted by
surname where both first name and surname are given.

Ted Lasso and Philosophy: No Question Is Into Touch, First Edition.
Edited by Marybeth Baggett and David Baggett.
© 2024 John Wiley & Sons, Inc. Published 2024 by John Wiley & Sons, Inc.

Carlson, Matt, *On the Condition of Anonymity* 180n2
Celeste, "Strange," 128–129
Cervantes, Miguel, *Don Quixote* 162
character 3, 4, 71, 158
  and comedy 127
  cowardice 57
  deformation of 206
  development/self-improvement 9, 56, 59–61, 63, 64, 93–95, 110, 194
  good or bad 79, 92, 207, 210
  maturation of xv–xvi
  moral 9, 38, 43n11, 132, 194
  music as a character 137
  portrayal in *Ted Lasso* 139n14, 201, 205–206
    progression 47–55
  strengths-focused approach to development 59, 60, 61–63
  television character arcs 94, 139n14, 201
  virtues of/virtuous 60–61, 79, 82
  see also bad character; characters in *Ted Lasso*; good character; virtue ethics
Character Strengths Profile (VIA Institute on Character) 60
characters in *Ted Lasso* xiv
  Edwin Akufo (Ghanaian billionaire) 8, 68, 111, 136, 167, 189
  Baz (AFC Richmond fan) xv, 7, 173
  Bex (Rupert's third wife) 40, 131, 189, 202, 205, 207–209
  George (Coach) Cartrick 80, 107, 117, 166, 186
  Raja Casablanca 68
  Coach Beard xvi, 21–22, 25, 39–41, 49, 64, 88, 90, 97, 98, 102, 146, 169, 195, 197
    books of 212–215
    delusions as to relationship with Jane 26, 72, 83, 98, 197

  history with Ted 198
  rift with Ted 120
  risky behavior 97
  self-loathing 154
  and simulation hypothesis 140, 142, 144, 147–148
Richard Cole, Dubai Airlines CEO 187
Flo "Sassy" Collins (Rebecca's friend) 28, 90–91, 128–130, 186, 202, 208, 209
  one-night stand with Ted Lasso 31, 128, 129
Trent Crimm (reporter) xv, 3, 4, 21–22, 39, 42, 67, 77, 79, 97, 175–178, 179, 198
  on character of Ted Lasso 36, 175–176
  The Lasso Way (manuscript) 39, 123, 180
  Rebecca's arrangement with to interview Ted/write article 116, 132
  revealing of sources 179, 181n6, 181n7
  see also journalism
Sharon M. Fieldstone (Dr), sports psychologist xv, 26–28, 38, 69, 105
  confrontational therapy style 49
  giving therapy to Ted 42, 48, 49–50, 51, 77, 97
  vulnerability, modeling of 111
Ronnie Fouch (child) xv, 24, 87, 201
Pep Guardiola 122
Leslie Higgins (Director of Football Operations) 21, 63, 64, 98, 112, 138n10, 189, 197, 203
  enabling of Rupert's infidelity 109
  frankness 26